THE SLANDER AND SOLACE OF JOB

An Exposition of the Book of Job

Kress Biblical Resources

The Slander and Solace of Job: An Exposition of the Book of Job

© copyright Eric Kress

Published by Kress Biblical Resources

www.kressbiblical.com

ISBN: 978-1-934952-91-7

Cover image generated by ChatGPT

Cover design: Stephen Williams

Except as noted, Scripture quotations are taken from the (**NASB**®) New American Standard Bible®, Copyright © 1960, 1971, 1977, 1995 by The Lockman Foundation. Used by permission. All rights reserved. lockman.org

Scripture quotations marked **CJB** are taken from the Complete Jewish Bible by David H. Stern. Copyright © 1998. All rights reserved. Used by permission of Messianic Jewish Publishers, 6120 Day Long Lane, Clarksville, MD 21029. www.messianicjewish.net.

Scripture quotations marked **CSB** have been taken from the Christian Standard Bible®, Copyright © 2017 by Holman Bible Publishers. Used by permission. Christian Standard Bible® and CSB® are federally registered trademarks of Holman Bible Publishers.

Scripture quotations marked **ESV** are from The ESV® Bible (The Holy Bible, English Standard Version®), © 2001 by Crossway, a publishing ministry of Good News Publishers. Used by permission. All rights reserved.

Scripture quotations marked **HCSB** are taken from the Holman Christian Standard Bible®, Copyright © 1999, 2000, 2002, 2003 by Holman Bible Publishers. Used by permission. Holman Christian Standard Bible®, Holman CSB®, and HCSB® are federally registered trademarks of Holman Bible Publishers.

Scripture quotations marked **NET** are from the NET Bible® https://netbible.com copyright ©1996, 2019. Biblical Studies Press, L.L.C. All rights reserved.

Scripture quotations marked **NIV** are taken from The Holy Bible, New International Version® NIV®. Copyright © 1973, 1978, 1984, 2011 by Biblica, Inc. Used with permission. All rights reserved worldwide.

Scripture quotations marked **NLT** are taken from the Holy Bible, New Living Translation, copyright ©1996, 2004, 2015 by Tyndale House Foundation. Used by permission of Tyndale House Publishers, Carol Stream, Illinois 60188. All rights reserved.

Scripture quotations marked **TNK** are taken from the Jewish Publication Society Tanakh (JPS, 1985).

BBE (The Bible in Basic English), The **Darby** Bible, **KJV** (King James Version) and **YLT** (Young's Literal Translation) are in the public domain in the USA.

For whatever was written in earlier times was written for our instruction, that through perseverance and the encouragement of the Scriptures we might have hope.

Romans 15:4

The grace of the Lord Jesus Christ, the love of God, and the fellowship of the Holy Spirit be with you all.

2 Corinthians 13:14

We count those blessed who endured. You have heard of the endurance of Job and have seen the outcome of the Lord's dealings, that the Lord is full of compassion and is merciful.

James 5:11

CONTENTS

Introduction to the Book of Job 7
Structure and Outline 15
Job 1:1-12 55
Job 1:13-22 67
Job 2:1-13 77
Job 3:1-26 93
Job 4:1-5:27 105
Job 6:1-7:21 123
Job 8:1-22 141
Job 9:1-10:22 151
Job 11:1-13:3 167
Job 13:4-14:22 185
Job 15:1-35 201
Job 16:1-17:16 213
Job 18:1-19:29 225
Job 20:1-21:34 239
Job 22:1-24:25 255
Job 25:1-27:23 271
Job 28:1-28 285
Job 29:1-31:40 295
Job 32:1-33:33 313
Job 34:1-35:16 329
Job 36:1-37:24 343
Job 38:1-38 355
Job 38:39-40:5 369
Job 40:6-42:6 379
Job 42:7-17 399
Postscript 412
Selected Bibliography 413

Introduction to the Book of Job

I. The author
A. The human author

The human author of the Book of Job is unnamed in Scripture and thus ultimately, we do not know who he was. Speculation about the authorship of Job includes figures such as Moses, Solomon, Ezra, Job, and Elihu, among many others. It would seem unlikely that Job himself authored the final form of this great work, as nothing in the text suggests that God ever revealed to him the reason for his suffering. It is clear, however, "the book reads as though an eyewitness of the events ... wrote it" (*Constable's Expository Notes on the Bible*).

The author may have been an Israelite, given the frequent use of the divine name "Yahweh" in the prologue, the divine discourse, and the epilogue (31 occurrences in Hebrew, cf. NIV Study Bible, p. 731). Interestingly, in the poetic dialogue section between Job and his counselors (chapters 3-37), "Yahweh" is mentioned only once (12:9).

The limited use of "Yahweh" in the poetic dialogue, along with Job's age (cf. 42:16; he is old enough at the beginning of the book to have ten grown children), his measurement of wealth (in livestock rather than money; cf. 1:3), and his role as family priest (1:5) suggest that the events of Job occurred in the patriarchal period, prior to the Mosaic law.

B. The divine Author (2 Tim. 3:16; 2 Pet. 1:20-21; cf. Rom. 11:35 [ref. Job 41:11]; 1 Cor. 3:19 [ref. Job 5:13])

Clearly God the Holy Spirit is the divine Author of all Scripture. It has been noted that much of the Book of Job is written in poetic form (most of chapters 3-41) and thus was either composed as such by the various participants in the debate, or more probably a stylized treatment of the argument written by the unnamed human author, his record inspired by the Holy Spirit.

II. The audience

A. The original recipients

The nation of Israel, though from an unspecified time period. Ezekiel references Job as if he were as well-known as Noah and Daniel (Ezekiel 14:14, 20). This suggests that the Book of Job likely dates to the pre-exilic period of Israel's history.

B. The current recipients

Believers today can greatly benefit from the Book of Job (cf. Rom. 15:4; James 5:11). The Apostle Paul quoted from Job twice—once in Romans 11:35 and once in 1 Corinthians 3:19.

III. The aim

A. The overarching biblical context

The summary purpose of the Bible itself is the reveal God's glory through His plan of redemption/salvation of sinners, which is through faith in Christ, resulting in love (see 2 Tim. 3:14-15; Matt. 22:34-40 [cf. 1 Tim. 1:5]; Eph. 1:6, 12, 14; 1 Pet. 2:9 [Faith; Love; Praise]).

B. The canonical placement within the "Writings" of the Jewish Scriptures

The Hebrew Bible is divided into three main sections: The Law, the Prophets, and the Writings (or Psalms; cf. Luke 24:44). The Writings include the Psalms, Job, Proverbs, Song of Solomon, Ruth, Lamentations, Ecclesiastes, Esther, Daniel, Ezra/Nehemiah, and Chronicles. These books particularly address the "godly individual/remnant" waiting for the consolation of Israel (the Messiah), contrasting with the more corporate and national focus found in the Law and the Prophets.

The Book of Psalms serves as a prayer guide for the godly remnant awaiting the Messiah, while Proverbs provides practical wisdom for the same. Strategically positioned between these two books, the Book of Job contributes to the consolation, perseverance, knowledge, and wisdom of the godly individual/remnant.

Many classify the Book of Job as wisdom literature, which emphasizes the theme and nuances of what it means to fear the Lord (the others being Proverbs and Ecclesiastes). Derek Kidner elaborates on this:

> ... in the Wisdom books the tone of voice and even the speakers have changed. The blunt 'Thou shalt' or 'shalt not' of the Law, and the urgent 'Thus saith the LORD' of the Prophets, are joined now by the cooler comments of the teacher and the often anguished questions of the learner. Where the bulk of the Old Testament calls us simply to obey and to believe, this part of it [the wisdom literature] (chiefly the books we have mentioned, although wisdom is a thread that runs through every part) summons us to think hard as well as humbly; to keep our eyes open, to use our conscience and our common sense, and not to shirk the most disturbing questions (Kidner, *The Wisdom of Proverbs, Job & Ecclesiastes*, IVP, p. 11).

Kidner also comments on the distinctions among Proverbs, Job, and Ecclesiastes:

> But now [the pilgrim] has to relate [his path] to the world at large, to the scene spread out on every side: from what lies right at his feet (shrewdly pointed out in Proverbs) to what is barely visible at the horizon—the dark riddle of how the world is governed (the book of Job) and how it should be valued (Ecclesiastes) (ibid.).

C. Specific biblical references to the man Job elsewhere in Scripture

The man Job is held up as an exemplary example of personal righteousness and perseverance in Ezekiel 14:14-20; James 5:11.

James 5:11 indicates that one of the purposes of Job is to encourage endurance and steadfastness while waiting for God's vindication when suffering; and to confirm that the Lord is full of compassion and is merciful (and inscrutably wise; see Rom. 11:25; 1 Cor. 3:19).

D. Specific references within the text of Job that help in understanding the theme and purpose

Job 1:6-12, 22 (notably, 1:9-11 serves as a central theme verse); 2:1-6, 10; 28:12-28; 42:1-10. *It is essential* to keep **1:9-11** and **42:7** in mind while interpreting the book (see also 1:1, 8; 2:3).

In the poetic dialogue section that comprises much of the book (chapters 4-31), Job makes several startling and to us, troubling statements about God (see, for instance, chapters 10 or 16; 24:12). Bill Cotton notes:

> The reader may often be puzzled by Job's fluctuating emotions. One moment he is plunged into despair, which leaves us convinced he cannot plumb the depths any deeper; the next he is expressing conviction of hope. In chapter 16 we sense a

state of near collapse, in which he portrays God as merciless, as a wild animal set to destroy him, yet by the end of the chapter he is speaking of God as his friend.

We need not be surprised by this. We can so easily forget the very real physical, mental and social catastrophe in which our hero finds himself, and which never leaves him, day or night. We can be so swept up into the argument of Job and his friends that we subconsciously think we are in a comfortable debating chamber.

We must constantly sit with Job on the dung heap. Only there can we understand why his emotions fluctuate so violently. We shall then be amazed that he has any hope at all, why he doesn't just give it up, curse God and die, as his wife had suggested (Cotton, p. 80).

This is why chapters 1-2 and **42:7** are crucial for properly interpreting the poetic dialogues throughout the book.

Job was right, but not self-righteous, to insist on his own integrity, to complain that his suffering was undeserved, and to demand from God Himself an explanation of how His justice was to be found in such unprovoked torture. The book of Job loses its point if the righteousness of Job is not taken as genuine (Andersen, p. 66).

Job may have spoken ignorantly (42:1-6), but he never cursed God, and in the end, God affirmed that Job spoke uprightly in relation to Yahweh (42:7).

The Book of Job illustrates that while wisdom—the fear of the Lord—promises blessings, there exists a place within God's sovereign wisdom for the innocent sufferer. In fact, we learn from the rest of Scripture that God Himself became the innocent Sufferer who would accomplish the greatest good—through suffering the greatest injustice. Theologically, while no man may receive all the suffering he deserves in this life, there can indeed be undeserved suffering, which accomplishes a greater good. This is evident in the lives of Abel, Joseph, Daniel, Jesus, the man born blind in John 9, and those listed in Hebrews 11:35b-38. Not all suffering is a result of personal sin, or a confirmation of the reaping and sowing principle outlined in Proverbs and elsewhere.

> [Job's friends] were uncomfortable when face to face with that which defied the logic of their own theological position. They had to proclaim the truth. They insisted on treating suffering only as a problem to be solved, rather than being willing to cope with the uncertainty of facing its mystery (Atkinson, p. 16).

It is noteworthy that though Satan is mentioned in chapters 1-2 as the main agent of Job's devastation, neither Job nor his counselors blame Satan. They all accept that God is ultimately sovereign over all creation, life, pain, and pleasure. Furthermore, in His speeches to Job, God never explicitly references Satan's role in the events that unfolded (even if Behemoth and Leviathan hint at death and the satanic realm, they are never identified as the agents of Job's suffering). The language of sovereignty is unmistakable, while Satan's hand is the agent of evil (1:8 [the LORD brought up Job], 11-12; 2:3, 5-6 [note the use of "hand" in 1:11-12; 2:5-6]).

Theme

The fear of the Lord is the source of wisdom and comfort in the midst of extreme suffering [contrast Proverbs—The fear of the Lord as wisdom in the midst of everyday life]. See Job 28:28 as the literary center of the Book of Job.

Titles that might capture the main ideas in Book of Job

God's Preface to Proverbs: The fear of the LORD does not depend on the temporal blessings that often accompany fearing the LORD

The Fear of the LORD—Tried and Triumphant

Heavenly Wisdom When All Hell Breaks Loose

The Book of Job—Consolation for Those Who Fear God for Nothing

Purpose

To encourage believers to trust God with the inscrutable pain, tragedies, and suffering that they may face; to endure in hope of God's vindication while waiting for the promised kingdom of God to come; and to confirm that those who fear the Lord, do so not ultimately for the temporal benefits of earthly blessing, but rather because of they find joy and satisfaction in having a real relationship with Him, trusting in His Person and His glorious character, which He graciously reveals to those who believe. As Francis Andersen writes:

> It plumbs the depths of human despair, the anger of moral outrage, and the anguish of desertion by God. From one man's agony it reaches out to the mystery of God, beyond all words and explanations. It is only God Himself who brings Job joy in the end. And, when all is done, the mystery remains. God stands revealed in His hiddenness, an object of terror, adoration and love. And Job stands before him 'like a man' (38:3; 40:7), trusting and satisfied (Andersen, p. 16).

In many respects, the Book of Job addresses the seemingly inexplicable exceptions to the general wisdom principles found in Proverbs. In Proverbs, the virtues and benefits of wisdom are extolled with promises of reward—often interpreted in terms of temporal blessings. In Job, the temporal benefits are replaced by suffering. But as seen in Job, the fear of the Lord does not depend on temporal blessings or even physical health; it hinges on a persevering (though not unquestioning or unwavering) trust in the Lord Himself and His ultimate vindication.

The Book of Job is an epic exploration of the fear of the Lord. It addresses the motivations behind saving faith. "Does Job fear God for nothing?" (1:9)—Yes, Job loved and served Yahweh, for nothing but the satisfaction of knowing Him! Like Peter, he realized he had nowhere else to go, only the Lord has the words of eternal life (cf. John 6:68-69).

The Book of Job does not directly answer "*why*" the righteous suffer (we may not always know, cf. Job 38-42), but it does instruct on "how" the righteous should suffer—even when tried to the limits of endurance—not necessarily without a word, but through prayer and in the end, in submission and persevering faith (adapted largely from unpublished notes taken in Old Testament Survey taught by Keith Essex at The Master's Seminary).

Structure and Outline

Structural Overview

Prologue (1-3)

Job's pain-filled curse: "I wish I had never been born" (3:1-26)

Job's passionate conflict with his three friends (4:1-27:23)

[Job's] poem considering divine wisdom (28:1-28)

Job's perspective concerning his suffering and pledge concerning his innocence, and Elihu's painstaking response (29:1-37:24)

Job's powerful Creator's cross-examination: "Whose wisdom is trustworthy—yours or Mine?"—and Job's proclamation of comfort (38:1-42:6)

Epilogue (42:7-17)

An Overview Outline

Prologue [in prose]: Job's faith withstood the test of total earthly devastation (1:1-2:13) [Devastation]

Dialogue [in poetry]: Job's faith withstood the test of theological debate/speculation and total spiritual isolation (3:1-42:6) [Debate]

Epilogue [in prose]: Job's faith withstood the test of forgiveness and restoration (42:7-17) [Deliverance]

Detailed Outline

<u>Prologue</u>: Job's faith [and God's character] withstood the test of total earthly devastation (1-2)

I. Job's life was characterized by faith and blessing (1:1-5)
    A. Job's character [faith] (1:1)
    B. Job's children [blessing] (1:2)
    C. Job's wealth [blessing] (1:3)
    D. Job's worship and witness [faith] (1:4-5)

II. Job's loss was characterized by divine approval but unimaginable earthly devastation (1:6-2:13)
    A. The heavenly dialogue—part 1 (1:6-12)
        1. The setting (1:6)
        2. The Sovereign questioning (1:7-8)
            a. *The question that revealed the character of the LORD's restless and rebellious servant (v. 7)*

Structure and Outline

      b.   The question that revealed the character of the LORD's righteous servant (v. 8)
- 3. The Satanic accusation (1:9-11)
    - a. Job's faith is mercenary (v. 9)
    - b. Job's God is money and family [earthly blessing] (vv. 10-11)
- 4. The Sovereign permission (1:12)

B. **The horrible loss of Job's children and wealth (1:13-22)**
- 1. The report of total devastation (1:13-19)
    - a. The day of feasting—the day of devastation (v. 13)
    - b. The devastation of Job's wealth and death of Job's children in one day (vv. 14-19)
        - i. A lone survivor recounts the loss of Job's oxen, donkeys and servants (vv. 14-15)
        - ii. A lone survivor recounts the loss of Job's sheep and servants (v. 16)
        - iii. A lone survivor recounts the loss of Job's camels and servants (v. 17)
        - iv. A lone survivor recounts the loss of Job's children (vv. 18-19)
- 2. The response of total devotion (1:20-22)
    - a. Proper expressions of grief (v. 20a)
    - b. Prayer and worship (vv. 20b-21)
    - c. Perseverance in faith (v. 22)

C. **The heavenly dialogue—part 2 (2:1-6)**
- 1. The setting (2:1)
- 2. The Sovereign questioning (2:2-3)
    - a. The question that revealed the character of the LORD's restless servant (v. 2)
    - b. The question that revealed the character of the LORD's righteous servant (v. 3)
- 3. The Satanic accusation (2:4-5)
    - a. Job's faith is still mercenary (v. 4)
    - b. Job's God is his own health (v. 5)
- 4. The Sovereign permission (2:6)

D. **The horrible loss of Job's health (2:7-10)**
- 1. The record of total physical devastation (2:7-8)
- 2. The response of Job's wife (2:9)
- 3. The response of devotion (2:10)

- E. The hopeful, but horrified response of Job's three friends (2:11-13)
  1. Their pedigrees (2:11a)
  2. Their purpose (2:11b)
  3. Their pain and perplexity (2:12)
  4. Their problematic silence (2:13)

<u>Dialogue</u>: Job's faith [and God's character] withstood the test of theological speculation and total spiritual isolation (3:1-42:6)

I. Job's pain-filled curse: "I wish I had never been born" (3:1-26)
   A. I wish I had never been born (3:1-10)
      1. Job cursed the day of his birth—but not his God (3:1)
      2. Let my birthday be destroyed (3:2)
      3. Let my birthday be darkened (3:4-6)
      4. Let my birthday be desolate (3:7)
      5. Let my birthday be damned and devoured (3:8)
      6. Let my birthday be deleted (3:9-10)
   B. I wish I had died at birth or in the womb (3:11-19)
      1. Why did I not die at birth? (3:11-15)
         a. *The poetic question (vv. 11-12)*
         b. *The pleasant hope (vv. 13-15)*
      2. Why did I not die in my mother's womb? (3:16-19)
         a. *The poetic question (vv. 16)*
         b. *The pleasant hope (vv. 17-19)*
   C. I wish I was dead (3:20-26)
      1. Why is life given to one who wishes he was dead? (3:20-23)
         a. *Life is wasted on me (v. 20)*
         b. *Death is treasured by me (vv. 21-22)*
         c. *The way is hidden to me (v. 23)*

Structure and Outline

    2. Why do I wish I was dead?—the sight of food makes me sick, my life is a nightmare come true, and I have no rest (3:24-26)
        a. *The sight of food makes me sick (v. 24)*
        b. *My life is a nightmare come true (v. 25)*
        c. *I have no rest (v. 26)*

II. **Job's passionate conflict with his three friends (4:1-27:23)**
   A. Eliphaz [the charismatic—the most gracious of all the speeches]— Job, you reap what you sow; if you seek God, you will be restored! (4:1-5:27)
      1. Patience, Job—don't get upset, but I feel compelled to speak (4:1-2)
        a. *Don't get upset because of what I'm about to say (vv. 1-2a)*
        b. *Does not your speech demand an answer (v. 2b)*
      2. Practice what you preached (4:3-6)
        a. *Remember how you instructed others (vv. 3-4)*
        b. *Receive instruction—if indeed you fear God and keep your integrity (vv. 5-6)*
      3. Plowing iniquity reaps a harvest of difficulty—remember, you reap what you sow (4:7-11)
        a. *The principle stated and restated (vv. 7-8)*
        b. *The punishment illustrated and re-illustrated (vv. 9-11)*
      4. Pay attention—my teaching comes from private revelation (4:12-16)
        a. *A secret word (v. 12)*
        b. *A special dream in the night (vv. 13-14)*
        c. *A spirit being before my face (vv. 15-16a)*
        d. *A spirit's silence, then a voice (v. 16b)*
      5. Private revelation confirmed depravity without the doctrine of grace—can a creature be righteous before the Creator? (4:17-21)
        a. *God is far more pure than man (v. 17)*
        b. *God is far more pure than angels (v. 18)*
        c. *God is eternal—man perishes (vv. 19-21)*
      6. Perceive who can really deliver man from the sowing and reaping principle—only the sower (5:1-7)

    a. Angels cannot deliver you from the sowing and reaping principle (v. 1)
    b. Anger slays the foolish man, his sons, and his wealth (vv. 2-5)
    c. Affliction doesn't just happen—man is the source of his own trouble (vv. 6-7)
7. Personally, I would seek God because proud men are punished, but the lowly are lifted (5:8-16)
    a. If I were you, I would seek God (v. 8)
    b. If you understand His ways of blessing the lowly and punishing the unrighteous (vv. 9-16)
        i. He can do miracles (v. 9)
        ii. He can providentially provide (v. 10)
        iii. He blesses the lowly (v. 11)
        iv. He punishes the shrewd (vv. 12-14)
        v. He rescues the helpless—and shuts the mouth of the unrighteous (vv. 15-16)
8. Prosperity and protection will be restored if you repent (5:17-27)
    a. Do not despise divine discipline (v. 17)
    b. Do not forget the benefits of repentance and turning to God's reproof (vv. 18-26)
        i. If you repent, He will bring relief (v. 18)
        ii. If you repent, He will deliver you from all trouble (v. 19)
        iii. If you repent, He will redeem you from death (vv. 20-22)
        iv. If you repent, He will bring you prosperity, security and long life (vv. 23-26)
    c. Do not reject the testimony of the wise (v. 27)
B. Job—What a disappointment you have been; Why me, O God? (6:1-7:21)
    1. I've spoken rashly because of the greatness of my torment and trial (6:1-7)
        a. You can't even fathom the grief and calamities that I've endured—therefore, my words have been rash (vv. 1-4)
            i. Job's answer (v. 1)
            ii. Weighed on the scales (v. 2)
            iii. Weightier than the sand of the seas (v. 3)
            iv. Wounded by the arrows of God (v. 4)
        b. Do I not have a reason to cry out? (v. 5)
        c. Perhaps voicing my complaint will make these things easier to swallow (vv. 6-7)

Structure and Outline

2. I long for God to answer my prayer for death (6:8-10)
   a. *My constant longing is for death (vv. 8-9)*
   b. *My comfort and concern is my faith (v. 10)*
3. My spiritual strength and hope are failing (6:11-13)
   a. *How can I go on? (v. 11)*
   b. *Am I not just flesh and bones? [I don't have the strength] (v. 12)*
   c. *Where is my help? (v. 13)*
4. A loyal friend is faithful, but you are like a dried-up river in summer [false hope and a great disappointment] (6:14-21)
   a. *A faithful friend should strengthen one's fear of the Almighty (v. 14)*
   b. *You have offered false hope (vv. 15-21)*
      i. The picture of a dried-up river in summer (vv. 15-18)
      ii. The picture of disappointed travelers (vv. 19-20)
      iii. The picture directly applied (v. 21)
5. I haven't asked you to "help me" (6:22-23)
   a. *I haven't asked you to help me financially (v. 22)*
   b. *I haven't asked you to deliver me (v. 23)*
6. You speak beautifully, but show me my sin [other than the frustrated words of a desperate man] (6:24-30)
   a. *Show me my sin (v. 24)*
   b. *What does your argument prove (v. 25)*
   c. *Are you so heartless that you would condemn me for words spoken in desperation (vv. 26-27)*
   d. *Look at me; I'm telling you the truth; have mercy on me (vv. 28-30)*
7. My days are like an endless cycle of futility; my flesh is rotting; my future is hopeless—I will voice my anguish (7:1-11)
   a. *My futility is experienced day after day (vv. 1-3a)*
   b. *My futility is experienced night after night (vv. 3b-4)*
   c. *My flesh is rotting (v. 5)*
   d. *My future is hopeless (vv. 6-10)*
      i. Soon the thread will run out (v. 6)
      ii. Soon the breath will be gone (v. 7)
      iii. Soon the eyes will not see (v. 8)

iv. Soon the cloud will dissipate (v. 9)
v. Soon the house will be empty (v. 10)
vi. So, I will not restrain my mouth (v. 11)

8. Who am I, O God? And what have I done that You have singled me out? (7:12-21)
   a. *Am I an unruly monster that you must constrain me? (v. 12)*
   b. *Leave me alone, I am nothing (vv. 13-19)*
      i. You terrorize me at night (vv. 13-14)
      ii. You have made death preferable to pain (v. 15)
      iii. Leave me alone, for my days are but a breath (v. 16)
      iv. What is man that you are concerned about him? (vv. 17-18)
      v. Leave me alone (v. 19)
   c. *How have I sinned? What have I done to You? Why do you not pardon my transgression? (vv. 20-21)*

C. Bildad [the religious traditionalist]—Job, repent! (8:1-22)
   1. You're a windbag, Job—shut up! (8:1-2)
   2. God is just—we must assume your family sinned and you've sinned; repent and be restored! (8:3-7)
      a. *God is just (v. 3)*
      b. *God dealt justly with your children (v. 4)*
      c. *God will deal compassionately and restore you if you seek Him (vv. 5-7)*
         i. If you seek God and beg for His compassion (v. 5)
         ii. If you are clean and upright (v. 6a)
         iii. Then He will bless you abundantly (vv. 6b-7)
   3. Wisdom from past generations teaches us—judgment comes to those who forget God (8:8-19)
      a. *The past generations confirm what I'm about to say (vv. 8-10)*
      b. *The prosperity of the godless is fragile, and is soon destroyed (vv. 11-19)*
         i. The papyrus soon dries out and withers (vv. 11-12)
         ii. So are the paths of all who forget God (v. 13)
         iii. Those who forget God experience a fragile prosperity and confidence, but are soon destroyed and forgotten (vv. 14-19)
            aa. The illustration of a spider's web (vv. 14-15)
            bb. The illustration of a plant—uprooted and forgotten (vv. 16-19)

4. Repent and you will be lifted up (8:20-22)
   a. God will not reject integrity—nor will He support evildoers (v. 20)
   b. God will restore your blessings—if you repent (vv. 21-22a)
   c. God will destroy the wicked (vv. 22b)

D. Job—I need an Umpire! God, what's going on? (9:1-10:22)
   1. How can a man be vindicated before God? (9:1-20)
      a. I know that God is just—but how can a man be vindicated before God? (vv. 1-2)
      b. If one wanted a legal hearing with Him—how would that go? (vv. 3-20)
         i. A man would have no answer (v. 3)
         ii. God is too skillful and too strong—who can safely argue with Him? (vv. 4-10)
            aa. The point stated (v. 4)
            bb. The point illustrated (vv. 5-10)
         iii. God is beyond comprehension (v. 11)
         iv. God is sovereign and thus who can question Him? (vv. 12-13)
            aa. His sovereignty is unquestionable (v. 12)
            bb. His sovereignty extends even over evil (v. 13)
         v. How could I then answer Him? (v. 14)
         vi. How could I ask for mercy—when I'm seeking vindication? (v. 15)
         vii. How could I believe He was even really listening to my case? (vv. 16-18)
            aa. The point stated (v. 16)
            bb. The picture of divine indifference (vv. 17-18)
         viii. How can I maintain my righteousness before Him? (vv. 19-20)
            aa. He is too strong for me to make my case before Him (v. 19a)
            bb. He is the Judge, so how can I cross-examine Him? (v. 19b)
            cc. He would hold anything I would say against me (v. 20)
   2. Let's consider God's justice in this world (9:21-24)
      a. It may cost me my life—but I plainly declare: I am guiltless (v. 21)
      b. Further—in God's sovereignty, He destroys the guiltless and the wicked (vv. 22-24)

3. Righteousness seems futile (9:25-31)
   a. My time is running out—and there is no court date in sight (vv. 25-26)
   b. If I dropped my case—You would still hold me guilty (vv. 27-31)
4. If only there were a mediator (9:32-35)
   a. The difference between a man and God makes vindication seem impossible (v. 32)
   b. The desire for mediator/arbiter expressed (v. 33)
   c. The desire for God's discipline and dread to be removed (v. 34)
   d. The direct communication that would occur if a mediator were found (v. 35)
5. God—why do You oppress me when You know I'm not wicked? (10:1-7)
   a. I will give full vent to my complaint, whatever the consequences (v. 1)
   b. Why do You contend with me? (v. 2)
   c. Is it right for You to oppress me and approve the schemes of the wicked? (v. 3)
   d. Are You not all-knowing? (vv. 4-6)
   e. You know I'm not guilty—yet there is no deliverance from Your hand (v. 7)
6. God—did You create me to destroy me? (10:8-17ab)
   a. The question posed (vv. 8-9)
   b. The creation of Job pictured (vv. 10-12)
      i. Conception (v. 10)
      ii. Clothed in skin, flesh—knit with bones and sinews (v. 11)
      iii. Created and cared for by God (v. 12)
   c. The concealed plan of God to destroy Job (vv. 13-17ab)
      i. Job's speculation assumed (v. 13)
      ii. Job's guilt would be punished (v. 14)
      iii. Job's righteousness challenged (vv. 15-16)
      iv. Job's counselors/accusers (v. 17ab)
7. God—leave me alone so that I may have some peace before I die! (vv. 17c-22)
   a. God—I still wish I had died in the womb (vv. 17c-19)
   b. God—withdraw from me that I may have some peace before I die (vv. 20-22)

Structure and Outline

E. Zophar [the fire and brimstone preacher]— Job, repent; God is incomprehensibly great and wise! (11:1-20)
   1. I must answer a fool as his folly deserves, lest he be wise in his own eyes (11:1-3)
      a. *Your multitude of words cannot go unanswered (vv. 1-2)*
      b. *Your boasts and scoffing deserve a rebuke (v. 3)*
   2. You're getting less than you deserve (11:4-6)
      a. *You claim to be innocent before God (v. 4)*
      b. *You would be surprised if God were to speak concerning you (vv. 5-6ab)*
      c. *You need to know that you're getting less than you deserve (v. 6c)*
   3. Do you really think you can comprehend the depths of God's greatness and wisdom? (11:7-12)
      a. *God's wisdom is beyond you (vv. 7-9)*
         i. You can't discover the deep things of God (v. 7)
         ii. You can't ascend to the heavens or plumb the depths of Sheol (v. 8)
         iii. You can't measure it by earth or sea (v. 9)
      b. *God's ways are beyond you (vv. 10-12)*
         i. You must understand that He does what He pleases (v. 10)
         ii. You must understand that He sees your sin (v. 11)
         iii. You must understand that you are an empty-headed, stubborn fool (v. 12)
   4. Repent and be blessed—don't, and you will die (11:13-20)
      a. *If you repent you will be blessed (vv. 13-19)*
         i. If you will seek God and pray to Him (v. 13)
         ii. If you will put away iniquity and sin (v. 14)
         iii. Then you will not be afraid (v. 15)
         iv. Then you will forget your trouble (v. 16)
         v. Then you will experience brighter days (v. 17)
         vi. Then you will experience rest and security (vv. 18-19a)
         vii. Then you will experience prosperity (v. 19b)
      b. *If you don't repent, you will die without hope (v. 20)*

F. Job—God is indeed incomprehensibly great and wise; thanks for the help; but I'm ridiculed and the wicked prosper! (12:1-14:22)
   1. Tell me something I don't already know—O wise ones (12:1-3)
      a. *What would the world do without your wisdom? (vv. 1-2)*
      b. *What have you said that I don't already know? (v. 3)*
   2. I am ridiculed and the wicked prosper (12:4-6)
      a. *I am a laughingstock for trusting God (v. 4)*
      b. *I am held in contempt by you who are at ease (v. 5)*
      c. *I declare that the wicked do prosper (v. 6)*
   3. Nature recognizes God's sovereignty—and so should you (12:7-12)
      a. *Ask the animals to teach you [Remember, I'm a donkey] (vv. 7-8)*
      b. *All creation knows that God is sovereign and does as He pleases (vv. 9-10)*
      c. *Are you listening and trying to understand what I'm saying? (v. 11)*
      d. *Age should bring wisdom [but you have proved otherwise] (v. 12)*
   4. I too can speak eloquently of God's infinite power, wisdom and sovereignty (12:13-25)
      a. *God is the source of wisdom, strength, counsel, and understanding (v. 13)*
      b. *God is the sovereign Whom no one can withstand (vv. 14-25)*
         i. He is sovereign over circumstances, which cannot be reversed (v. 14)
         ii. He is sovereign over the weather (v. 15)
         iii. He is sovereign over the deceived and the deceiver (v. 16)
         iv. He is sovereign over making fools of the wise (v. 17)
         v. He is sovereign over the decisions of kings (v. 18)
         vi. He is sovereign over who is honored and dishonored (v. 19)
         vii. He is sovereign over advisers (v. 20)
         viii. He is sovereign over the mighty (v. 21)
         ix. He is sovereign over mysteries (v. 22)
         x. He is sovereign over the rise and fall of nations (v. 23)
         xi. He is sovereign over the bad decisions of the rulers of the earth (vv. 24-25)

5. **I understand these things—therefore, I want a hearing with Him (13:1-3)**
    a. *I have witnessed the inscrutable wisdom and unrivaled sovereignty of God (v. 1)*
    b. *I know what you know about God's wisdom and power (v. 2)*
    c. *I still want to speak to and argue my case with God (v. 3)*
6. **You are worthless counselors who distort the truth in the name of God (13:4-12)**
    a. *You misrepresent the truth and mistreat your patients (v. 4)*
    b. *You ought to stay quiet and actually listen to my argument (vv. 5-6)*
    c. *You cannot win favor with God by misrepresenting justice to make Him look better (vv. 7-11)*
        i.   Will you misrepresent justice for God's sake? (vv. 7-8)
        ii. Will it be well with you when He examines you? (v. 9)
        iii. Will not He reprove you? (vv. 10-11)
    d. *You offer worthless advice (v. 12)*
7. **It may cost my life, but I will maintain my righteousness (13:13-19)**
    a. *Be quiet so I can speak—then I will face the consequences (v. 13)*
    b. *Why would I speak like this if I were not innocent? (v. 14)*
    c. *My hope is in God—no matter the consequences—this will be my salvation; a godless man has no such hope (vv. 15-19)*
        i.   My hope issues in the confidence to argue my ways (v. 15)
        ii. My salvation (Yeshua) is in Him—such is not the confidence of the godless (v. 16)
        iii. My case is prepared—listen carefully; I will be vindicated (vv. 17-18)
        iv. My mouth will be silent and I will die if someone can successfully prosecute the charges against me (v. 19)
8. **God—please show me my sin; why am I treated like Your enemy? (13:20-27)**
    a. *You must enable our relationship (vv. 20-22)*
        i.   Only You can change the reality that I'm terrified of You (vv. 20-21)
        ii. Only You can open the avenues of our communication (v. 22)
    b. *You must reveal why our relationship seems broken (vv. 23-24)*
        i.   How have I sinned? (v. 23)

Structure and Outline

        ii. Why is our relationship broken? (v. 24)
    c. *You must see what you've done to me (vv. 25-27)*
        i. I am frail and at your mercy (v. 25)
        ii. I am suffering bitterly (v. 26)
        iii. I am a prisoner of your sovereignty (v. 27)

9. **Life is hard and then you die! What else is there? (13:28-14:12)**
   a. *The brevity of life (13:28-14:6)*
      i. Man wears out (v. 28)
      ii. Man is short-lived and full of turmoil (v. 1)
      iii. He is like a flower or a shadow (v. 2)
      iv. You are sovereign over this (vv. 3-6)
         aa. You are the Judge (v. 3)
         bb. Man is depraved (v. 4)
         cc. You are Sovereign (v. 5)
         dd. You are Master (v. 6)
   b. *The finality of death (vv. 7-12)*
      i. A tree that is cut off can grow back (vv. 7-9)
      ii. A man does not grow back, or have a new start after he dies (vv. 10-12)

10. **Oh, to die and live again—I will wait for it (14:13-17)**
    a. *Job's honest longing for the refuge of the grave (v. 13)*
    b. *Job's hopeful longing for the resurrection from the grave (vv. 14-17)*
       i. I will wait for my change (v. 14)
       ii. You will call, and I will answer You (v. 15)
       iii. You will pay attention to my steps, but not my sin (v. 16)
       iv. You will put an end to my sin (v. 17)

11. **But in this life, there is nothing but hopelessness and the inevitable (14:18-22)**
    a. *The inevitable illustrated (vv. 18-19a)*
       i. Mountains wither (v. 18)
       ii. Stones wear away (v. 19ab)
    b. *The inevitable declared (vv. 19bc-22)*
       i. Hope is this life is inevitably destroyed (v. 19c)
       ii. Death is the inevitable end of this life (vv. 20-22)
          aa. At death, a man departs and decays (v. 20)
          bb. At death, a man does not know his legacy on earth (v. 21)

cc. At death, a man does not know the pain of others—only his own (v. 22)

G. Eliphaz—Who do you think you are, Job? (15:1-35)

1. Job, you're a fool whose own words prove the wickedness of your heart (15:1-6)
   a. *Does a wise man belch hot air—and argue with vain and unprofitable words? (vv. 1-3)*
      i. Eliphaz's second answer (v. 1)
      ii. Eliphaz's vulgar analogy—you excrete hot air from your belly (v. 2)
      iii. Eliphaz's assessment of Job's argument—you use vain and unprofitable words (v. 3)
   b. *Your words do away with the pursuit of proper worship—and thus they reveal your guilt (vv. 4-6)*
      i. You distract from the fear of God, and proper perspective of God (v. 4)
      ii. You testify to your own guilt by the way you speak (vv. 5-6)

2. Who do you think you are to reject God's wisdom through us? (15:7-16)
   a. *Are you somehow wiser than everyone else in the world? (vv. 7-10)*
      i. Have you lived longer than any other person ever? (v. 7)
      ii. Is wisdom limited to you? (v. 8)
      iii. What do you know that we do not know? (v. 9)
      iv. We are older and wiser than you (v. 10)
   b. *Is God's wisdom [as spoken through us] not enough for you? (vv. 11-13)*
      i. Are not our words of consolation adequate to minister to you? (v. 11)
      ii. Why do you turn to anger and speak such foolishness (vv. 12-13)
   c. *How can you claim to be righteous in light of the doctrine of depravity? (vv. 14-16)*
      i. Men are born sinners (v. 14)
      ii. God is holier than you could ever imagine; therefore how could a man be pure in his sight? (vv. 15-16)

3. Wisdom tells us that the wicked inevitably suffer, even if they seem to prosper for a time—therefore repent of your vain hope (15:17-35)
   a. *I will speak wisdom confirmed by men of old (vv. 17-19)*

      b. *The wicked inevitably suffer for their sins (vv. 20-35)*
          i. The wicked is tormented now because of his rebellion against God (vv. 20-26)
              aa. He is tormented by fear (vv. 20-22)
              bb. He is tormented by the reality that today is all he has, because he is an enemy of God (vv. 23-25)
              cc. He is too stubborn to repent—rather he continues to fight God (v. 26)
          ii. The wicked will inevitably suffer for their sins (vv. 27-35)
              aa. He may have enjoyed the prosperity of the wicked for a time (v. 27)
              bb. He will not escape temporal devastation (vv. 28-30)

                  His wealth will not endure (vv. 28-29)

                  He will not escape the darkness (v. 30)

              cc. He must repent of his false trust and self-deception—or suffer an untimely death (vv. 31-35)

                  Repent of your empty hope (v. 31)

                  Or emptiness and an early death will be your reward (vv. 31c-33)

                  The godless have no children and lose all their wealth, because they are pregnant with iniquity (vv. 34-35)

H. **Job—God has forsaken me, yet He alone is my witness that I am innocent (16:1-17:16)**
    1. You are sorry comforters (16:1-5)
      a. *Why do you keep repeating yourselves? (vv. 1-3)*
          i. I've heard your troublesome counsel before (vv. 1-2)
          ii. When will you stop talking? (v. 3)
      b. *If the tables were turned, I could talk like you—or I could strengthen and comfort (vv. 4-5)*
          i. If I were in your place (and you in mine), I too could be condescending and judgmental (v. 4)
          ii. Or I could strengthen and comfort you (v. 5)
    2. God has attacked me though I am innocent (16:6-17)
      a. *Whether I speak or I hold back, I find no relief from my pain (v. 6)*
      b. *God, You have worn me out and wrecked my family (v. 7)*
      c. *God, You have emaciated my body (v. 8)*
      d. *He has become my adversary (v. 9)*
      e. *God has handed me over to those who mock and oppose me (vv. 10-11)*

Structure and Outline

    f.   God has declared war on me (vv. 12-14)

    g.   I have humbled myself and mourned—though I am innocent and my prayer is pure (vv. 15-17)

3. **Yet God [or a Heavenly Mediator who is a companion of God's] is my only Advocate and hope (16:18-21)**
    a. I don't want my case to be forgotten, even if I die (v. 18)
    b. Yet even now my Witness and Advocate is in heaven (vv. 19-21)
        i. Job's confidence—my Witness is in heaven and my Advocate on high (v. 19)
        ii. Job's case—my friends scoff; God is my only recourse (v. 20)
        iii. Job's desire—that a man might plead with God as with his neighbor (v. 21)

4. **God—defend me from these mockers (16:22-17:5)**
    a. The cemetery is not far off (16:22-17:1)
    b. The contempt of mockers is upon me (v. 2)
    c. God—only You can ultimately prove my innocence (vv. 3-5)
        i. Only You can verify my innocence (v. 3)
        ii. But You have kept their heart from understanding (v. 4)
        iii. Yet they are in danger of judgment (v. 5)

5. **The righteous will hold to his way, though mockers may mock, and all hope seems gone (17:6-16)**
    a. In God's sovereignty, I am held in contempt (vv. 6-8)
        i. I am a byword and the object of scorn (v. 6)
        ii. I am grieved and diseased (v. 7)
        iii. I should be defended by the upright (v. 8)
    b. Nevertheless, the righteous will hold his way and grow stronger—though mockers may continue to mock, and all hope seems gone (vv. 9-16)
        i. The righteous will hold his way and grow ever stronger (v. 9)
        ii. Take another shot at me, for I do not find a wise man among you (v. 10)
        iii. My life and hopes are torn apart, and they keep trying to tell me that everything will be fine if I repent (vv. 11-12)
        iv. Even if I long for death, I will not give up my hope of God's vindication (vv. 13-16)

Structure and Outline

I. Bildad—Let me tell you again! (18:1-21)
   1. Stop talking and start thinking (18:1-4)
      a. How long before you stop talking and show some sense? (vv. 1-2)
      b. Why do you regard us as stupid animals, rather than wise counselors? (v. 3)
      c. You're destroying yourself in anger (v. 4a)
      d. Do you expect the world to be turned upside down for you? (v. 4b)
   2. The wicked live in terror and die desolate [so think about it, Job, why are you suffering?] (18:5-22)
      a. The wicked man is terrorized (vv. 5-14)
         i. In darkness (vv. 5-6)
         ii. In danger of stumbling and being captured (vv. 7-10)
         iii. In fear, failing health, and terror (vv. 11-14)
      b. The wicked man and his house perish (vv. 15-22)
         i. No possessions (v. 15)
         ii. No hope (v. 16)
         iii. No honor (v. 17)
         iv. No fellowship (v. 18)
         v. No offspring (v. 19)
         vi. Only infamy (v. 20)
         v. Such are the wicked, who do not know God (v. 21)

J. Job—I am rejected, but not forever (19:1-29)
   1. You are against me without shame (19:1-6)
      a. How long will you torment me with words? (vv. 1-3)
      b. Even if I've mistakenly sinned, it's my error—not yours (v. 4)
      c. If you seek to exalt yourselves and make my humiliation an argument against me—then know that God has bent me and gone to battle against me (vv. 5-6)
   2. God is against me (19:7-12)
      a. He does not answer my prayer for help (v. 7)
      b. He has considered me His enemy (vv. 8-12)
         i. No escape (v. 8)
         ii. No honor (v. 9)
         iii. No hope (v. 10)
         iv. No escape (vv. 11-12)

3. Have mercy—everyone has forsaken me (19:13-22)
   a. *Everyone has forsaken me (vv. 13-19)*
      i. Relatives and friends (vv. 13-14)
      ii. Servants (vv. 15-16)
      iii. Wife and brothers (vv. 17)
      iv. Children (vv. 18)
      v. Loved ones (vv. 19)
   b. *Have mercy, O you my friends (vv. 20-22)*
      i. I'm wasting away—pity me, O you my friends (vv. 20-21)
      ii. Why do you persecute me, and are not satisfied with my current distress? (v. 22)
4. Write it down forever. Be careful, my friends—my Redeemer lives, and He will bring justice (19:23-29)
   a. *Job's conviction and confession of faith/hope (vv. 23-27)*
      i. Write it on my tombstone forever (vv. 23-24)
      ii. I know my Redeemer lives, and in the end He will take His stand on the earth (v. 25)
      iii. Even after I die—in my flesh, I will see God; oh, how I long for it (vv. 26-27)
   b. *Job's caution to his accusers (vv. 28-29)*
      i. If you condemn me for all of this (v. 28)
      ii. Be afraid of being condemned yourselves (v. 29)

K. Zophar—The wicked prosper for only a moment, then they get what they deserve (20:1-29)
   1. I must speak wisdom though you insult me (20:1-3)
      a. *I am concerned and thus compelled to answer (vv. 1-2)*
      b. *I am insulted but will answer with insight (v. 3)*
   2. The wicked triumph only for a moment then they get what they deserve (20:4-29)
      a. *The wicked may rejoice for a time, but their triumph is short (vv. 4-5)*
      b. *The wicked may be exalted beyond measure, but he will soon come to an ignoble end (vv. 6-11)*
         i. Though he is momentarily exalted, he will be destroyed like his own dung (vv. 6-7)
         ii. He will vanish like a vision or dream in the night (vv. 8-9)
         iii. He will leave a legacy to his sons of having to pay restitution for his wickedness (v. 10)
         iv. He will die and lie down in the dust—no matter how strong he was (v. 11)

- c. The wicked loves ill-gotten gain, but will not be able to enjoy the spoil (vv. 12-19)
    - i. He savors his wicked ways (vv. 12-13)
    - ii. He is poisoned and sickened by them (vv. 14-16)
    - iii. He cannot enjoy the wealth he has attained through his wickedness (vv. 17-19)
- d. The wicked will be fully repaid for his wickedness (vv. 20-29)
    - i. He has no enduring satisfaction (vv. 20-21)
    - ii. He will be suddenly judged, in the midst of his success (vv. 22-23)
    - iii. He may run, but he will not be able to escape (vv. 24-25)
    - iv. He will lose his wealth, his health, and his family in the day of God's anger (vv. 26-28)
    - v. He will be fully repaid by God (vv. 29)

L. Job—face reality (21:1-34)
  1. Consider my condition and what I've been through (21:1-6)
      - a. Since you are so concerned, let this be your comfort (vv. 1-3)
          - i. Listen to my words and let this be your comfort (vv. 1-2)
          - ii. Let me speak and then you can mock (v. 3)
      - b. Stop talking and look at me—how have I offended you? (vv. 4-6)
          - i. Is my rambling against man? (v. 4)
          - ii. Is not my condition enough to make you shut up? (v. 5)
          - iii. Contemplating the reality about the prosperity of the wicked makes me disturbed and horrified (v. 6)
  2. Actually, the wicked do prosper in spite of their rebellion against God (21:7-16)
      - a. My question is—Why do the wicked live, grow old, and become powerful? (v. 7)
      - b. My observation is—The wicked do live long and prosper (vv. 8-15)
          - i. They see their children established (v. 8)
          - ii. They are safe from fear (v. 9)
          - iii. They prosper materially (v. 10)
          - iv. They have fun and enjoy their lives (vv. 11-12)
          - v. They don't suffer in life or death (v. 13)
          - vi. They reject God and yet they prosper (vv. 14-15)
      - c. My perspective is—I still do not envy the wicked, and their prosperity did not come from their own hand (v. 16)

3. Some live and die in prosperity, some die bereft—God's wisdom is inscrutable (21:17-26)
   a. Do the wicked always suffer in this life? (vv. 17-18)
   b. Do wicked people care if after they die their sons must make restitution for their iniquity? (vv. 19-21)
      i. A proverb asserted and challenged (v. 19)
      ii. What does a wicked man care about his children suffering once he's gone?—may he himself drink of the wrath of the Almighty (vv. 20-21)
   b. Do people have the ability to instruct God on how He deals with the wicked? (v. 22)
   c. One dies in prosperity and another in pain—but both die (vv. 23-26)
4. Face reality, friends, sinners don't always suffer in this life (21:27-33)
   a. It is clear what you think about me—that I'm wicked (vv. 27-28)
   b. But ask those who have seen the world if the wicked always suffered (vv. 29-33)
      i. Recognize the testimony of those who have been around (v. 29)
      ii. The wicked is kept from calamity [or perhaps he is reserved for judgment after death] (v. 30)
      iii. The wicked does not always get what he deserves (v. 31)
      iv. In fact, he often gets a glorious funeral when he does die (vv. 32-33)
   b. Your counsel has proved comfortless and false (21:34)

M. Eliphaz—I've heard enough/Repent and Be Saved (22:1-30)
   1. Your "righteousness" and "integrity" are of no concern to God (22:1-3)
      a. Man's power and wisdom is of no benefit to God (vv. 1-2)
      b. Man's righteousness or integrity is of no benefit to God (v. 3)
   2. You are a despicably wicked man, Job—that's why you are suffering (22:4-11)
      a. Is it because of your reverence that you are suffering? (v. 4)
      b. No, it is because of your endless iniquities (vv. 5-9)
         i. The statement (v. 5)
         ii. The sampling of iniquity (vv. 6-9)
      c. This is why you are suffering, terrified, in darkness and danger (vv. 10-11)

3. You don't seem to think that God sees your sin (22:12-20)
   a. *Do you think God doesn't see? (vv. 12-14)*
   b. *Do you continue to ignore the evidence that God sees and judges the wicked? (vv. 15-16)*
   c. *Will you think lightly of the kindness and common grace He extends to the wicked? (vv. 17-18)*
   d. *The righteous rejoice when the wicked are judged (vv. 19-20)*
4. Repent and know the blessings of God! (22:21-30)
   a. *Repent now, and God Himself will be your treasure (vv. 21-25)*
      i. Submit to God and good will come to you (v. 21)
      ii. Listen to God's Word and repent—and you will be restored (vv. 22-23)
      iii. Regard riches as nothing compared to knowing God and He will be your treasure (vv. 24-25)
   b. *Receive the blessings of repentance (vv. 26-30)*
      i. You will have a relationship with God (vv. 26-27)
      ii. He will direct your paths in blessing (v. 28)
      iii. You will become a minister of blessing and salvation for others (vv. 29-30)

N. Job—I can't find God, but I believe; I'm terrified but I speak (23:1-24:25)
   1. If I could find God, I would argue my case—but I can't find Him (23:1-9)
      a. *I am still contentious in my complaint (vv. 1-2)*
      b. *I wish I could argue my case before God (vv. 3-5)*
      c. *I know He would pay attention, and I would be delivered (vv. 6-7)*
      d. *But I can't find Him (vv. 8-9)*
   2. I believe God knows what He's doing, and I will ultimately be vindicated (23:10-12)
      a. *God knows what He's doing [and where I'm going], and I will shine forth as gold (v. 10)*
      b. *I have walked in His ways (v. 11)*
      c. *I have delighted in His Word (v. 12)*
   3. God does whatever He pleases, and it terrifies me (23:13-17)
      a. *God is sovereign—He does whatever He wants and does not turn from it (vv. 13-14)*
      b. *God's sovereign presence would terrify me (v. 15)*

Structure and Outline

      c. *God's sovereign ways terrify me now—but I am not cut off (vv. 16-17)*

  4. Why do the wicked prosper and others get oppressed—and God doesn't seem to do anything? (24:1-17)

      a. *Why doesn't God set a court date, so His people will see Him act in judgment? (v. 1)*

      b. *Look at the injustice (vv. 2-12)*

          i. Thieves and oppressors (vv. 2-3)

          ii. The plight of those they oppress (vv. 4-8)

          iii. Slave masters (v. 9)

          iv. The plight of those they enslave (vv. 10-12)

      c. *Look at the iniquity (vv. 13-17)*

          i. Rebels against the light (v. 13)

          ii. The murderer (v. 14)

          iii. The adulterer (v. 15)

          iv. They do not know the light, but operate in darkness (vv. 16-17)

  5. [But you say,] "The wicked get their just reward" (24:18-24)

      a. *The wicked are short-lived and not blessed (v. 18)*

      b. *The wicked are overtaken by death (vv. 19-20)*

      c. *The wicked may feel secure in their wickedness, but God sees and cuts them off (vv. 21-24)*

          i. The violence of the wicked (v. 21)

          ii. The justice of God [or the violence of the wicked continued] (vv. 22-23)

          iii. The justice of God in regard to the wicked summarized (v. 24)

  6. Who can prove me a liar [that God's friends don't always get to see Him act in judgment, but He will judge the wicked]? (24:25; cf. 24:1)

O. **Bildad—God is infinitely majestic, and man is a filthy maggot (25:1-6)**

  1. God is infinitely majestic (25:1-3)

      a. *God's rule is absolute and awesome (vv. 1-2)*

      b. *God's resources are limitless and His glory universal (v. 3)*

  2. Man is a filthy maggot (25:4-6)

      a. *How then can a man be just with God? (v. 4)*

- b. Heavenly light in the darkness cannot begin to compare with God's glory—much less, man who is a maggot by comparison (vv. 5-6)

P. Job—Thanks for the help; I know God is awesome; I swear I am innocent; and may God do to my enemies as you have described (26:1-27:23)
  1. How in the world has your instruction helped, and where in the world did it come from? (26:1-4)
     a. How in the world has your instruction helped? (vv. 1-3)
     b. Where in the world has your instruction come from? (v. 4)
  2. I too can describe God's amazing power and majesty (26:5-14)
     a. God's power and majesty extends not only in the heavens, but also in Sheol (vv. 5-6)
     b. God created space, the atmosphere, and the celestial phenomena (vv. 7-10)
     c. God controls the storms and their origins (vv. 11-13)
     d. God's power and majesty are beyond our full comprehension (v. 14)
  3. I know I am innocent, and will go to my grave holding fast my integrity (27:1-6)
     a. Job continued (v. 1)
     b. Job continued to maintain his innocence (vv. 2-6)
        i. Under oath (v. 2)
        ii. For as long as I live (v. 3)
        iii. In utter honesty (v. 4)
        iv. I maintain my righteousness with a clean conscience (vv. 5-6)
  4. May God do to my enemy as you have all described (27:7-23)
     a. May my enemy be as the wicked (vv. 7-10)
        i. The imprecation (v. 7)
        ii. The implications (vv. 8-10)
           aa. The wicked will not escape God's justice (vv. 8-9)
           bb. The wicked have no relationship with God (v. 10)
     b. May I remind you of what you have seen concerning the end of the wicked (vv. 11-23)
        i. This you have seen—it is your instruction and mine to you (vv. 11-12)

ii. This is the portion of the wicked man from God (vv. 13-23)
   aa. The wicked man will have an inheritance from the Almighty (v. 13)
   bb. The wicked man will lose all his family (vv. 14-15)
   cc. The wicked man will lose all his wealth (vv. 16-19)
   dd. The wicked man will be taken away in sudden terror (vv. 20-22)
   ee. The wicked man will be the object of ridicule and scorn [or perhaps the wind claps its hands and hisses him from his place] (vv. 23)

III. Job's poem considering divine wisdom (28:1-28)

A. Wisdom is harder to obtain than precious metals and priceless jewels [God's wisdom is beyond human effort and ingenuity] (28:1-12)

1. Man, through human effort and ingenuity, has found the source of all that it precious in the temporal realm (28:1-11)
   a. *The minerals man seeks after (vv. 1-2)*
      i. Silver and gold (v. 1)
      ii. Iron and copper (v. 2)
   b. *The mines where treasure is found (vv. 3-6)*
      i. The mine and mining pictured (vv. 3-4)
      ii. The produce of the earth (vv. 5-6)
   c. *The manmade genius of finding such treasures (vv. 7-11)*
      i. The keenest and strongest animals could never find such hidden treasures (vv. 7-8)
      ii. The cleverness and strength of man is incredible in finding precious, earthly treasure (vv. 9-11)
2. Man, through human effort and ingenuity, has not found the source of wisdom (28:12)

B. Wisdom is more valuable than precious metals and priceless jewels [God's wisdom is beyond price] (28:13-22)

1. The price of wisdom is beyond human comprehension (28:13-19)
   a. *Man does not know wisdom's value (vv. 13-14)*
      i. Wisdom's value is not understood (v. 13a)
      ii. Wisdom is not found in man's realm—in earth or sea (vv. 13b-14)

  b. *Nothing can compare to the surpassing value of true wisdom (vv. 15-19)*
    i. Not pure gold nor the price of silver (v. 15)
    ii. Not the gold of Ophir, onyx, or sapphire (v. 16)
    iii. Not gold or glass, or gold jewelry (v. 17)
    iv. Not coral and crystal or pearls (v. 18)
    v. Not topaz from Ethiopia or pure gold (v. 19)
 2. The place of wisdom is beyond human discovery (28:20-22)
  a. *Where does wisdom come from? (v. 20; cf. v. 12)*
  b. *The answer is not found with the living, even from the vantage point of the birds of the sky (v. 21)*
  c. *The answer is not found in death—though there is a report of it there (v. 22)*

C. Wisdom is found only in God, and known only in the fear of the Lord [God's wisdom is begotten only in God, and revealed to man as inextricably bound to the fear of the Lord] (28:23-28)
 1. Wisdom is known by God alone (28:23-27)
  a. *The reality—God knows wisdom (v. 23)*
  b. *The reasons (vv. 24-27)*
    i. He sees everything (v. 24)
    ii. He created everything (vv. 25-26)
    iii. He established wisdom (v. 27)
 2. Wisdom is made known by God in the proverb: "Behold, the fear of the Lord, that is wisdom; and to depart from evil is understanding" (12:28)

IV. Job's perspective concerning his suffering and pledge concerning his innocence, and Elihu's painstaking response (29:1-37:24)

A. Job—His closing testimony (29:1-31:40)
 1. I long for the days and honor of the past (29:1-25)
  a. *I was blessed by God (vv. 1-6)*
    i. The longing expressed (vv. 1-2a)
    ii. The love-relationship described (vv. 2b-4)
    iii. The life of blessing described (vv. 5-6)
  b. *I was respected by others (vv. 7-10)*
    i. The respect of young and old (vv. 7-8)

Structure and Outline

    ii. The respect of princes and nobles (vv. 9-10)
   c. *I was a blessing to others (vv. 11-25)*
    i. My godliness and wisdom were obvious (v. 11)
    ii. My compassion brought blessing to the orphan and widow (vv. 12-13)
    iii. My justice brought blessing to those who were oppressed (vv. 14-17)
    iv. My outlook was hopeful and confident (vv. 18-20)
    v. My words were respected and brought hope (vv. 21-24)
    vi. My leadership was unquestioned (v. 25)
 2. **I lament the degradation and humiliation of the present (30:1-31)**
   a. *I'm not respected—I'm an object of ridicule (vv. 1-15)*
    i. The description of those who now mock Job (vv. 1-8)
     aa. Their fathers were worthless men (v. 1)
     bb. They are without strength and food (vv. 2-4)
     cc. They are without a home (vv. 5-7)
     dd. They are without any honor (v. 8)
    ii. The description of their mocking attacks (vv. 9-15)
     aa. They sing and talk about me (v. 9)
     bb. They spit at my face (v. 10)
     cc. They are unrestrained in their abuse (v. 11)
     dd. They join together to attack me (v. 12)
     ee. They are unrestrained—no one stops them (vv. 13-15)
   b. *I'm afflicted, opposed, alone and dying (vv. 16-31)*
    i. I am afflicted and dying (vv. 16-19)
    ii. I cry out to You, O God, for help—but You oppose me (vv. 20-23)
    iii. I am not suffering due to my own lack of compassion (vv. 24-26)
    iv. I am agitated, without comfort, alone, sick, and full of sorrow (vv. 27-31)
 3. **I legally testify to my honesty and innocence under oath (31:1-40)**
   a. *I'm innocent of lust, deceit and adultery (vv. 1-12)*
    i. I am not guilty of lust (vv. 1-4)
     aa. I have made a covenant with my eyes (v. 1)
     bb. Because God sees—and there are devastating consequences (vv. 2-4)

ii. I am not guilty of deceit (vv. 5-8)
    aa. If I have walked with deceit—God knows the truth (vv. 5-6)
    bb. If I have strayed—then let me face the consequences (vv. 7-8)
iii. I am not guilty of adultery (vv. 9-12)
    aa. If I have committed adultery—may my wife serve others (vv. 9-10)
    bb. I have not committed adultery, for that would bring death and the loss of everything (vv. 11-12)

b. I'm innocent of injustice (vv. 13-23)
    i. If I have committed injustice in business, how could I answer to God (vv. 13-15)
    ii. If I have withheld charity from the needy ... (vv. 16-21)
    iii. Let my arm be broken off by God, because I did nothing to help those with outstretched arms (vv. 22-23)

c. I'm innocent of greed and idolatry (vv. 24-28)
    i. I have not turned to the idolatry of wealth (vv. 24-25)
    ii. I have not turned to the idolatry of paganism (vv. 26-28)

d. I'm innocent of hatred, blame shifting, and bad stewardship (vv. 29-40ab)
    i. I have not rejoiced in the calamity of my enemy (vv. 29-30)
    ii. I have not refused hospitality to anyone (vv. 31-32)
    iii. I have not covered my sin—but rather confessed it publicly (vv. 33-34)
    iv. I have confidence I can refute any indictment before God (vv. 35-37)
    v. I have not defrauded the land or its tenant farmers (vv. 38-40ab)

e. I rest my case—the words of Job are ended (vv. 40c)

B. Elihu—The angry young man, full of words (32:1-37:24)

1. Elihu's introduction—the angry young man and his opinion (32:1-22)
    a. The explanation of Elihu's motive in prose (vv. 1-5)
        i. The absence of an answer that solicited the young man to speak (v. 1)
        ii. The anger that motivated his speech (vv. 2-5)
            aa. His anger toward Job (v. 2)
            bb. His anger toward Job's three friends (v. 3)
            cc. His attention to cultural protocol (v. 4)

Structure and Outline

              dd. His anger over the absence of an answer (v. 5)
       b. *The exhortation of Elihu in poetry—listen to my unbiased opinion (vv. 6-22)*
           i. Listen to me—I too will tell you what I think (vv. 6-10)
              aa. I waited because of my youth and your age (vv. 6-7)
              bb. But God hasn't given you wisdom (vv. 8-9)
              cc. Now listen to me and I too will tell you what I think (v. 10)
           ii. You never refuted Job's arguments (vv. 11-14)
              aa. I waited and listened carefully (vv. 11-12)
              bb. Don't claim that you have answered Job, and now God will rout him (vv. 13-14)
           iii. I am full of words—let me speak, and I will answer without bias (vv. 15-22)
              aa. Words have failed them—but not me (vv. 15-16)
              bb. I too will give my opinion (vv. 17-18)
              cc. I must speak or burst (vv. 19-20)
              dd. I will be partial to no one (vv. 21-22)

2. **Elihu's first speech: Here's where you're wrong, Job—God is gracious [in allowing you to suffer] (33:1-33)**
       a. *I'll speak for God (vv. 1-7)*
           i. Listen to me now Job (vv. 1-2)
           ii. I speak honestly and sincerely (v. 3)
           iii. I'll speak for God—and you try to refute me (vv. 4-7)
              aa. I'm a creature—try to refute me if you can (vv. 4-6)
              bb. I should not scare you since I'm a man and not God (v. 7)
       b. *Job, you claim you are sinless [innocent] and that God is acting unjustly [opposing you without cause] (vv. 8-11)*
           i. I've heard you claim that you are sinless [innocent] (vv. 8-9)
           ii. I've heard you claim that God opposes you [without cause] (vv. 10-11)
       c. *God is greater than man, yet He graciously reveals Himself (vv. 12-18)*
           i. You are not right in your claims—because God is greater than man (v. 12)
           ii. Why do you complain that God does not give an account of His actions, when He is gracious to reveal Himself to man at all (vv. 13-18)
              aa. The question (v. 13)

Structure and Outline

- bb. The revelation (vv. 14-16)
- cc. The reason for God's revelation (vv. 17-18)
- d. *God hears those who hear His voice in pain, come to realize their sin, and then turn to Him in prayer (vv. 19-30)*
  - i. When chastening comes (vv. 19-22)
  - ii. If there is a messenger-mediator to turn him to repentance and bring restoration (vv. 23-26)
  - iii. Then the chastened one will sing praise and confess his sin (vv. 27-28)
  - iv. God chastens man oftentimes to bring him to repentance (vv. 29-30)
- e. *Hold your peace and I will teach you wisdom (vv. 31-33)*
  - i. Pay attention Job—listen to me (v. 31)
  - ii. Respond to my instruction—I want to help you (v. 32)
  - iii. If not—keep silent and I will teach you wisdom (v. 33)

3. **Elihu's second and third speeches: Here's where you're wrong, Job—God is righteous (34:1-35:16)**
   a. *Hear my words, you wise men (vv. 1-4)*
      - i. The Elihu speeches continue (v. 1)
      - ii. The exhortation to listen (v. 2)
      - iii. The evaluation of what is right and good (vv. 3-4)
   b. *Job claims it profits a man nothing to delight in God (vv. 5-9)*
      - i. The quote from Job (vv. 5-6)
      - ii. The question that condemns Job (vv. 7-8)
      - iii. The quote used to support that conclusion (v. 9)
   c. *God is not wicked (vv. 10-15)*
      - i. He is perfectly just (vv. 10-12)
      - ii. He is the sovereign Creator and Sustainer of all (vv. 13-15)
   d. *God judges sinners (vv. 16-30)*
      - i. Wise men will listen to the sound of my words (v. 16)
      - ii. Would you condemn the righteous mighty One? (vv. 17-20)
        - aa. The implicit judgment against Job (v. 17)
        - bb. The impartiality of the righteous mighty One (vv. 18-20)
      - iii. Wicked men cannot hide and do not escape His judgment (vv. 21-30)
        - aa. He sees everything—nothing escapes His omniscience (vv. 21-22)
        - bb. He does not need to have a court hearing to establish the facts (vv. 23-24)

Structure and Outline

    cc. He deals justly with the wicked (vv. 25-28)
    dd. He does this in His own way and timing—not always discerned by men (vv. 29-30)
  e. *God does not answer to rebellious fools like you, Job (vv. 31-37)*
    i. The proper approach to God suggested (vv. 31-32)
    ii. The problem of Job's approach (v. 33)
    iii. The prudent will agree with me—Job speaks ignorantly and rebelliously (vv. 34-37)
  f. *Job claims to be more righteous than God and that it is worthless to be righteous [The third speech—but continues the defense of God's righteousness] (35:1-3)*
    i. Another speech (v. 1)
    ii. Another interpretative paraphrase of Job (vv. 2-3)
  g. *Man's righteousness or wickedness is relative to others—but God's ways are higher than man's (vv. 4-8)*
    i. You and your friends have too low a view of God (vv. 4-5)
    ii. Your sin and your righteousness do not influence God (vv. 6-7)
    iii. Your wickedness or righteousness is relative to other men (v. 8)
  h. *Oppressed people's prayers are not answered because of pride, empty talk, and lack of patience (vv. 9-14)*
    i. Some cry for help, but not in faith (vv. 9-11)
      a. Because of their circumstances (v. 9)
      b. But not because they trust God (v. 10)
      c. And not out of humility (v. 11)
    ii. Surely God will not listen to an empty cry (vv. 12-13)
    iii. So it is with your supposed faith and hope in Him (v. 14)
  i. *Because God is patient, Job increases his foolish talk (vv. 15-16)*
    i. Because God is patient (v. 15)
    ii. Job multiplies words without knowledge (v. 16)

4. **Elihu's fourth speech: Here's where you're wrong Job—God is compassionate and Almighty, not uncaring or impotent (36:1-37:24)**
  a. *Bear with me a little longer, because I speak for God (vv. 1-4)*
    i. Wait—there is more to be said in God's behalf (vv. 1-2)
    ii. My words are the very truth of God (vv. 3-4)

Structure and Outline

- b. *God is compassionate, even in affliction (vv. 5-21)*
    - i. He uses affliction to instruct and lead men to repentance (vv. 5-11)
        - aa. God is mighty, but not uncompassionate or unjust (vv. 5-7)
        - bb. God uses affliction to teach men of their pride and lead them to repentance (vv. 8-11)
    - ii. If men refuse to see His compassion and repent, they die—so be careful how you to respond to affliction (vv. 12-21)
        - aa. Those who harden their hearts die in their sin (vv. 12-14)
        - bb. If you listen you will be saved and restored (vv. 15-16)
        - cc. Your zeal for "justice" is blinding you to God's compassion (vv. 17-21)
            - You are consumed with your idea of justice (v. 17)
            - Your anger has turned you aside (v. 18)
            - Your own resources cannot deliver you (v. 19)
            - You must not long for vengeance (v. 20)
            - You must not turn to evil, but rather let affliction teach you humility (v. 21)
- c. *God is almighty, thus you should exalt His work (36:22-37:24)*
    - i. Who are you to question Him? (vv. 22-23)
    - ii. Rather, you should exalt His work (vv. 24-26)
    - iii. His power demonstrated in the storm—introduced (vv. 27-33)
        - aa. God's power over the rain (vv. 27-28)
        - bb. God's power over the clouds (vv. 29-30)
        - cc. God's power to use them for His purposes (vv. 31-33)
    - iv. His power demonstrated in the storm—expanded (vv. 1-13)
        - aa. Elihu's personal response to God's power (37:1)
        - bb. God's power demonstrated in the thunder (vv. 2-5)
        - cc. God's power demonstrated in the snow (vv. 6-10)
        - dd. God's purpose in directing the storm (vv. 11-13)
    - v. His power demands that men fear Him (vv. 14-24)
        - aa. Listen and stand in awe, O Job (v. 14)
        - bb. Can you explain God's almighty ways? (vv. 15-20)
            - Can you explain the inner workings of the clouds? (vv. 15-16)
            - Can you change the weather? (vv. 17-18)

Can you really instruct God? (vv. 19-20)

dd. Men cannot even look directly at the sun—let alone God—He is to be feared, not challenged by men (vv. 21-24)

God is more awesome than the sun in full strength (vv. 21-22)

God is almighty and perfectly just (v. 23)

God is to be feared, and He does not regard the proud (v. 24)

V. Job's powerful Creator's cross-examination: "Whose wisdom is trustworthy—yours or Mine?" (38:1-42:6)

A. God's first cross-examination and Job's response of conviction (38:1-40:5)

1. The LORD's call for Job to instruct Him (38:1-3)

    a. *The LORD answered Job out of the storm (v. 1)*

    b. *The LORD questioned who it was that spoke without knowledge (v. 2)*

    c. *The LORD called on Job to instruct Him (v. 3)*

2. The LORD's challenge concerning Job's wisdom to rule creation (38:4-39:30)

    a. *Were you there at the creation of the earth? (vv. 4-7)*

        i. Explain how I created the earth (vv. 4-6)

        ii. Examine the response of angels to such wisdom and power (v. 7)

    b. *Were you there at the creation of the sea? (vv. 8-11)*

        i. Explain the creation of the sea (vv. 8-9)

        ii. Explain the control of the sea (vv. 10-11)

    c. *Can you control the morning light? (vv. 12-15)*

        i. Have you ever been in control of the morning? (v. 12)

        ii. Can you see the topography of the earth without the light of day? (v. 14)

        iii. Can you stop the wicked by the making the light shine? (vv. 13, 15)

    d. *Have you ever seen what's under the earth and sea—or over the expanse of earth? (vv. 16-18)*

        i. Do you know what is in the depths of the sea? (v. 16)

        ii. Do you know what is in the depths of the earth? (v. 17)

        iii. Do you know what is on the entirety of the earth? (v. 18)

e. Do you understand the way of light and darkness? (vv. 19-21)
   i. Do you understand light and darkness, and can you control them? (vv. 19-20)
   ii. Do tell me, because of your great wisdom? (v. 21)
f. Can you comprehend and control the elements of a storm? (vv. 22-30)
   i. Do you understand the origin and divine weaponry of snow and hail? (vv. 22-23)
   ii. How is lightening dispersed, or the east wind? (v. 24)
   iii. Who has ordered the place and uses of the rain? (vv. 25-28)
   iv. Can you give birth to ice and imprison the deep? (vv. 29-30)
g. Can you rule the stars? (vv. 31-33)
   i. Can you order the stars? (vv. 31-32)
   ii. Do you fix the heavenly laws? (v. 33)
h. Can you control the weather? (vv. 34-38)
   i. Can you command the rain? (v. 34)
   ii. Can you command the lightening? (v. 35)
   iii. Can you communicate the weather to animals? (v. 36)
   iv. Can you cure a drought? (vv. 37-38)
i. Do you feed the lion and the raven? (vv. 39-41)
   i. Do you give lions the ability to hunt and satisfy their hunger? (vv. 39-40)
   ii. Do you give ravens their instincts to feed their helpless children? (v. 41)
j. Do you know the birthing and nurturing of wild goats and deer? (39:1-4)
   i. Do you know the birth cycle of wild goats and deer that live in places man cannot travel? (vv. 1-3)
   ii. Do you know when their young are no longer dependent on their mother? (v. 4)
k. Do you set the wild donkey free? (vv. 5-8)
   i. Who untied the ropes of the wild donkey? (vv. 5-6)
   ii. Who released him from the hustle and bustle of the city? (vv. 7-8)
l. Will the wild ox agree to serve you? (vv. 9-12)
   i. Can you get a wild ox to serve you and let you take care of him? (v. 9)
   ii. Would you trust him enough to let him walk behind you in the field, or pull your wagon? (vv. 10-12)
m. Consider the silly ostrich (vv. 13-18)
   i. Consider her anatomy (v. 13)

                ii. Consider her habits in regard to her young (vv. 14-16)
                iii. Consider Who made her unique (v. 17)
                iv. Consider her speed (v. 18)
            n. *Do you give the horse his might? (vv. 19-25)*
                i. Do you give the horse his strength, beauty? (v. 19)
                ii. Do you give the horse his agility? (v. 20)
                iii. Do you give the horse his courage in battle? (vv. 21-25)
            o. *Is it by your wisdom that the hawk flies and the eagle provides for its young? (vv. 26-30)*
                i. Is it by your wisdom the hawk soars? (v. 26)
                ii. Is it by your wisdom the eagle protects and provides for its young? (vv. 27-30)
    3. The LORD's challenge concerning Job's complaint against God (40:1-2)
        a. *The culmination of the first cross-examination signaled (v. 1)*
        b. *The challenge issued—answer Me (v. 2)*
    4. Job's response to such revelation of the LORD [The LORD's incontestability revealed in Job's first response] (40:3-5)
        a. *I am small, and I will be silent (vv. 3-4)*
        b. *I've already said more than I should have (vv. 5)*
B. God's second cross-examination and Job's response of consolation (40:6-42:6)
    1. The LORD's call for Job to instruct Him (40:6-7)
        a. *The LORD again answered Job out of the storm (v. 6)*
        b. *The LORD again called on Job to instruct Him (v. 7)*
    2. The LORD's challenge concerning Job's complaint against God (40:8-14)
        a. *Do you still hold to your case? (v. 8)*
        b. *Do you have the power and authority to prosecute your case? (vv. 9-14)*
            i. The question concerning Job's power and authority (v. 9)
            ii. The commands for Job to demonstrate divine power and authority (vv. 10-13)
            iii. The confession that will come if Job can prove himself able to press his case (v. 14)

Structure and Outline

3. The LORD's challenge concerning Job's wisdom to rule the land and sea creatures (40:15-41:34)
   a. *Are you wise and powerful enough to capture Behemoth? (vv. 15-24)*
      i. The description of Behemoth (vv. 15-18)
         a. He is a creature (v. 15a)
         b. He is not a carnivore (v. 15b)
         c. He is colossal (vv. 16-18)
      ii. The dependence of Behemoth as a creature in God's creation (vv. 19-23)
         aa. He is a creature under the authority of God alone (v. 19)
         bb. He is a creature, dependent on creation (vv. 20-22)
         cc. He is colossal and confident in his habitat (v. 23)
      iii. The demonstration of Job's limitations of power and authority in regard to Behemoth (v. 24)
   b. *Are you wise and powerful enough to catch Leviathan? (41:1-34)*
      i. The demonstration of Job's limitations of power and authority in regard to Leviathan (vv. 1-10)
         aa. Can you catch him? (vv. 1-2)
         bb. Can you tame him? (vv. 3-5)
         cc. Can you sell him? (vv. 6)
         dd. Would you even dare to try? (vv. 7-9)
      ii. The deduction that God alone has sufficient power and authority to judge creation (vv. 10-11)
      iii. The description of Leviathan (vv. 12-34)
         aa. His body (vv. 12-17)
         bb. His breath (vv. 18-21)
         cc. His impenetrability (vv. 22-29)
         dd. His agility (vv. 30-32)
         ee. His incomparability (vv. 33-34)

4. Job's response to the revelation of the LORD [The LORD's consolation revealed in Job's final response] (42:1-6)
   a. [You've called me to answer You—] <u>I know You can do all things and nothing is beyond Your discernment</u> *(vv. 1-2)*
      i. The call of God to answer, finally answered (v. 1)
      ii. The confession of Job concerning God's power and discernment (v. 2)

b. [You've asked, "Who is this that hides counsel without knowledge"?—] <u>I have spoken about things I did not know or understand</u> (v. 3)
      i. The question of God summarized (v. 3a)
      ii. The confession of Job concerning His own wisdom (v. 3b)
   c. [You've called me to instruct you—now that I see] <u>I reject my complaint and I am consoled in dust and ashes</u> (vv. 4-6)
      i. The question of God restated (v. 4)
      ii. The change in Job's perspective described (v. 5)
      iii. The consolation of Job declared (v. 6)

Epilogue: Job's faith [and God's character] withstood the test of forgiveness and restoration (42:7-17)

I. The LORD's rebuke and plan of reconciliation for Job's friends—Job's vindication (42:7-9)
   A. The LORD's rebuke of Eliphaz and his three friends (42:7)
      1. The record of Yahweh's rebuke (42:7a)
      2. The reason for Yahweh's rebuke (42:7b)
      3. The rightness of Job's speech and reminder of Job's position as Yahweh's servant (42:7c)
   B. The LORD's remedy for their sin—sacrifice and the intercessory prayer of God's suffering servant (42:8)
      1. The requirement of a sin offering and repentance (42:8a)
      2. The restoration of forgiveness and intercession of God's servant (42:8b)
      3. The rightness of Job's speech and reminder of Job's position as Yahweh's servant (42:8c)
   C. The LORD's reception of Job's intercessory worship on behalf of his three friends (42:9)
      1. The faith of Job's friends (42:9a)
      2. The fellowship of Job's intercession—divine and human (42:9b)

II. The LORD's record of compassion, in the exaltation of His servant—Job's exaltation (42:10-17)
   A. The LORD revealed His compassion and mercy when He turned Job's captivity, as he prayed for his friends [note the connection between forgiveness and freedom from captivity] (42:10-11)
      1. Yahweh's compassion is revealed in the connection between forgiveness and freedom (42:10)
      2. Yahweh's compassion is revealed in the coming of Job's family and friends to comfort and care for him (42:11)
   B. The LORD revealed His compassion and mercy in doubling Job's fortune, granting him a new family, and an extraordinary life (42:12-17)
      1. Yahweh's compassion is confirmed to others in the doubling of Job's fortune (42:12)
      2. Yahweh's compassion is confirmed to others in the grace of a new family (42:13-15)
      3. Yahweh's compassion is confirmed to others in the grace of an extraordinary life (42:16-17)

Exposition

Wisdom & Warfare in the Heavenlies
Job 1:1-2:13

While the Book of Job chronicles Job's suffering, its primary focus is on the vindication of God's character and the surpassing value of knowing Him. God does not buy worshippers through the temporal benefits of wisdom. Believers find their ultimate satisfaction and rest in knowing Him.

In Job 1, the prologue consists of two sections that reveal how those who walk in wisdom do not always receive earthly blessings as perceived from a human viewpoint. These scenes illustrate divine wisdom and sovereignty, which can help us maintain our faith when faced with inexplicable and even devastating trials. The first chapter summarizes Job's life before he experienced the loss of everything dear to him.

Prologue: Job's faith endured the test of complete earthly devastation (1-2)

I. Job's life was marked by faith and blessing (1:1-5)
A. Job's character [faith] (1:1)

Ezekiel 14:14 and 20 affirm that Job was indeed a historical figure, alongside Noah and Daniel. The "land of Uz," as indicated in verse 3b, was located to the "east" of Israel.

Genesis 10:23 and 22:21 associate "Uz" with the Aramean tribes—essentially cousins to Israel.

Lamentations 4:21 explicitly identifies "Uz" with Edom, where the descendants of Esau lived (cf. 1 Chron. 1:35-42). Remarkably, this unique individual—this blameless and upright man who feared the LORD and was divinely blessed— does not appear to be Jewish. Rather, his origins typically considered outside the covenant promises of Yahweh (Jer. 25:20). God cares for all people and understands their ways, both Jew and Gentile.

The term "blameless" literally means "complete," referring to his integrity or wholeness. Job lived according to what he professed to believe. The word "upright" means "straight." Job exemplified sincerity and honesty, walking in a manner that was pleasing to God. See Proverbs 3:5-6 for the faith that undergirds a straight path.

The phrase "fearing God and turning away from evil" serves as biblical shorthand for living in divine wisdom (28:28; see also Ps. 34:11-14; Prov. 3:7; 14:16; 16:6, 16-17). Job was a man of genuine faith who adhered to biblical wisdom, even if his friends doubted this during his suffering (cf. 8:20). Job himself acknowledges that no man is without sin, yet he asserts that he has no secret sins that have led to his calamities (9:1; 14:4; cf. 7:20-21; 13:26). As the Psalmist states: "If You, LORD, should mark iniquities, O Lord, who could stand? But there is forgiveness with You, that You may be feared" (Ps. 130:3-4).

Job feared God—undoubtedly, in part because he understood God's forgiveness (Ps. 32). We can assume, like Abraham, that Job believed God, and this faith was counted as righteousness (cf. Gen. 15:6; Rom. 4:5). God's affirmation of Job's faith-based righteousness is evident not only in this inspired introduction but also in His dialogue with Satan in 1:8 and 2:3—both before and after Job's calamities. Job was indeed a man of genuine faith who walked in accordance with biblical wisdom. Francis Andersen provides valuable insight here:

> The fact of Job's genuine righteousness is essential to the book. It begins with a clash of opinion between Yahweh and the Satan on this point. The slanderer denies it; Yahweh sets out to prove it. This insistence on Job's uprightness should not be weakened in the interests of a dogma of universal human depravity. Job is not considered to be ... sinless. All the speakers in the book, including Job himself, are convinced that all men are sinful. Job's first recorded act is to offer sacrifices for sin. This is not the point. It is possible for sinful men to be genuinely good. It may be rare, but it is possible for a man who loves and obeys God. It requires effort, but Job had made that effort. ... Job was as faultless as a man can be. He is not Everyman; he is unique. God boasts that 'there is none like him on the earth' (1:8, 2:3). As such he presents the case of the innocent sufferer in what is almost the acutest form. In one Life only is Job excelled, in both innocence and grief: in Jesus, who sinned not at all, but who endured the greatest agony of any man. In His perfection of obedience and of suffering the questions of Job and of all of us have their final answer (Andersen, p. 79; G. Campbell Morgan, *The Answers of Jesus to Job* (1950)).

Simply put, Job's character is defined by faith.

B. Job's children [blessing] (1:2)

"Seven sons" signifies a superlative blessing from God, as seen in Ruth 4:15 (cf. 1 Sam. 2:5; Jer. 15:9). Psalm 127:3-5 and Psalm 128:1, 3-4 speak generally of the divine blessing of children and associate it in the latter Psalm with the blessing of those who fear the LORD. Children, in some respects, served as the ancient social security system, and most would assume Job would be well taken care of in his later years. The mention of "three daughters," who are invited to their brothers' celebrations in verses 4-5, suggests that Job's family was not only extremely wealthy (as confirmed in verse 3) but also highly unified in their relationships. Job lived a life of faith and wisdom, blessed with an ideal family.

C. Job's wealth [blessing] (1:3)

Job's possessions included 7,000 sheep, 3,000 camels, 500 yoke of oxen, 500 female donkeys, and very many servants. The holdings of "sheep, camels, oxen, donkeys, and very many servants" are reminiscent of Genesis' descriptions of Abraham, Isaac, and Jacob's wealth in Genesis 12:16; 24:35; 26:12-14; 30:43.

The term "yoke" refers to a "pair," suggesting that Job had 1,000 oxen. These would likely be used for plowing, indicating that Job was also involved in farming. The numbers presented here will gain further significance in 42:12, when Job's fortunes are not only restored but doubled.

As the greatest of all the men of the east, Job was likely the wealthiest of all the men of the east. However, it may also reflect his righteousness, wisdom, genuine faith, as well as the temporal blessings bestowed upon him by God.

D. Job's worship and witness [faith] (1:4-5)

His sons would hold feasts in each other's houses on their respective days, inviting their three sisters to eat and drink with them. Some suggest these were birthday parties for each son that lasted a week. The "three sisters" may have lived at home but were permitted to join their brothers for the weeklong celebrations. This indicates an extremely wealthy family.

After the days of feasting had completed their cycle, Job would send and consecrate them. This could mean that seven times a year, "Job would send and consecrate" his children—or possibly once a year after each annual cycle of celebrations. The idea seems to be that after each feast, Job would gather his children and dedicate them to God. As the next phrase indicates, he did this through the worship of blood sacrifice—an innocent animal gives its life for the worshipper to be acceptable before God

"Rising up early" conveys the idea of diligent and conscientious worship. Job no doubt explained the significance of the burnt offerings, teaching his family about fearing God and turning away from evil. He urged them to live by faith, emphasizing the importance of their "hearts" rather than merely external ceremonies or rules, as seen in the latter part of 1:5. Job was not aware of any specific blasphemies, but he recognized the danger of "blessing God" in vain if one's heart is not fully dedicated to Him.

His faith encompassed not only his own life and piety but also worship and witness. It was deeply rooted in both heart and holiness. Verses 1-5 clearly convey that Job's life was marked by faith and blessing.

II. Job's loss was characterized by divine approval but unimaginable earthly devastation (1:6-2:10)

A. The heavenly dialogue—part 1 (1:6-12)

1. The setting (1:6)

The phrase "sons of God" appears in Genesis 6:2, 4 (a debated passage regarding its reference), here, and in 2:1. In Psalm 82:6, a similar expression refers specifically to men—rulers: "I said, 'You are gods, and all of you are sons of the Most High.'" It is possible that this is speaking of "a day" when men "came to present themselves before Yahweh." The only other mention of "sons of God" in the Old Testament is found in Job 38:7, which speaks of the angelic host who "sang together and ... shouted for joy" at creation. Thus, this scene appears to be set in the heavenly realm, where the angelic host "came to stand before the LORD."

Notably, Satan also came among them. In 1 Kings 22:19-23, another angelic scene depicts the presence of evil messengers:

> Micaiah said, "Therefore, hear the word of the LORD. I saw the LORD sitting on His throne, and all the host of heaven standing by Him on His right and on His left. The LORD said, 'Who will entice Ahab to go up and fall at Ramoth-gilead?' And one said this while another said that. Then a spirit came forward and stood before the LORD and said, 'I will entice him.' The LORD said to him, 'How?' And he said, 'I will go out and be a deceiving spirit in the mouth of all his prophets.' Then He said, 'You are to entice him and also prevail. Go and do so.' Now therefore, behold, the LORD has put a deceiving spirit in the mouth of all these your prophets; and the LORD has proclaimed disaster against you."

Here in Job 1:6, the Hebrew term "Satan" includes the definite article—"the Satan/the Adversary." He "came in the midst" of the sons of God but stands somewhat apart from them. This sets the stage for the heavenly dialogue that follows.

2. The Sovereign questioning (1:7-8)
   a. *The question that revealed the character of the LORD's restless servant (v. 7)*

Yahweh speaks first, addressing "the Adversary." The omniscient, eternal LORD asks: "From where do you come?" When God poses a question to a creature, it is not for His own knowledge but to reveal something about that creature.

Satan answered the LORD, saying, "From roaming about on the earth and walking around on it." The Adversary's response to Yahweh reveals both rebellion and restlessness. While it is not a lie, it is evasive. One paraphrase has been suggested: "Nowhere in particular and everywhere in general" (Alden, p. 54). Perhaps the Apostle Peter drew on this imagery when he wrote:

> *Be of sober spirit, be on the alert. Your adversary, the devil, prowls around like a roaring lion, seeking someone to devour. But resist him, firm in your faith, knowing the same experiences of suffering are being accomplished by your brethren who are in the world. After you have suffered for a little while, the God of all grace, who called you to His eternal glory in Christ, will Himself perfect, confirm, strengthen, and establish you (1 Pet. 5:8-10).*

Using New Testament language, the god of this age (John 12:31; 2 Cor. 4:4) was roaming freely in his realm. The LORD's question revealed Satan's restlessness and rebellion. The LORD is sovereign, while Satan is a subordinate servant—even if he is dissatisfied with that role and restless in his rebellion.

b. *The question that revealed the character of the LORD's righteous servant (v. 8)*

Once again, Yahweh initiated this line of questioning: "Have you set your heart upon My servant Job?" Notably, Job is explicitly identified as Yahweh's "servant." The LORD wanted the Adversary to "consider" Job. This was an act of kindness, mercy, and judgment! This rebellious servant could observe a righteous servant. Satan is subservient to God, not out of love and trust, but because of God's absolute authority and freedom as the eternal, infinite, transcendent Creator.

Here, the LORD Himself brings up the subject of Job. The LORD describes him further: "For there is no one like him on the earth, a blameless and upright man, fearing God and turning away from evil." Job serves God because he recognizes God's compelling majesty—as we will see by the end of the book. Although Satan had been roaming "on the earth," he had not found anyone like Job. How so?

The Sovereign questioning revealed a wicked servant and a wise servant—restless Satan and righteous Job. Next, we see the Adversary's response to God's servant, Job.

3. The Satanic accusation (1:9-11)
   a. *Job's faith is mercenary (v. 9)*

"Does Job fear God for nothing?"—As stated in the introduction, this is the underlying question for the rest of the book. Do men love and serve God for the earthly benefits and blessings He provides, or do they do so because they see God as intrinsically worthy of their love and obedience? Essentially, Satan's accusation is: "Job's love and service are purely mercenary!" Job seeks, loves, and worships the gifts—not the Giver.

Proverbs 19:23 states, "The fear of the LORD leads to life, so that one may sleep satisfied, untouched by evil." Proverbs 22:4 reads, "The reward of humility and the fear of the LORD are riches, honor, and life." Job was living proof of these proverbs. However, Satan is ever the cynic. He focused on the temporal benefits rather than the Benefactor. He assumed Job's motives for worshipping, serving, obeying, and loving God were driven by greed. In short, Satan claims, "Job's faith is mercenary." Verses 10-11 further detail the Adversary's accusation further.

b. *Job's God is money and family [earthly blessing] (vv. 10-11)*

Here, the Adversary subtly accuses God of buying Job's love—hiring people to worship Him. Satan says in essence: "You protect Job, his family, and their possessions—why wouldn't he 'fear' You and follow Your commands? You have blessed the work of his hands, and his possessions have multiplied in the land—You have made Job rich and prospered all that he does. Why wouldn't he 'fear' You?"

> Cynicism is at the core of the satanic. The Satan believes nothing is genuinely good—neither Job in his disinterested piety

nor God in His disinterested generosity. Faith in God's goodness is the heart of love, hope, joy, and all other radiant qualities; cynicism is studied disbelief, and a mind turned in on its own malice represents the final horror of the diabolical (Andersen, p. 84).

The Adversary becomes bold enough to issue a command to God. The grammar is not only demanding but also audacious. The syntax can imply an oath: "But now send out Your hand, I pray, and strike all that he has; and [I'll be damned] if he does not curse You to Your face" (Andersen, p. 85).

In simpler terms, does Job fear God because of God's good and glorious character—His intrinsic majesty—or does Job's true god lie in his money and family, with fearing God simply a means to secure earthly blessings? This is the essence of Satan's idolatry—self-interest. He believed Job to be fundamentally like him. The satanic accusation is that those who fear God do so only for the earthly benefits they receive. God is not worthy of men's love unless it is purchased.

With perhaps the heavenly host watching, in the next verse, God sets out to vindicate His character and that of His righteous servant Job—who has been grievously slandered in this heavenly court.

4. The Sovereign Permission (1:12)

Satan had commanded the LORD to stretch forth His "hand" in verse 11. However, the Sovereign LORD—in no way tempted by or the author of evil—grants permission to Satan by stating, "Behold, all that he has is in your hand; only do not put forth your hand on him." Notably, in verse 10, Satan referenced God's protection over Job's person, house, and possessions. At this moment, Yahweh withheld "Job" himself from Satan's attack. This will be a key point in the next heavenly dialogue in chapter two. For now, we see the Sovereign granting limited permission to the Adversary, with the ultimate purpose of vindicating both God's character and Job's.

Satisfied with a significant portion of his demand, the Adversary "departed from the face of Yahweh." He left the "face" of the LORD, believing he could provoke Job to curse the LORD to His "face."

Application

Job's life was characterized by wisdom, faith, and blessing. Job's loss—as we've begun to see and will explore more fully next time—is marked by divine approval but unimaginable earthly devastation. Here are a few thoughts in closing:

It is possible to be pleasing to God. Job was a believer who truly lived out his faith.

Yes, he was unique in his generation (1:8)—singularly devoted to the LORD. However, we must remember that Ezekiel 14:14 and 20 also mention Noah and Daniel, who lived out their faith in exemplary ways. Perhaps every generation has a believer who serves as a model for the angelic realm to contemplate. Why not strive, by faith and relying solely on grace, to be that one? Is not Christ, our Creator and Savior, worthy of such devotion? As stated in Romans 12:1-2:

> *Therefore I urge you, brethren, by the mercies of God, to present your bodies a living and holy sacrifice, acceptable to God, which is your spiritual service of worship. And do not be conformed to this world, but be transformed by the renewing of your mind, so that you may prove what the will of God is, that which is good and well-pleasing and perfect.*

In Hebrews 13:15-16, we read:

> *Through [Christ], then, let us continually offer up a sacrifice of praise to God, that is, the fruit of lips that give thanks to His name. And do not neglect doing good and sharing, for with such sacrifices God is pleased.*

Hebrews 11:6 states: "And without faith it is impossible to please [God], for he who comes to God must believe that He is and that He is a rewarder of those who seek Him."

There are spiritual realities that are not visible to the eye yet are nonetheless active in this age.

The New Testament supports this in Ephesians 6:10-18 (cf. Eph. 3:10) and 1 Peter 1:12. Importantly, we are not called to vain curiosity or speculation about this spiritual realm and its warfare, but we should not be completely ignorant of it either. Instead, we are to embrace sincerity and practical righteousness, remembering the gospel that secures our footing, hiding behind the shield of faith, and always contemplating our glorious salvation in Christ and His return. We should use specific passages from the Word of God to fight the good fight of faith, taking every thought captive to the obedience of Christ (2 Cor. 10:3-5).

Let us remember the promise of Romans 16:20: "The God of peace will soon crush Satan under your feet. The grace of our Lord Jesus be with you."

Suffering, if not a consequence of walking in folly, is a sign of God's approval rather than His anger. It is a divine prize, not divine punishment.

Perhaps Job's pain was intended to help us see what was hidden from him. If he had been aware of the spiritual battle and the Adversary's slander against God's character and his own, Job might have been more encouraged to endure. Nevertheless, Job persevered even without knowing he was vindicating God's character and his own faith—or rather, God was vindicating them through him. The LORD has revealed this to us so that we may be more encouraged to endure suffering, if called to it, for the glory of God.

May our great God and Savior grant us the grace to trust Him as we await the return of His Son.

Worship & Warfare in the Heavenlies
Job 1:13-22

When we experience deep hurt or devastation, how do we respond? Do we chase every emotion until we find one that suits us? Do we allow ourselves to lose control of our hearts—our thoughts, our feelings, our words? Or do we intentionally and prayerfully seek to honor God in that situation? By examining Job's response to perhaps the greatest loss in human history, aside from our Lord Jesus', we can see wisdom expressed through worship—even amid an unseen spiritual battle. Wisdom manifests worship, even in the throes of spiritual warfare.

In Job 1, we will explore two major sections that reveal that those who walk in wisdom do not always receive temporal blessings as defined from a human perspective. Instead, these scenes reveal divine wisdom and sovereignty, which call us to persevere in faith during inexplicable trials and devastation.

II. Job's loss was characterized by divine approval yet resulted in unimaginable earthly devastation (1:6-2:10)

B. The horrible loss of Job's children and wealth (1:13-22)
1. The report of total devastation (1:13-19)
a. The day of feasting—the day of devastation (v. 13)

This verse establishes the setting for the day that changed Job's life forever. What began as a day of celebration and feasting in the "oldest brother's house" would soon turn tragic. It appears that all ten of Job's children had gathered to celebrate (cf. 1:2, 4-6). Some suggest this was the day Job offered burnt offerings for his children (Smick, p. 882; Delitzsch), based on the definite article and the prior reference in verse five. While we cannot confirm this, the setting underscores Job's love and concern for his children.

We are not informed how long Satan waited to strike Job with the calamities that followed, but his timing was chillingly calculated. He chose to destroy all that Job cherished a single day—a celebration day. From 1:5, we know this day was a source of parental concern for Job.

b. The devastation of Job's wealth and death of Job's children in one day (vv. 14-19)
i. A lone survivor recounts the loss of Job's oxen, donkeys, and servants (vv. 14-15)

If all the "oxen" were plowing in pairs, it would have required at least 500 servants to manage them (cf. v. 3). Nearby were the "donkeys"—potentially all 500 females (v. 3) along with a few males necessary to maintain the herd. The term "Sabeans" refers to people descended from Ham's son, Cush, as noted in Genesis 10:7 (see also Gen. 10:28; 25:3). They were from southern Arabia—modern-day Yemen—and were more commonly known as traders than raiders (cf. 6:19), but not on this fateful day. On this day, the "Sabeans fell upon and took" Job's oxen and donkeys.

On this day of satanic destruction, the Sabeans "struck down the young men with the edge of the sword." This exact phrase will be repeated in verse 17. It is likely that over 500 servants died in this raid. Consider the devastation faced by hundreds of families who lost a father, brother, or son. What a massacre it must have been.

And I alone have escaped to tell you. This phrase will be repeated exactly by four different messengers in quick succession (vv. 16, 18, 19). "Fully and literally it would read: 'And I have escaped! Only me! I alone to tell you!'" (Alden, p. 59). In verse 15, we see a lone survivor recounting the loss of Job's oxen, donkeys, and servants.

> ii. A lone survivor recounts the loss of Job's sheep and servants (v. 16)

While he was still speaking, another also came and said. This phrase ties each report together in a rapid chain of horrifying news and will be repeated in verses 17 and 18. Before the news of the loss of hundreds of lives under Job's care, and the destruction of his agricultural livelihood with the oxen and donkeys, could even fully register, "another" messenger "also came" with another unthinkable report.

"The fire of God from heaven" could refer to lightning or perhaps a "great fire"—the fire to end all fires. The same phrase is used in 2 Kings 1:12, regarding God's judgment on two groups of 50 soldiers dispatched by King Ahaziah, seeking to take Elijah into custody. As Robert Alden writes:

> It was the "fire of the LORD" that struck the grumbling Israelites in the wilderness (Num 11:1). It also kindled Elijah's sacrifice on Mount Carmel (1 Kgs 18:38)... The expression "fire of God" may be the equivalent of "a great fire" or "fire from the sky," that is, lightning, but it should not be taken to imply that

the Satan had some kind of control over God since these are the words of the messenger (Alden, p. 59).

The Hebrew says literally, "The fire of God fell down from the heavens and burned up the sheep and the young men and ate them." Again, it is likely that many families were devastated—not just Job's. Yet it is the man Job that God chose to vindicate His majesty and the indestructibility of saving faith.

As in verse 15, there was only one survivor. If Satan had not spared even one, the report would not have come at the same time as the others. So, we see a lone survivor recounting the loss of Job's sheep and servants.

> iii. A lone survivor recounts the loss of Job's camels and servants (v. 17)

Again, the symmetry of the lone survivors and their reports coming successively, while the previous servant was still speaking, suggests supernatural coordination. Job would soon confess the sovereignty of God as the one in control of these events—and worthy of worship, even in the face of them.

"Chaldeans" refers to semi-nomadic people from what is now southern Iraq. "Three bands" denotes some organization, perhaps necessary to capture and manage Job's 3,000 camels (v. 3).

Just as in verse 15, the "young men/servants" were struck down "with the edge of the sword." Thus far, Job had heard of two deadly and devastating raids and a great fire that had decimated everything he owned, along with all the servants he cared for, except for the three survivors who brought back the horrifying news. Again, the symmetry and organization of these disasters are unmistakable. As in verses 15-16, there was one lone survivor who "escaped to tell" Job.

Job 1:13-22

As indescribably devastating and painful as the combined news from these three messengers must have been, we cannot imagine how the final messenger's news impacted Job—already in shock, no doubt.

> iv. A lone survivor recounts the loss of Job's children (vv. 18-19)

Again, as in verses 16 and 17, the reports overlap. This time, the news was even more devastating.

Verse 18 recalls the introductory information given in verse 13. This description brackets the entire section. The celebration that at some level concerned Job (v. 5), now must have only added to Job's grief.

The climax of this section is introduced with the interjection "behold." Notably, the word "struck" is the same word used in verse 11, reflecting Satan's desire for God to "touch" or "strike" all that Job has. God did not "touch" or "strike" Job's children, but He did allow Satan to influence the weather patterns so that "a great wind came from across the wilderness" and it "touched/struck the four corners of the house" of Job's eldest son—where all of Job's children were celebrating.

In verse 15: "the Sabeans *fell* upon the donkeys and took them"; in verse 16: "the fire of God ... *fell* upon" the sheep and servants. Now, the "great wind" that came across the desert touched the four corners of the house, and that house "*fell* on the young people and they died." Again, the term for "young people" is the same word used previously to describe the servants, emphasizing the symmetry and obvious supernatural organization of these disasters. The servants were "young people" who were killed—and now Job's own children, who were also "young people," were struck down and killed.

As in verses 15, 16, and 17, here too—there was a lone survivor to report the calamity. In rapid-fire sequence, in a matter of minutes—Job learned that all he had—and all he held dearest (except for his wife)—was no more. His servants died in battle or by fire—and his children died in a tornado. His wealth was completely gone. Had his children survived, he might have been able to rebuild his wealth. But they too were gone. Thus, we see in verses 13-19 the report of total devastation. Would Job curse God as the Adversary had charged (v. 9)?

2. The response of total devotion (1:20-22)

   a. Proper expressions of grief (v. 20a)

The Hebrew has five verbs in rapid succession: "Job arose, he tore ... he shaved ... he fell ... and he worshipped." The act of tearing one's robe is a common expression of appropriate grief in many other passages (Gen. 37:29, 34; 44:13; Num. 14:6; Josh. 7:6; 2 Sam. 1:11; 13:19, 31; 2 Kings 5:7; 6:30; 19:1; Ezra 9:3; Is. 36:22; 37:1; Jer. 41:5; cf. Alden, p. 61). While shaving one's head in grief is often associated with pagan worship in the Old Testament (Lev. 21:5; Deut. 14:1; Is. 15:2), there are instances that portray it as an appropriate response to total devastation (Is. 22:12; Micah 1:16). The inspired commentary in 1:22 confirms that Job's "shaved ... head" was a suitable expression of his profound grief.

However, Job did not simply enter into the proper expressions of grief and then lose control of his emotions.

   b. Prayer and worship (vv. 20b-21)

The Sabeans "fell" upon Job's servants, oxen, and donkeys (v. 15); the fire of God "fell" from heaven and consumed more servants and all Job's sheep (v. 16); the house, propelled by a whirlwind, "fell" upon his children. Now Job "fell to the ground and worshiped." The grammar indicates a repeated act of "bowing down" (Alden, p. 62). He did not simply collapse but intentionally and repeatedly bowed in worship. The words Job uttered were deliberate and clearly crafted. He did not cry out, "O my God!" or "Why me?" or "How can this be?" Instead, he expressed his anguish with poetic words that reveal an intentional and practiced faith.

Naked I came from my mother's womb, and naked I shall return there—The poetic thought is that Job entered this temporal world with nothing—not even clothes—and he would take nothing with him when he departed.

> A man may stand before God stripped of everything that life has given him, and still lack nothing. His essential being came into life naked from his mother's body, and in that ... birth into another world which is death, he will pass in similar nakedness (Andersen, p. 88).

> When Adam discovered he was naked, he hid from the Lord. But when Job was faced with his nakedness he worshiped, and this is what sets the fallen man apart from the redeemed man. Even Christ after all, when he came into the world, came naked. And He died naked too (Mason, Mike, *The Gospel According to Job*, Crossway, p. 38).

The next phrase confirms that Job's reaction was not mere stoicism or resignation. Rather, he actively blessed "Yahweh"—the covenant name of the ever-living God—the One who is uncreated, eternal life Himself. Three times in verse 21, Job uses the name "Yahweh." Whether Yahweh gives or takes away, He is worthy of worship. Andersen is again helpful here:

> Job sees only the hand of God in these events. It never occurs to him to curse the desert brigands, to curse the frontier guards, to curse his own stupid servants, now lying dead for their watchlessness. All secondary causes vanish. It was the Lord who gave; it was the Lord who removed; and in the Lord alone must the explanation of these strange happens be sought (Andersen, p. 88).

In the end, the answer to our devastation lies solely in the LORD. This is how the book begins and how it concludes with God's revelation to Job. God was and is enough. In the final phrase, "Yahweh" is vindicated before both the sons of God and Satan himself. Rather than curse God, Job blesses him.

The "name of Yahweh" encapsulates all that He is in His character. Praise be to all that Yahweh is! In verse 11, Satan challenges, "But put forth Your hand now and touch all that he has; he will surely 'bless/curse' You to Your face." However, Job chose to praise the LORD.

> After the Prologue Job will appear to us to move very far away from these clear and simple statements of faith. Often he will seem even to repudiate them. Nevertheless, because he shows himself at the outset to be a man for whom worship is second nature, his faith is justly celebrated. Worship is his initial response, worship is the spontaneous reaction to tragedy that wells up out of his soul, and somehow everything he says later on must be judged in the light this fact. For we know that under such circumstances worship does not come to a person naturally or spontaneously, but rather it is a practiced response, a fruit of long faith and discipline. Job could never have reacted as he did unless he had been practicing for this moment all his life (Mason, p. 35).

We must not view Job as superhuman or impervious to pain; he suffered greatly. Yet, he made a conscious decision to bless the name of the LORD and turn away from sin.

Job's response of total devotion is affirmed not only through his external actions and words but also by the Holy Spirit's commentary on Job's inner man in verse 22.

c. Perseverance in faith (v. 22)

Mark it down, "through all this Job did not sin." The phrase "nor did he blame God" refers to ascribing foolishness or moral impropriety to God.

...The chapter ends with "the greatest man among all the people of the East" destitute, childless, and broken. In...a brief span of time, he went from being the greatest to being the least of men. We the readers know something that Job did not, and so we cannot enter into his sorrow. Like God, we know the end from the beginning [in Job's case]. We know...that Job had been chosen as a test case. Because of his godliness God selected him for this trial. Job was unaware that his troubles were a great honor. Would Job remain faithful? Will we? (Alden, p. 62)

Application

What is our "default" response when difficulties arise in our lives? Do we turn to worship or anger? God is gracious and compassionate toward our weaknesses and sins. Yet He is worthy of our worship even amid our grief. Job believed that! It is irrelevant to claim that my suffering is minor compared to Job's or Jesus's. Perhaps it is. But difficulty, pain, and suffering are still real, no matter how minor or major. It is just as important to honor God in the grocery store as it is at the guillotine—"the corner store [or] the concentration camp" (Mason, p. 34).

> The real question is whether I myself, in my own unique set of circumstances, am giving glory and thanks to God from my heart. If I am not, then it makes no difference whether the problem I face is a big thing or little thing. For the smallest complaints can spoil fellowship with God. Just one (Mason p. 34).

May God direct our hearts toward steadfast trust in our trials, so that He is glorified in both worship and warfare in the heavenlies!

Misery & Warfare in the Heavenlies
Job 2:1-13

Mike Mason, in his book *The Gospel According to Job*, is eminently quotable in describing Job's plight, helping us to be perhaps a little less critical of Job's words in chapters 3-31. He writes:

> When it comes to the topic of physical pain, people who are not actually experiencing such pain can entertain all kinds of noble theories about it. As long as it is happening to someone else, pain is but an abstraction, a theological conundrum, an unfortunate blight on an otherwise fairly tolerable world. But as soon as [pain] so much as touches a person's own body, the whole picture changes. Then suffering becomes the very opposite of an abstraction: it becomes an enormity, a concrete reality so overwhelming that it has the power to engulf all other reality, to eclipse all other thought except the thought of itself. ... At its deepest level, much of the meaning of Job revolves around the distinction between these two vastly different perspectives on suffering: on the one hand, the coolly considered outsider's view, and on the other hand, the view from inside the furnace. As for the latter, it is not really a "view" at all and even to call it that is do the sufferer an injustice. One does not hold rational, articulate opinions when one is writhing in pain. Pure suffering has a consciousness, a tongue, a heart all its own, and even the memory of it is a pale unreality when compared with the actual experience. Only the sufferer himself, in the moment of piercing torment, knows what it is

really like. And his knowing is of a sort that drastically alters the very meaning of the verb "to know."

It could almost be said that the sufferer's knowledge of pain is of the same order as the believer's knowledge of God and that this why the Devil exploits pain as a prime vehicle of temptation. Restlessly he casts about for something that will prove more compelling, more absorbing, more real than God Himself, for he believes that to find that something (and in this he is perhaps partly right) would be to dislodge God from His throne. After surveying all the possibilities, his final choice lights on physical pain. It is no accident that the place where the Lord and the Devil themselves join [in] ultimate battle—the cross—is a rack of torture. So the stakes are very high when Satan afflicts Job with "painful sores form the soles of his feet to the top of his head" (2:7). At this point the central question of the book subtly shifts from, "Can a man lose everything he has and still bless God?" to "Can a man lose even what he is and still remain under God's blessing?" For enough agony, like enough joy, can alter a person's most basic makeup. How much pain can a human being take and still nurse the fond notion that "nothing in all creation can separate us from the love of God" (Rom. 8:39)? (Mason, p. 41-42)

In this lesson, we will examine the final three scenes of the prologue to Job, prior to the commencement of the poetic debate. These scenes will deepen our understanding of the profound loss and pain that serve as the backdrop for the ensuing theological debate that follows. This was not a seminary classroom or an air-conditioned church auditorium; rather, Job was on death's door, in constant, unbearable pain, and totally isolated from meaningful and helpful fellowship. Even though his wife and friends were present, they could not truly enter into his suffering.

In Job 2:1-13, we encounter three additional scenes that confirm the truth that those who walk in wisdom do not always receive temporal blessings as perceived from a human perspective. In fact, God's blessing may genuinely rest on someone who appears to be entirely abandoned by Him. In this light, Job may serve as a foreshadowing of our Savior's blessed status before God, even while others perceive Him as cursed by God.

C. The heavenly dialogue—Part 2 (2:1-6)
1. The setting (2:1)

As in 1:6, this verse establishes the setting for the ensuing scene. As previously noted in our commentary on 1:6, this scene appears to take place in the heavenly realm when the angelic host "came to stand before the LORD." The wording in verses 3-5 indicates that this is a different heavenly dialogue than the one depicted in chapter one. As well, here we are told explicitly that the Adversary is accountable to Yahweh and must stand before Him.

Thus, once again, we see the setting for the heavenly dialogue that follows, resembling an angelic courtroom where angels provide an account of their activities to the eternal God, Yahweh.

2. The Sovereign questioning (2:2-3)
a. The question that revealed the character of the LORD's restless and rebellious servant (v. 2)

Yahweh's question closely resembles 1:7, although it uses slightly different wording. In 1:7, the question was: "From where did you come?" Here, it is phrased literally as: "Where from this have you come?" This second question may carry a stronger emphasis—possibly suggesting that Satan's roaming in Job's direction had failed, and they both knew it. Though perhaps this interpretation might be too nuanced to assert definitively, the varied wording indicates that this is not merely a repetition from chapter one, but a new conversation initiated by the LORD.

Again, as in 1:7, the Adversary's response reflects his rebellious and restless character. While it was not a lie, it also did not constitute a confession of sin or an acknowledgment that Job exemplifies the truth that people fear Yahweh for His intrinsic worthiness rather than for temporal blessings.

b. The question that revealed the character of the LORD's righteous servant (v. 3)

Once more, "Yahweh" initiated the question about Job (cf. 1:8). The presentation of Job to "the Adversary" by God Himself reveals that God's ways are higher than ours. He is working in and through Job in ways that can only be understood through divine revelation, not human reasoning. As in 1:8, Job is here explicitly identified as Yahweh's "servant."

Note the LORD's description in the remainder of the verse. *For there is no one like him on the earth, a blameless and upright man fearing God and turning away from evil.* Even after suffering the devastating loss of all his children, servants, and wealth, Yahweh's assessment of His servant Job remains unchanged from 1:8, which aligns with the narrator's assessment in 1:1. Job was a believer who walked in wisdom. However, the final phrase of verse three introduces a new element to this discussion.

The issue of Job's "integrity," and his commitment to it, will recur throughout the book (cf. 2:9; 8:20; 27:5-6; 31:6). One caution from the book as a whole may be to warn innocent sufferers against slipping into the mindset that their own integrity can become the paramount concern—rather than trusting God.

Although you incited Me against him to ruin him without cause. Here, Yahweh identifies Satan as the one responsible for Job's devastation, while also acknowledging His own sovereignty over Job's "ruin." The LORD literally tells Satan, "and you incited Me against him to swallow him—for nothing."

Many commentators interpret this final phrase to mean that Job had done nothing to deserve such calamities. However, it is possible that God was making a very specific and ironic point—divine sarcasm, if you will. In 1:9, the same root for "without cause" was used in Satan's accusation: "Does Job fear God for nothing?" Now, God tells Satan that his challenge regarding Job was all "for nothing." "Satan's experiment was all for nothing" (Andersen, p. 90), because Job did fear God for nothing other than the surpassing value of knowing Him.

Verses 2-3 reveal this sovereign questioning. Satan was a rebellious and restless servant, while Job remained the righteous servant—even in the face of great suffering. His suffering was "for nothing"—except for the vindication of God's glory and Job's faith. But notice Satan's cynical and unbelieving response.

3. The Satanic accusation (2:4-5)

   a. Job's faith is still mercenary (v. 4)

The phrase "skin for skin!" is likely a cynical proverb or cliché, which is further clarified by Satan's words in verses 4-5. It is clear that Satan was still accusing Job of having mercenary faith. Perhaps Job did not curse God over the loss of his children, servants, and wealth, but he still retained his health—money and even children cannot buy health. The implication is that Job did not curse God to save his own skin—his personal well-being.

As we often say today, as long as we have our health, what more can we really ask for? Proverbs 19:23 highlights the benefits of walking in wisdom: "The fear of the LORD leads to life, so that one may sleep satisfied, untouched by evil." The adversary accuses Job of fearing God solely for his own benefit—not for the profound value of knowing and loving the LORD. Verse five presents another challenge from Satan, suggesting that all creatures are fundamentally idolaters, driven by self-interest rather than true love for God.

b. Job's God is his own health (v. 5)

Satan calls upon to Yahweh take away Job's health. "The Satan wished Job to be diseased totally, thoroughly racked with pain, and plagued in every physical dimension. Later Elihu said, 'His flesh wastes away to nothing, and his bones, once hidden, now stick out' (33:21)" (Alden, p. 64-65).

As in 1:11, Satan makes a bold assertion: "But now send out Your hand, I pray, and strike his bone and his flesh... [and I'll be damned] if he will not, against Your face, curse You." The term "curse" here is the same word typically translated as "bless," but is used facetiously in this context. It is clear that Satan believed Job's true "god" was self-preservation; he would abandon Yahweh once his health was compromised.

4. The Sovereign permission (2:6)

Satan had commanded the LORD to stretch out His hand and strike Job. But the LORD replied, "Behold, he is in *your hand*, only spare his life." It is Satan, not Yahweh, who will inflict pain on Job—but only with the sovereign permission of the LORD. Once again, we see that Yahweh is neither tempted by evil nor the author of evil; however, He is inscrutably sovereign over it.

"Only spare his life" was the one boundary that Satan could not cross regarding Job's physical condition. This very boundary would bewilder and torment Job, as he remained unaware of the satanic challenge occurring in the heavenly realm. Chapter three serves as a poetic expression of Job's longing for death, which would not come (see also 7:15). Thus, the heavenly dialogue concludes. And the scene moves to the earthly pain of the LORD's prized, but pain-riddled servant, Job.

D. The Horrible loss of Job's health (2:7-10)
1. The Record of Total Physical Devastation (2:7-8)

In 1:13, there may have been a delay in Satan's actions, waiting for the most strategic moment to destroy Job's wealth and family. However, here the grammar suggests an immediate assault on Job's body, intending to undermine his faith and ruin his soul. This is the last mention of "the Satan" in this book. He departed from before Yahweh and "struck Job." This was all he could do.

Certainly, the responses of Job's friends and remaining family aligned with Satan's scheme. He is after all the ruler of this world (John 12:31), and the world lies in the power of the evil one (1 John 5:19). Job's wife and friends unwittingly served Satan's purposes, yet ultimately their actions only validated God's assessment of Job.

From a literary standpoint, after afflicting Job as described in verses 7-8, Satan's work was done. Only God could intervene to alleviate Job's pain. Interestingly, when God did intervene, He chose to reveal Himself to Job rather than heal him first. It was this revelation of God that healed Job's pain, even before addressing his physical suffering.

Job's total physical devastation under Satan's assault is well documented. He suffered from eruptions of the skin, sores from the sole of his foot to the crown of his head. The term "boils" is used in Exodus 9:9-10 to describe the sixth plague on the Egyptians, which preceded the Exodus. In Deuteronomy 28:27, 35 it is used as a warning to Israel regarding God's judgment for neglecting covenant obedience. Leviticus 13:18-23 refers to it in the context of a skin disease that resembles leprosy. Hezekiah had a "boil" that was nearly fatal until God graciously intervened, as noted in 2 Kings 20:7ff and Isaiah 38:21. Some have suggested it could be a form of skin cancer, but we cannot be certain. What is clear is that Job was covered with these painful eruptions and sores, making him unrecognizable, as stated in 2:12.

The symptoms and consequences of his condition can be seen in 7:5; 19:14-22; and 30:30. Andersen describes it as:

> Some kind of acute dermatitis spreading everywhere and developing infections with darkened (Jb. 30:28) and peeling (30:30) skin and constantly erupting pustules (7:5b) ... Other symptoms may be the results of complications in the wake of such a severe malady: anorexia, emaciation (19:20), fever (30:30b), fits of depression (7:16; 30:15f.), weeping (16:16a), sleeplessness (7:4), nightmares (7:14). These and other general sufferings, such as putrid breath (19:17cf. 17:1), failing vision (16:16b), rotting teeth (19:20) and haggard looks (2:12) are less direct clues. They add up to a hideous picture of a man tortured by degrading disfigurement (Is. 52:14) and unendurable pain, a bleak reminder that a man is flesh, made out of soil from the ground (Andersen, p. 91-92).

Job's first recorded response to this satanic attack on his body is poignant: "And he took a potsherd to scrape himself while he was sitting among the ashes." This imagery depicts a man living in an ash heap—an outcast from society, deemed unclean, and desperately seeking relief from his incurable sores. He was either scratching his sores to ease the itch or lacerating them to allow them to drain. "Sitting among the ashes" suggests he lived in a garbage dump or perhaps in a designated area of "ashes" on his own property (if he still owned property), symbolizing the waste of his current existence. It is that verses 7-8 are the record of total physical and social devastation.

2. The response of Job's wife (2:9)

Job's wife now enters the narrative. She had not perished in the earlier attack by Satan; perhaps she was spared for this moment. Giving her the benefit of the doubt, she may have wanted to see her husband's suffering come to an end. She too had lost everything, with no record of sin on her part up to now. However, witnessing her husband's health totally decimated, she said: "Do you still hold fast your integrity?" This echoes the expression used by God to commend Job in 2:3, where it was confirmed as true. Here, however, Job's wife urges him to forsake it.

Mrs. Job's suggestion/command—"Curse God and die!"—reflects Satan's desire for Job as well. Perhaps she knew that her husband would maintain his "uprightness" even if everything around him declared otherwise (Barrick, William D. Messianic Implications in Elihu's "Mediator Speech" (Job 33:23-28); ETS paper Nov. 19, 2003).

Indeed, Job would eventually seem to imply some questionable things about God's justice in light of his own "integrity." However, the angelic realm knows, and Job believes, that his integrity is indeed without question. Job's wife, on the other hand, interprets his immense suffering as necessitating a solution. Her exasperated suggestion is for him to abandon his piety and escape his misery. Although Job rebukes her suggestion, it becomes the foundation for his torment in the subsequent chapters before God reveals Himself to Job. Ultimately, Job champions his own integrity, which leads him to speak words he will later rescind (42:1-6). Nonetheless, Job's response to his wife here is remarkably loving and gracious.

3. The response of devotion (2:10)

Job does not label his *wife* a fool; rather, he indicates that her *words* reflect the foolishness of those who reject wisdom. The term "foolish" denotes godless folly—wicked senselessness, which is captured in Psalm 14:1 and 53:1: "The fool has said in his heart, 'There is no God.'" Job lovingly conveys to his wife that her command to abandon the fear of the LORD is contrary to wisdom; it is godless, wicked, self-destructive, and demonic. She too has suffered immense loss—her husband, her love, her security, and their future are now unrecognizable and teetering on the brink of death, leading her to tempt him to forsake the truth, whether out of bitterness or misguided compassion.

Unlike Adam, Job chooses to fear God rather than heed his wife's voice. In love and grace, he tells her the truth, asking rhetorically, "Shall we indeed accept good from God and not accept adversity?" He clings to God's sovereignty amid his suffering and wishes for his wife to do the same.

As the isolation from any true fellowship deepens during the ensuing debates, Job's words at times seem to convey (or at least are often interpreted by sermonizers and certainly his three friends as filled with) self-pity, self-righteousness, and self-vindication. However, he does not focus on secondary causes; he acknowledges that God is the Giver of both "good" and "adversity." He understands sin and evil in a fallen world, but he remains confident in God's sovereignty over it all. As Andrew Blackwood notes, "Faith knows that there are many purposes, not God's, at work in the world. Faith claims, though, that all these ultimately serve the purpose of God" (Blackwood, p. 42). Verse 10 serves as an inspired commentary on Job's response to the complete devastation of his health, his status as an outcast, and his appearance as one under divine judgment.

The statement "In all this Job did not sin with his lips" is both encouraging and enigmatic. After losing his children, servants, and all his possessions, it is noted in 1:22 that "Through all this Job did not sin nor did he blame God." Here, it simply states, "In all this Job did not sin with his lips." We know that "the things that proceed out of the mouth come from the heart" (Matt. 15:18). As Jesus stated in Matthew 12:34b-37:

> *For the mouth speaks out of that which fills the heart. The good man brings out of his good treasure what is good; and the evil man brings out of his evil treasure what is evil. But I tell you that every careless word that people speak, they shall*

give an accounting for it in the day of judgment. For by your words you will be justified, and by your words you will be condemned.

Despite all of the physical pain and social isolation—along with the lack of marital support—"in all this Job did not sin with his lips." As James 3:2 says, "If anyone does not stumble in what he says, he is a perfect man, able to bridle the whole body as well." Yet, in the next chapter and the ensuing debate, we will see Job express his vexation "with his lips." Ultimately, Job will lay his hand over his mouth and acknowledge that he spoke words without knowledge. For now, however, we see that Satan was mistaken; Job did not curse God, nor did he err in anything he said.

Beyond this, we cannot definitively know Job's thoughts. Did he wrestle with the temptation to sin in his mind? Perhaps. But up to this point, he managed to take such thoughts captive to the obedience of Yahweh.

E. The hopeful yet horrified response of Job's three friends (2:11-13)

1. Their pedigrees (2:11a)

When Job's three friends heard of all the adversity that had come upon him, they each came from their own place. This indicates that Job was a man of international reputation, with "three friends" from different countries (Andersen, p. 94). The report of Job's "evil/adversity/misery" reached them in their respective locations. The three "friends" are introduced along with their backgrounds.

"Eliphaz," meaning "My God is pure gold," is a name first found in Scripture in Genesis 36:4, as the firstborn son of Esau by a Canaanite woman. According to Genesis 36:11, Eliphaz's firstborn son was Teman. In the Book of Job, "Eliphaz the Temanite" is evidently a descendant of Esau—an Edomite—who carried the namesake of his notable ancestry. For Israel, the Edomite lineage would likely not have been viewed positively, potentially casting him in an unfavorable light. As we will see, he is the most gracious of the three "friends."

The name "Bildad" appears nowhere else in the Bible. It may mean "loved of the Lord" or perhaps "loved of Bel," a pagan god. Again, this may not be a favorable name, but we cannot be certain. "Shuah" was a son of Abraham by his wife Keturah after Sarah's death (Gen. 25:2). However, "Shuah" was also the name of Judah's Canaanite father-in-law, according to Genesis 38:2.

"Zophar" is mentioned only here in the Scriptures. There is a woman named "Naamah," born to the infamous "Lamech" of Genesis 4, from the cursed lineage of Cain (Gen. 4:22). Though not a direct relation, this association is again not favorable.

These men appear to have been of considerable stature and semi-famous lineage. Although their spiritual backgrounds may be questionable, they were the "three friends" who came to comfort Job in his misery.

2. Their purpose (2:11b)

These three gathered with the intent of sharing in Job's sorrow and offering him consolation. The term "sympathize" originates from a word meaning to shake or nod back and forth, which conveys the idea of lamenting or mourning alongside someone in their grief. The term "comfort" can denote either "to console" or in some cases English translators have rendered it "to repent" depending on the context. Ironically, while they came to comfort Job, they ultimately found themselves needing to repent and change their thinking about suffering, sin, and God's sovereignty (42:7-9; cf. Alden, p. 69). Their stated goal here was to grieve with and comfort Job.

3. Their pain and perplexity (2:12)

Job's three friends did not find him among the leading men at the city gate; instead, they saw him in an ash heap, covered from head to toe with oozing, bloody sores. His skin had darkened, he appeared emaciated, possibly toothless, and he lacked fine clothing. According to chapter 30, young men insulted him, drunkards sang songs celebrating his misfortune, and people spat on him as they passed by (Cotton, p. 16). It is no wonder that his three friends initially did not recognize him. When they did, they wept loudly, shocked by what they saw. Each man tore his robe and threw dust over his head toward the sky. These actions were appropriate expressions of grief; Job had torn his robe upon hearing of his children's deaths in 1:20. "Though not as common as ashes, dust is another sign of mourning (Josh. 7:6; 2 Sam. 1:2; Ezek. 27:30; Micah 1:10)" (Alden, p. 70). However, given Job's silent demeanor, the intensity of the three men's response may have seemed excessive. From a human perspective, Job showed all the signs of having been cursed by God, and his friends were genuinely perplexed and pained by his suffering.

4. Their problematic silence (2:13)

Their silence is commendable in many ways. While others mocked Job, sang perverse songs about him, and some spit on him—Eliphaz, Bildad, and Zophar chose to sit with him on the ground. In doing so, they entered into his humiliation and remained silent. As the rest of the book illustrates, this was their shining moment. Their purpose was noble, and their silence was preferable to the taunts and disparaging songs of mockers and drunks. Notably, their silence lasted for "seven days and seven nights." According to Genesis 50:10, 1 Samuel 31:13, and Ezekiel 3:15, "seven days" was the traditional mourning period for the deceased (Reitman, p. 69, citing Zuck).

In Job 2:1, however, it is noted that this was a "day" after the death of Job's children. It is possible that the men were mourning for Job himself, as they knew him—or perhaps Job perceived it that way. In the next chapter, Job curses the day of his birth and expresses a wish for death. Initially, their silence may have provided Job with a measure of peace, as he was now the target of mockery and derision from others.

How different things might have been if Eliphaz, Bildad, and Zophar had remained silent and remembered just how "very great" Job's "pain" was. As we will explore in the next lesson, Job eventually broke the silence with words that shocked those who did not fully grasp the extent of his suffering. His friends thus felt compelled to speak, driven by their own theological suppositions.

Application

In this prologue to Job, we have witnessed how Job's faith withstood the test of total earthly devastation. It began with a heavenly dialogue; followed by the devastating loss of Job's children and wealth; then another heavenly dialogue; culminating in the tragic loss of Job's health; and finally, the hopeful yet horrified response of his friends. This sets the stage for the bizarre and disturbing debate that follows.

We must not overlook the profound misery Job experienced as he spoke the words that follow and the poetic argument that ensues. He was a man devoid of both physical and emotional solace. No one could fully comprehend his suffering—not even his wife, let alone his friends.

In 3:1-42:6, we will see how Job's faith—and God's character—withstood the test of theological speculation and total spiritual isolation. Job's faith may seem to wobble—at least in some of his seemingly shocking statements, but he never cursed or abandoned God. He longed for an audience with

God to seek vindication and consolation. Eventually, Job received what he sought, but not in the manner he expected.

For now, we recognize that a believer can experience total devastation, both physically and emotionally, to the point of appearing to others as cursed—and yet still possess God's approval, favor, and blessing. In fact, such a believer may be a testament to God's majesty. If Job had known he was chosen to vindicate God's character and reveal Satan as the liar he is, he might have found some solace in his suffering. But Job remained entirely unaware of the spiritual battle taking place in the heavens. This ignorance served to demonstrate that believers fear God not for personal gain, but because of who He is.

The LORD has revealed these truths to us. We are called to persevere in faith, trusting that God will vindicate His majesty and our faith in Him. Thus, we are to endure whatever suffering He deems necessary for His glorious purposes and our good.

Blessed By God and Wishing You Were Dead
Job 3:1-26

Why do people believe in [fear] God? Is it to get what they want from Him, or is it because they have a relationship with Him that is infinitely more important to them than anything else? When a true believer feels abandoned by God, how does he respond? Will he curse God and forsake the faith?

The Book of Job illustrates that a believer can lose perspective and even the will to live. He may curse the day of his birth and question God's wisdom, both implicitly and explicitly. To others, such an embattled believer can seem not only forsaken by God but also rebellious and disrespectful. At that point, his despair can only be resolved through revelation from God Himself, regardless of how well-meaning friends may attempt to help.

In Job 3:1-26, we will explore three movements in Job's poetic speech depicting his desire for death, which reveal that God's blessing may still rest on a believer, even when they feel (and appear to others to be) abandoned by Him. Recognizing this should encourage us to persevere in faith, trusting that despite our longing for death, God is accomplishing something glorious beyond our full comprehension.

Dialogue: Job's faith [and God's character] withstood the test of theological speculation and total spiritual isolation (3:1-42:6)

I. Job's pain-filled curse: "I wish I had never been born" (3:1-26)

A. I wish I had never been born (3:1-10)

1. Job cursed the day of his birth—but not his God (3:1)

"Afterward" connects us back to the events of chapters 1-2, specifically to the "seven days and seven nights" of silence observed by Job's three friends, recorded in 2:13. Job himself broke the silence. Following the loss of his wealth, the death of his servants, and even his own children, Job had previously uttered, "Blessed be the name of the LORD" (1:21). After being brought to the brink of death, he stated, "Shall we indeed accept good from God and not accept adversity?" (2:10).

Now, after seven days of silence from his friends, Job may have recognized a connection to a week of mourning for the dead. Regardless of how the silence was interpreted, Job was the first to speak. He did so not by directly addressing his friends, but rather with a curse and a lament for death. The term "cursed" refers to "lowering" or treating "lightly" something in terms of its significance. In Hebrew, the word for "honor" or "glorify" means literally to give weight to something. The opposite of honor is to speak "lightly"—to give something no weight; to "curse."

Specifically, here Job "cursed his day," meaning his birthday, as the following poem confirms. Remember, Satan boldly claimed that if Job's "skin" were destroyed, he would curse God to His face. Instead, Job's unrelenting pain and devastation led him to curse his own birthday. He essentially expresses a wish that he had never been born—so profound was his pain and despair.

2. Let my birthday be destroyed (3:2)

Literally, "Job answered and said". Verse two is Job's response to his unbelievable plight and perhaps to the seven-day silence of his friends. If they were mourning the death of their friend as they knew him, Job mourned the day of his birth.

The word "perish" could also be translated as "be destroyed." The parallelism between the phrases "the day ... on which I was to be born" and "the night which said, 'A boy is conceived'" is significant. Job wanted the day of his birth to "be destroyed," wanting it to no longer exist. To emphasize his desire, he wished for even the "night" of his conception to perish. He clearly saw a connection between his life and his conception. "Job cursed not only the day he emerged from his mother's womb but the night nine months earlier when the spark of his life was kindled" (Alden, p. 73). Job's despairing cry was essentially—"let my birthday, and even my conception, be destroyed."

3. Let my birthday be darkened (3:4-6)

In verses 4-6, the word "darkness" appears three times in the NAS, representing two Hebrew words. The emphasis of the poetry in these verses is evident: "May that day be darkness; Let not ... light shine on it ... Let darkness and black gloom claim it; Let a cloud settle on it; Let the blackness of the day terrify it. As for that night, let darkness seize it ..."

In verses 4-5, Job seems to reference the "day" of his birth introduced in verse 3a. In verse 6, he speaks of "that night," referring to the night of his conception mentioned in verse 3b. Job wanted "God" to abandon that day. His life felt God-forsaken, prompting him to cry out for the day of his birth to be God-forsaken—i.e., that he would have died. "Black gloom" is the same term translated as "shadow of death" in Psalm 23:4. "Darkness" poetically signifies "death"—as "light" and "life" are paralleled in 3:16, 20 (Alden, p. 73).

Job employed the word "redeem" in verse 5, suggesting that darkness and black gloom should redeem the day of his birth; his death could somehow redeem the terrible day he came into the world. It is important to remember that Job spoke in poetic form here. His words express despair—not just spontaneous outrage. Instead, these were carefully considered expressions of outrage stemming from his unending pain and feelings of utter abandonment. In verse 6, Job wished for the night of his conception to be erased from the calendar, as if it had never existed.

4. Let my birthday be desolate (3:7)

Job may be referencing the "night" of his birth or still speaking of the "night" of his conception. Either way, such a "barren" night would never hear a "joyful shout." Job wanted his birthday to be desolate—barren.

5. Let my birthday be damned and devoured (3:8)

"Those ... who curse the day" may refer to professional prophets for hire—professional cursers, like Balaam in Numbers 22:5-6; people who accepted money to pronounce curses upon something or someone. "Leviathan" is more fully described in chapter 41, as the mightiest sea monster or dragon ever known to man (cf. Ps.104:26; Is. 27:1). This reference may allude to the unseen spiritual forces of Satan, the ultimate dragon of old (cf. Fyall, Robert S., *Now My Eyes Have Seen You*, IVP. 2002). The New Living Translation captures this verse well: "Let those who are experts at cursing—whose cursing could rouse Leviathan—curse that day." In essence, Job wished for his birthday to be damned and devoured by a sea monster—a creature so fierce that it symbolized Satan himself.

6. Let my birthday be deleted (3:9-10)

In verses 9-10, Job uses vivid language to express his wish that the sun never rose on the day he was born. He explains his reasoning in verse 10: "Because it did not shut the opening of my mother's womb, or hide trouble from my eyes." The sunrise symbolizes the opening of a womb, bringing light and life to the world. However, as Andersen writes, "For Job the soft beauty of the sunrise mocks the ugliness it makes visible" (Andersen, p. 105). By wishing for the sun to never rise on that day, Job desired his birthday to be delayed forever, erased from existence, signifying total deletion from history. He wanted the day and night that brought him life to be destroyed, darkened, damned, devoured, and ultimately deleted from history. Throughout verses 1-10, Job says with great imagery and passion: "I wish I'd never been born".

B. I wish I had died at birth or in the womb (3:11-19)

1. Why did I not die at birth? (3:11-15)

a. The poetic question (vv. 11-12)

Job now poses the next logical question: "Why did I not die in the womb, come forth from the body and expire?" The tone in verses 1-10 resembles a curse, while in verses 11-19, it shifts to one of longing (Alden, p. 75). This imagery is shocking, but it reflects Job's intense pain and loss. He questions why he could not have died during childbirth or at least have drawn his last breath immediately after birth. Here, "knees" poetically refer to birth. Essentially, Job is asking, "Why was I delivered and then fed at my mother's breasts?"

b. The pleasant hope (vv. 13-15)

In verse 13, it is clear that Job views death as a pleasant alternative to his current existence. Now he was weeping, but if he had died, he "would have lain down and been quiet." Job longs for death, but it eludes him. Had he died at birth, he "would have slept" and "been at rest" (cf. v. 26; 7:13-14).

The meaning of Job's enigmatic poetry here is debated. Some interpret it to suggest that even these "kings and counselors of the earth"—those in esteemed positions with grand building projects—along with those who have "gold" and "silver," ultimately find rest in the grave. They cease their futile pursuits and find peace. Job, exhausted physically, yearns for rest. In 3:11-15, he essentially asks: "Why did I not die at birth?" If he had, there would be rest—even the great men of the earth find lasting peace there.

2. Why did I not die in my mother's womb? (3:16-19)

   a. The poetic question (v. 16)

The New Living Translation clarifies this as: "Why wasn't I buried like a stillborn child, like a baby who never lives to see the light?" Again, we must remember that Job feels and appears to be—from every human perspective—utterly abandoned by God. Those around him believe, and perhaps even he wonders if he is under God's temporal judgment (though he knows it is not for some willful transgression on his part). He longs for death to ease his suffering, dramatically recounting the blessings of those who are dead. Here, he shifts from the blessings of dying at birth to the blessings of babies who died in the womb.

   b. The pleasant hope (vv. 17-19)

Notice that in the pleasant hope of death, "the wicked cease from raging"—the wicked can no longer oppress the righteous. Additionally, "the weary are at rest." The Geneva Bible translates this as: "There the wicked ceased from their tyrannies, and there they that labored valiantly, are at rest." Job deeply desires "rest." For the believer, death brings "rest" from the burdens that weary the righteous soul.

Those who were captive escape their captors in death. In death, Job perceives freedom. "The small and the great are there, and the slave is free from his master"—this line depicts freedom and equality in a world no longer marked by injustice. Job's calculated song of outrage began with the sentiment: I wish I'd never been born (3:1-10); then moved to—I wish I had died at birth or in the womb (3:11-19); and finally, in 3:20-26, he plainly states his point.

C. I wish I was dead (3:20-26)

1. Why is life given to one who wishes he was dead? (3:20-23)

a. Life is wasted on me (v. 20)

As previously mentioned, "light" and "life" are parallel here, as are "him who suffers" and "the bitter of soul." Clearly, Job is the sufferer—the one "bitter of soul." Most translations use the term "misery." Job is in misery, and his "soul" or "life" is "bitter." The thrust of his question is really an assertion—life is wasted on me.

b. Death is treasured by me (vv. 21-22)

Job "waits for death, but there is none." He "digs for it more than for hidden treasures." Notably, Proverbs 2:4 uses the term "hidden treasures" in regard to searching for wisdom and the knowledge of God: "For if you cry for discernment, lift your voice for understanding; if you seek her as silver and search for her as for hidden treasures; then you will discern the fear of the LORD and discover the knowledge of God."

Temporarily, Job's heart of wisdom (1:1, 8; 2:3) was preoccupied with his search for death. However, Job never speaks of suicide as an alternative to life. He continued to fear God and trusted that only He holds the power of life and death.

Three different terms for "joy" or "rejoicing" are employed here to depict the man who treasures the grave when he finds it. Death would bring unspeakable joy to Job as he sat in the ashes, surrounded by appalled friends, a misguided wife, and unending pain.

c. The way is hidden to me (v. 23)

Job wondered why life was granted to someone who had no understanding of the path he was on. Job further described himself as one "whom God has hedged in"—"fenced from behind." Satan had previously stated in 1:10, using a synonym, that God had placed a protective "hedge" around Job. Now, after Satan's assault, Job perceived a different "hedge" surrounding him. God had sovereignly fenced him in. Job felt trapped, unsure of how to navigate life, which fueled his longing for death.

Life is wasted on me; death is treasured by me; the way is hidden to me. *Why is life given to one who wishes he was dead?* Finally, in 3:24-26, Job answers the question.

2. Why do I wish I were dead? (3:24-26)

a. The sight of food makes me sick (v. 24)

"Groaning" and "cries" are parallel, as are "food" and "water." The word "cries" may be better translated as "roaring." Job groans when food is presented to him, and his roaring spills out like water. One might consider the sound of dry heaving, but that may be too limited for the poetic expression. Whether groaning and crying are his food or drink, or whether they are a response to food and drink, the outcome is the same. Job was either too sick to eat or repulsed by the sight of his food.

b. My life is a nightmare come true (v. 25)

We are not explicitly told what Job feared and dreaded that he now experiences. We know he was concerned for the spiritual well-being of his children, who died on a day of feasting. However, as the rest of the book suggests, Job perceived his circumstances as tangible evidence that God had seemingly abandoned him. There seemed to be a rupture in his relationship with God. Whatever the exact nature of Job's fear, it is clear he was expressing: "My life is a nightmare come true."

Finally, Job concludes with what he has repeatedly emphasized in this poem and what he longs for in death—the issue of rest.

c. I have no rest (v. 26)

The word "turmoil" conveys "shaking" or "agitation"—perhaps even "raging." He was neither "at ease, nor ... quiet ... [nor] at rest." He was in "turmoil." "I have no rest" is Job's final cry. See note on 42:6.

Job wanted to die because he believed he would find rest there.

Application

Chapter three encapsulates Job's pain-filled curse: "I wish I had never been born." Do believers actually entertain such audacious thoughts? Does this shock us? It certainly shocked Job's friends, who felt compelled to address his outrage and correct him.

Several verses in Job are important to consider. Recall Satan's challenge in 2:5: "... put forth Your hand now, and touch his bone and his flesh; he will curse You to Your face." Job's wife, in 2:9, foolishly urged him to curse God and die. However, when Job spoke, he did not curse God, himself, or anyone else. Instead, he cursed the day of his birth and expressed a deep longing for death. Perhaps many of us have known someone suffering through a long trial who craved relief in death.

Throughout the painful, poetic debate that follows, we should remember God's words to Eliphaz and his companions: "My wrath is kindled against you and against your two friends, because you have not spoken of Me what is right as

My servant Job has" (42:7). God confirmed that Job had spoken rightly in some senses before Him, while Eliphaz, Bildad, and Zophar had not. The specific words of Job that God referenced have been widely debated. We must be cautious when evaluating Job and his words—lest we too accuse Job of things that God does not. Was it wrong for Job to curse the day he was born and long for death? The text does not condemn him for this, but then again neither does it commend him; it merely records his painful lament.

Job later acknowledged that he spoke in ignorance. Yet God affirmed Job's essential righteousness regarding his relationship to Him. A believer can always be honest with God while clinging to Him in faith. Job teaches us that our pain may tempt us to vent our ignorance. While God does not prohibit this, He may eventually correct us—for our good and in love.

James 5:11 reminds us of another aspect of Job's suffering that we ought to remember: "We count those blessed who endured. You have heard of the endurance of Job and have seen the outcome of the Lord's dealings, that the Lord is full of compassion and is merciful." Job endured; he continued to trust Yahweh in tenacious (and sometimes wavering) faith despite his suffering. He longed for death and felt abandoned by God, yet he persevered, seeking vindication before God.

As we will explore in the next lesson and for many more to come—Job's friends believed they needed to set Job straight. They needed to fix his situation—more for the sake of vindicating their theological suppositions, than for the sake of their devastated friend it would seem. Can a believer feel utterly abandoned by God and still hold on to faith? Moreover, can a believer appear to be, and feel absolutely abandoned by God—and yet be the object of God's love and favor, ultimately? Job teaches us that both can be true. A believer fears God not for the temporal benefits but for the surpassing value of knowing Him (cf. 1:9; Phil. 3:7-14). The ultimate test, however, is keeping the faith even when it seems God has abandoned you.

A believer may speak candidly about his pain; he may curse the day of his birth or wish for death. But the believer will not abandon the One who seems to have abandoned him; instead, he will continue to take his case to God. Such revelation may give fresh insight into Jesus' words on the cross: "My God, My God, why have You forsaken Me?" (Mark 15:34) and His final words, "Father, into Your hands I commit My spirit" (Luke 23:46). Jesus, in His humanity, undoubtedly learned from Job that a believer trusts and endures in hope of vindication from God, even when feeling completely abandoned by God—and everyone else seems to confirm it. As those who see Job's innocent suffering—and that of our Savior—we are encouraged to persevere in faith, even while expressing our pain, looking to God for ultimate deliverance and vindication.

Eliphaz— "You Know the Sowing and Reaping Principle"
Job 4:1-5:27

As we explore the poetic arguments and speeches found in chapters 3-37, it is crucial to keep in mind the setting and circumstances surrounding them. These men were not engaged in theological debate in a classroom or through journal articles; they were seated in an ash heap, with Job, who was financially bankrupt, bereft of his children, alienated by his wife, and covered in oozing, painful sores. He was taunted and ridiculed by the society that once regarded him as the greatest of men. From a human perspective, he bore every evidence of having been cursed by God.

In chapter three, Job expressed his pain and anger, wishing he had never been conceived or, at the very least, that he had died in the womb or at birth. In his despair, he longed for death. Job's words of agony and bitter despair were evidently offensive to his three friends. *He* had broken the silence. *He* was the one now implying that God makes mistakes—at least that was how they interpreted his speech in chapter three. In response, these presumably wise and respectable friends felt it was their duty to help Job navigate his crisis. Thus, Eliphaz speaks in chapters 4-5.

Job 4:1-5:27

In Job chapters 4-5, we will observe eight summary sections in Eliphaz's speech. While his points often touch on truth in the abstract, they fail to appropriately relay the truth of God to Job and thus comfort him and strengthen his relationship with God. Eliphaz's first speech warns against making rash judgments about comments made by those who are suffering.

A. Eliphaz [the charismatic—the most gracious of all the speeches]—Job, you reap what you sow; if you seek God you will be restored! (4:1-5:27)

  1. Patience, Job—don't get upset, but I feel compelled to speak (4:1-2)

    a. Don't get upset because of what I'm about to say (vv. 1-2a)

"Eliphaz the Temanite" was evidently recognized as the leader among Job's three friends and possibly the eldest (32:6-7). In 42:7, Yahweh Himself will address Eliphaz directly, rebuking him for not speaking "what is right" about God. Here, this esteemed descendant of Esau responds to Job's painful lament.

Eliphaz's first speech stands out as the most gracious in tone among the men who offer their words to Job. In this initial attempt to help, he does not *directly* accuse his friend of wrongdoing. However, as we will see, his words strongly suggest that some unrecognized sin must be present in Job's life that requires repentance. But we, as readers of the inspired text, are privy of the real issue, which is recorded in chapters 1-2—that Job's blamelessness is precisely why he is so afflicted.

In 3:26, Job had exclaimed, "... I am not at rest ..." Eliphaz here echoes this sentiment by asking, "If one tests a word with you, will you become weary?" The implication is that Job may already be feeling "impatient," and Eliphaz worries that addressing Job's complaints could exacerbate this impatience. This rhetorical question serves to encourage Job to listen, as Eliphaz essentially says: *Don't get upset because of what I am about to say.*

b. *Does not your speech demand an answer? (v. 2b)*

This second rhetorical question presupposes the answer: "No one can resist responding to such a death wish as Job has just expressed." In verses 1-2, Eliphaz says: *Patience, Job—don't get upset, but I feel compelled to speak.*

2. Practice what you've preached (4:3-6)

   a. *Remember how you instructed others (vv. 3-4)*

Eliphaz began with kind words of encouragement, acknowledging Job's ministry to others. Job had "admonished" or "corrected" many and "strengthened weak hands," helping those who were "tottering" or "stumbling." However, the implication from Eliphaz is that *Job* now needs correction and is the one who is stumbling.

   b. *Receive instruction—if indeed you fear God and keep your integrity (vv. 5-6)*

In verse 5, once again, Eliphaz uses the terms "impatient" or "weary" in reference to Job. The underlying message is that Job needs patience and strength. This holds some truth, as the Book of James ultimately praises Job for his endurance. However, here, Eliphaz begins with a subtle rebuke of Job's perceived lack of strength, in spite of the fact that Job had lost all his wealth, lost all of his children, and his physical health was completely destroyed.

Job indeed *feared* God and turned away from evil (1:1, 8; 2:3). The term "integrity," which describes Job in the earlier verses, translates to "blameless." God was the source of Job's "confidence" and "hope," establishing him as a man of godly "fear" and "integrity."

However, in verses 5-6, there is a subtle accusation embedded in Eliphaz's question. If Job genuinely feared God, would he compose a passionate lament cursing the day of his birth? If he were truly a man of "integrity," could he express such hopeless sentiments? Eliphaz implies that Job's words and the calamities he faces serve as evidence against him. This is the subject of Eliphaz's next point. The elder statesman tries to counsel Job by reminding him of how Job himself used to correct those who faltered, suggesting that Job now needs to apply his own instructions.

3. Plowing iniquity reaps a harvest of difficulty—remember, you reap what you sow (4:7-11)

    a. The principle stated and restated (vv. 7-8)

Here, Eliphaz called Job to "remember" the principle of sowing and reaping. And he poses two rhetorical questions intended to instruct Job. The expected answers are that "no one" ever perished being innocent; and "nowhere" can we find the upright destroyed. Eliphaz seems either unaware of or has overlooked the murder of Abel, as recorded in Genesis 4.

Job, along with the psalmist and the writer of Ecclesiastes, will challenge the absoluteness of this maxim in a fallen world (Eccl. 7:15; 8:12). Nevertheless, the Scriptures generally affirm that there is a divine principle regarding sowing and reaping. Proverbs 5:22 states: "His own iniquities will capture the wicked, and he will be held with the cords of his sin" (cf. Prov. 1:31-32; 11:5-6; 12:13-14; 26:27). The Apostle Paul echoes this in Galatians 6:7-9:

> *Do not be deceived, God is not mocked; for whatever a man sows, this he will also reap. For the one who sows to his own flesh will from the flesh reap corruption, but the one who sows to the Spirit will from the Spirit reap eternal life. Let us not lose heart in doing good, for in due time we will reap if we do not grow weary.*

In verse eight, Eliphaz refers to his personal observations. His words are reminiscent of Psalm 37:25: "I have been young and now I am old, yet I have not seen the righteous forsaken or his descendants begging bread." Proverbs 22:8 also supports the principle Eliphaz is stating here. But Eliphaz seems to be suggesting it applies directly to Job: "He who sows iniquity will reap vanity ..."

The concept of sowing and reaping is reiterated as a maxim that applies to Job's horrifying situation. But Job's experience (similar to the man born blind in John 9) reveals that there are divinely ordained exceptions to the principle of sowing and reaping—at least in man's estimation. No doubt, God's perfect laws are and will always be perfectly fulfilled in His sovereign timing, goodness, and wisdom.

Given the heavenly challenge described in chapters 1-2, Eliphaz's counsel misses the mark in regard to Job. Directly in front of Eliphaz's eyes sat a man for whom the general maxim did not directly apply. Jesus, Job's Savior and ours, would know the scorn of those who believed He was cursed by God for sin and pride. Yet He was perfectly innocent, and actually accomplishing God's sovereign will in His suffering.

b. The punishment illustrated and re-illustrated (vv. 9-11)

The phrase "by the breath of God they perish" recalls Proverbs 22:8: "He who sows iniquity will reap vanity, and *the rod of his fury will perish.*" The term translated as "blast" in verse 9 literally means "wind" or "spirit" (*ruach*). It is uncertain whether this allusion is intentional, but the same word is used to describe the great "wind" that took the lives of his children in 1:19.

Verses 10-11, with their repeated references to the "lion," illustrate that even the strongest can be silenced, rendered helpless, and perish when God's judgment arrives because of their iniquity. The implication is that Job—no matter his previous status or perceived strength—could not protect his own children. True in the abstract, but truly inappropriate, unhelpful, and misapplied in regard to Job.

4. Pay attention—my teaching comes from personal revelation (4:12-16)

   a. *A secret word (v. 12)*

After appealing to wisdom that Job would perhaps accept in principle, Eliphaz now turns to a mystical experience to bolster his counsel. The New Living Translation captures the essence well: "This truth was given to me in secret, as though whispered in my ear." Eliphaz claimed to have received *a secret word* intended to guide him in instructing Job.

   b. *A special dream in the night (vv. 13-14)*

These verses recount a dream or vision that left Eliphaz feeling "disquieted," filled with "dread" and "trembling." It occurred "at night when deep sleep falls on men." Eliphaz experienced *a special dream in the night* that deeply troubled him. The subsequent verses reveal the reasons behind his distress.

   c. *A spirit-being before my face (vv. 15-16a)*

Again, the term "spirit" can also mean "wind." It is unclear whether a "spirit" actually passed by his "face" or if it was merely the "wind." However, based on the following context, it appears Eliphaz interpreted it as a spirit being. In essence, he had an experience that caused his hair to stand on end.

This spirit stood still, but Eliphaz could not discern its appearance, even though it was before his eyes.

   d. *A spirit's silence, then a voice (v. 16b)*

The term translated as "silence" is used in 1 Kings 19:12 in conjunction with the term "voice," where it is rendered as "still small voice" in the KJV. The Jewish Bible translates the phrase here as: "I heard a murmur, a voice."

Eliphaz states: *Pay attention—my teaching comes from private [supernatural] revelation.* What message did this spirit convey?

5. Private revelation confirmed depravity without the doctrine of grace—can a creature be righteous before the Creator? (4:17-21)

   a. *God is far purer than man (v. 17)*

In what could be seen as anticlimactic, this supernatural "word" from the spirit merely reaffirmed the doctrine of human depravity—and if anything, it overstated it so that it would be misapplied to Job's situation. Romans 3:10-18 serves as a New Testament confirmation of the doctrine of depravity. But this is not really at issue in the context of Job.

Ironically, the spirit's doctrine of depravity, as revealed to Eliphaz (though most certainly a consequence of sin and the fall) fails to consider the clear teachings of Scripture concerning justification by faith. From Genesis 3 onward, the biblical narrative indicates that mankind *can* be just before God and made clean before Him—not through man's own merit, but rather by grace, through faith. Abel's offering was accepted by God because it was made in faith (Gen. 4); Enoch walked with God and was pleasing to Him (Gen. 5:22, 24; Heb. 11); Noah was described as a righteous man, blameless in his time, because he found grace in the eyes of the LORD (Gen. 6:8-9); Abraham believed God, and it was credited to him as righteousness (Gen. 15:6).

We see from Job 1:1, 8, and 2:3 that Job was "right" before God. Yet, Eliphaz employed the general truth that God is infinitely more righteous and purer than man to persuade Job to reassess his own integrity. However, if Job were to do so, it would actually validate Satan's claims. Agreement with the spirit's message would be tantamount to abandoning the doctrine of justification by faith. Job himself begins to question his understanding about faith and righteousness in 9:2. But in the end, his faith and righteousness would be strengthened and confirmed (42:7ff).

Verse 17 records the spirit's supposed private revelation to Eliphaz: *God is far purer than man.* The implication is that one cannot truly be "right" or "pure" before Him. This inferred conclusion is unbiblical error that damns people and misrepresents God. It can rightly be classified as a doctrine of demons, as the context bears out. Eliphaz would later be rebuked for it (42:7).

b. God is far purer than angels (v. 18)

Using a logical argument of greater to lesser, this spirit claimed that God "puts no trust even in His servants; and against His angels He charges error." The term "His servants" seems to parallel "angels" in this context. Yes, *God is far purer than angels*, but does this implication necessitate that "He puts no trust" in them? Is this spirit referring to fallen angels charged with "folly" or "error"?

In Genesis 3, God entrusted two angels with guarding the entrance to the Garden after the fall. In Genesis 18, He entrusted the rescue of Lot to two angelic servants. Eliphaz's spirit-visitor emphasized the transcendence, holiness, and righteousness of God, neglecting His grace, tender mercies, and condescension.

c. God is eternal—man perishes (vv. 19-21)

If angels are deemed untrustworthy and flawed in God's assessment (according to the distorted theology of this spirit), then how much more so is man—who is mortal, described as "those who dwell in houses of clay, whose foundation is in the dust, who are crushed before the moth!" God is eternal, whereas man exists briefly, "between morning and evening"—in a single day. Like a "tent," which collapses when a string is pulled, so too is the brevity and fragility of man's life. In line with his hopeless message of transcendence, wisdom, and holiness, without grace—men "die without wisdom." Ultimately, God's ways are unknowable. This is a logical conclusion, yet He does graciously reveal Himself to His own, as Job will ultimately find out (chaps 38-41; cf. Deut. 29:29).

In 4:17-21, Eliphaz asserts that his *private revelation confirmed depravity without the doctrine of grace—can a creature be righteous before the Creator?* In chapter five, he returns to his main point about the principle of sowing and reaping as he addresses Job directly once again.

6. Perceive who can really deliver man from the sowing and reaping principle—only the sower (5:1-7)
   a. *Angels cannot deliver you from the sowing and reaping principle (v. 1)*

As previously noted, Eliphaz shifts back to addressing Job directly—aiming to educate him rather than recounting his private vision. Here, his direct assessment of Job becomes more evident.

The expected answer to Eliphaz's two rhetorical questions is that "no one" will respond to Job, and not even one of the "holy ones" or angels can liberate him from the principle of sowing and reaping.

   b. *Anger destroys the foolish man, his sons, and his wealth (vv. 2-5)*

Here Eliphaz implies that Job's folly is now catching up with him. Was Job now being accused of harboring "anger" and unjust "zeal" or "envy"? Very likely, his longing for death in chapter three is now framed as "anger" and ungodly "zeal." Eliphaz would position himself as the righteous man (at least in his own estimation) to "curse" the dwelling of the foolish (v. 3).

The fool's "sons are far from safety ... and there is no deliverer." This could point to the legal repercussions of the father's folly—or perhaps more directly to their destruction due to the father's sins. Verse five might subtly reference the raids that led to Job's financial ruin.

   c. *Affliction doesn't just happen—man is the source of his own trouble (vv. 6-7)*

Again, note the terminology of "sowing" with "sprout from the ground." You do not reap "affliction" unless you have sown it; it does not arise spontaneously. The idea is that trouble has a source. In Genesis 3:17-18, the ground was cursed because of Adam's sin, but here Eliphaz is clearly suggesting that *Job* is the source of his own troubles—which we know, and Job believes, is not true.

For man is born for trouble, as sparks fly upward—This statement is brilliantly articulated and, as a standalone maxim, is proverbially true. However, in this context, Eliphaz urges Job to consider himself as the source of his "trouble." Just as fire produces sparks that "fly upward," there must be something in Job's life that has led to these overwhelming signs of judgment.

7. Personally, I would seek God, because proud men are punished, but the lowly are lifted (5:8-16)
   a. *If I were you, I would seek God (v. 8)*

Bildad will suggest something similar in 8:5, and actually Job desires this more than either of them, as seen in 23:3-5 (cf. Alden, p. 93). Ultimately, God would respond—but not in the way any of them expected—even though Job's righteousness was vindicated (cf. chapters 38-41).

Eliphaz counsels Job by saying, "*If I were you, I would seek God.*" He then paints a beautiful and theologically rich picture of God's power, justice, and mercy. However, Eliphaz has already assumed Job's guilt, which undermines his theological insights and fails to truly help Job.

> b. *If you understand His ways of blessing the lowly and punishing the unrighteous (vv. 9-16)*
>> i. He can do miracles (v. 9)

Indeed, God performs what the NIV describes as "wonders that cannot be fathomed, miracles that cannot be counted." Eliphaz tells Job, whom he suspects to be the cause of his own misery, that God is capable of miracles. However, the context suggests that God will only perform a miracle *if* Job repents of his hidden sin and seeks Him.

>> ii. He can providentially provide (v. 10)

Jesus affirmed that God causes the sun to shine on both the evil and the good and sends rain on the righteous as well as the unrighteous (Matt. 5:45). This theology is sound and quite biblical in summary, but its application falls short regarding Job's need to confess his guilt. God is indeed good! However, the implication in Eliphaz's statement is that Job must repent of some hidden fault to experience God's good providence.

>> iii. He blesses the lowly (v. 11)

Proverbs 3:34b states that God "gives grace to the afflicted," while Proverbs 29:23b declares, "a humble spirit will obtain honor." Isaiah 57:15 emphasizes this further: "For thus says the high and exalted One who lives forever, whose name is Holy, 'I dwell on a high and holy place, and with the contrite and lowly of spirit in order to revive the spirit of the lowly and to revive the heart of the contrite.'" While Eliphaz is theologically correct in principle, he misjudges the source of Job's troubles.

iv. He punishes the shrewd (vv. 12-14)

Proverbs 3:34a points out that God "scoffs at the scoffers." Similarly, Psalm 33:10 states, "The LORD nullifies the counsel of the nations; He frustrates the plans of the peoples."

Ironically, verse 13 is quoted by the Apostle Paul in 1 Corinthians 3:19 to illustrate that "the wisdom of this world is foolishness before God. For it is written: 'He is the one who catches the wise in their craftiness.'" Eliphaz, who considered himself a sage, fell victim to his own shrewdness. He believed he was wise but failed to speak what is right in regard to God, and to address the true nature of *Job's* situation.

In verse 14, Eliphaz depicts the proud, who mistakenly believe themselves wise and perceptive but are, in fact, blind. Tragically, he was a living example of the truth he attempted to convey to Job. Misapplied theology can blind the loveless theologian, reminiscent of a man with a large beam protruding from his eye trying to assist another with a small speck in his. Eliphaz was correct—*God punishes the shrewd*—but quite incorrect that God was punishing Job.

v. He rescues the helpless—and shuts the mouth of the unrighteous (vv. 15-16)

Psalm 72:12-14 supports the essence of Eliphaz's declaration here, reflecting a common theme in many psalms. The concluding phrase of verse 16 here in Job may be a veiled response to Job's speech in chapter three—"And unrighteousness must shut its mouth." Job would later confess that he had spoken without knowledge (42:3), but God will render an even more unfavorable verdict on Eliphaz's words in 42:7-8.

8. Prosperity and protection will be restored if you repent (5:17-27)

   a. Do not despise divine discipline (v. 17)

Eliphaz here echoes Proverbs 3:11-12: "My son, do not reject the discipline of the LORD or loathe His reproof. For whom the LORD loves He reproves, even as a father corrects the son in whom he delights." Hebrews 12:5-6 quotes from Proverbs 3, and ends with an encouraging message in Hebrews 12:11: "All discipline for the moment seems not to be joyful, but sorrowful; yet to those who have been trained by it, afterwards it yields the peaceful fruit of righteousness." Additionally, Psalm 94:12 states, "Blessed is the man whom You chasten, O LORD ..." Jesus Himself affirmed this in Revelation 3:19: "Those whom I love, I reprove and discipline; therefore be zealous and repent."

In this context, Eliphaz emphasizes—*do not despise divine discipline*. Great advice if he hadn't already insinuated that this discipline was a result of Job's sin—rather than part of God's inscrutable plan. In verses 18-26, Eliphaz lists the benefits of repentance and heeding God's reproof—though this is a valuable summary, it is entirely misplaced in Job's situation. Job was suffering *because* he feared God, not because he had abandoned the fear of God.

   b. Do not forget the benefits of repentance and turning to God's reproof (vv. 18-26)

   i. If you repent, He will bring relief (v. 18)

Eliphaz's words align with God's declaration in Exodus 32:39: "See now that I, I am He, and there is no god besides Me; It is I who put to death and give life. *I have wounded and it is I who heal* ..." Hosea 6:1 states: "Come, let us return to the LORD. For He has torn us, but He will heal us; He has wounded us, but He will bandage us." Similarly, Eliphaz asserts, *If you repent, He will bring relief.*

ii. If you repent, He will deliver from all trouble (v. 19)

This x + 1 formula is characteristic of several proverbs (Prov. 6:16; 30:18, 21, 29; Alden, p. 96). The number "seven" is often used to express the ideal number. In this case, Eliphaz asserts that if Job repents and seeks God, He will deliver him from every "evil" and all his "troubles." Verses 20-23 illustrate deliverance from death.

iii. If you repent, He will redeem you from death (vv. 20-22)

Eliphaz boldly asserts that the curses of "famine ... war ... the scourge of the tongue ... violence ...[and] wild beasts" would pose no danger if Job simply turned to God and away from his hidden sins. Job had no money; his children had been killed in a war-like raid; he was the object of ridicule; and he sat in a refuse heap—a place frequented by jackals, so to speak. Yet, Eliphaz told him, *If you repent, [God] will redeem you from death.*

iv. If you repent, He will bring you prosperity, security, and long life (vv. 23-26)

The phrase "in league with the stones of the field" may reference the stony ground that does not hinder crops from thriving. Therefore, verse 23 might suggest that agricultural prosperity will follow repentance, or perhaps even signify conditions akin the Kingdom—similar to the imagery of a lion lying down with a lamb.

Verse 24 promises security at home, while verse 25 promises many children, and verse 26 speaks of a peaceful death after a long life. "At this point in the book, little did Eliphaz or Job realize the accuracy of [these verses]. Job lived after this trial, most likely 'in full vigor' for 140 (more?) years ..." (Alden, p. 97). However, in the present context,

> It is hardly appropriate to be telling someone who has lost his house and all his descendants in terrible circumstances, that

his tent will be secure, and that he will have many children. Nor is it particularly helpful to be saying to someone who wants to die that his remaining years will be full of life (Atkinson, p. 47).

c. Do not reject the testimony of the wise (vv. 27)

Eliphaz is now urging Job to regain his perspective and agree with him.

The word translated "investigated" appears 13 times in the book, most notably in 28:27-28, where it describes God's inquiry into the nature of true wisdom: "Then He saw [the place where wisdom is found] and also *searched it out*. And to man He said, 'Behold, the fear of the Lord, that is wisdom; and to depart from evil is understanding'."

In this instance, however, Eliphaz speaks on behalf of his friends, states, "we have investigated it, and so it is." Deuteronomy 19:15 teaches that a matter is confirmed by the mouth of two or three witnesses. Eliphaz, Bildad, and Zophar collectively assert that the only answer to Job's problems is to seek God's blessing and repent of the iniquity he has sown. But we know from chapters 1-2, Job was blameless and upright—a man of genuine faith.

Eliphaz concludes with two commands to his distressed friend: "Hear it and know it for yourself." "Listen and learn"—addressing him as a father would a child, rather than as a comforter to a friend. *Prosperity and protection will be restored if you repent* (5:17-27).

Application

This is the first of eight speeches from Job's three friends, aimed at persuading him to accept their belief that he has committed some sin, which has led to his suffering. As Job listens, he becomes increasingly agitated, emotional, and defiant in his responses, both defending himself and trying to restore his seemingly fractured relationship with God. His words at times may appear to support his friends' view that he was indeed a rebellious fool at heart. However, the prologue and epilogue reveal that Job is a man of genuine faith.

We must remember the central theme of the book and Satan's challenge in 1:9: "Does Job fear God for nothing?" Do believers love and trust God because of the temporal blessings He gives them in return—or do they love and trust Him because of the surpassing value of knowing God Himself? Job's test has now entered a new phase, the most difficult of all. He was now beginning to be tested by theological speculation and complete spiritual isolation.

29:2-4 reveals that Job's greatest anguish stems from the absence of God's "light" and "friendship." He feels utterly abandoned by God and is unsure why. His friends attribute this abandonment to some hidden sin in Job's life, which he knows is not true. Consequently, Job begins to question and speculate himself, adding to his suffering. After each speech, his friends reiterate their message: repent, you've sinned; you're reaping what you've sown.

What can we glean from Eliphaz's eloquent, yet misguided poem filled with true statements horribly misapplied to Job's situation? To Job, Eliphaz was akin to a clanging cymbal and a noisy gong (1 Cor. 13:1). Regarding Job's situation, he did not endeavor to believe all things, hope all things, and endure all things (1 Cor. 13:7). Furthermore, while his theology emphasizes God's transcendence and man's depravity—at least in theory—it falls woefully short in understanding God's wisdom and grace. Eliphaz kept the focus on *Job*, suggesting that he alone holds the key to unlocking divine blessing, rather than encouraging Job to cling to God in his pain. In truth, fearing God is a source of divine blessedness regardless of one's circumstances. As Mason notes:

The essential error of Eliphaz, and of Job's other friends, is in trying to shift Job's focus away from the roots of faith and onto its flowers and fruit. Even as they talk loftily of God, what they are really doing is distracting Job's full attention from the Lord and tempting him to concentrate instead on himself and his sin (Mason, p. 70).

We should learn to be more restrained in what we say when we or others are suffering. James 1:19 captures this sentiment well in light of Eliphaz's speech: "This you know, my beloved brethren. But everyone must be quick to hear, slow to speak and slow to anger, for the anger of man does not achieve the righteousness of God."

However, this does not mean we should never offer counsel or confront sin with love. Romans 15:14 says of believers: "And concerning you, my brethren, I myself also am convinced that you yourselves are full of goodness, filled with all knowledge and able also to admonish one another." The Book of Job serves as a caution against speaking too quickly or assuming we understand the causes of others' difficulties based solely on circumstantial evidence.

The Scriptures indeed encourage us to "counsel" and "admonish" each other using the Word of God. Matthew 7:1-5 and 18:15-18 affirm that believers should help one another concerning sin and confront each other when it's necessary. Nonetheless, the loss of wealth, children, or health is not necessarily due to sin, and the bold words of someone in pain (as seen in Job 3) do not necessarily confirm our assumptions about hidden sin.

Finally, our Savior—the innocent Sufferer, *par excellence*—must have Himself been strengthened in His faith by the Book of Job as He endured suffering for our sins, abandoned by everyone. First Peter 2:21-23 states:

> *For you have been called for this purpose, since Christ also suffered for you, leaving you an example to follow in His*

steps, who committed no sin, nor was any deceit found in His mouth; and while being reviled, He did not revile in return; while suffering, He uttered no threats, but kept entrusting Himself to Him who judges righteously.

When we are confronted with the test of total spiritual isolation, and we are steadfastly convinced that there is no hidden sin in our lives, then there is only one recourse: to keep entrusting ourselves to Him who judges righteously. God is our only hope and consolation. Friends may not provide any genuine compassion, and God may not offer immediate relief (cf. Reitman, p. 83). Yet, He remains our sole hope as we wait for Him to reveal Himself to us in our pain or in death.

Job—What a Disappointment You "Friends" Have Been
Why Me, O God?
Job 6:1-7:21

From the prologue, we understand that Job was a godly man, a believer—being tested to demonstrate that those who fear God do so not for temporal benefits, but because of the profound worth of a relationship with God Himself. After losing everything, Job, in chapter three, expresses his wish that he had never been born. In chapters 4-5, Eliphaz, Job's friend, begins to instruct him, essentially telling Job that he needs to seek God, as everyone knows—you reap what you sow. In this lesson, we will examine Job's response to Eliphaz's poetic counsel.

In Job 6-7, we will explore eight movements in Job's speech, which serve as both a reply to Eliphaz and a prayer to God, calling us to trust God even when others misjudge us.

B. Job—What a disappointment you "friends" have been; why me, O God? (6:1-7:21)

1. I've spoken rashly because of the greatness of my torment and trial (6:1-7)

a. You cannot fathom the grief and calamities I've endured; therefore, my words have been rash (vv. 1-4)

i. Job's Answer (v. 1)

"Then Job answered" will be repeated in 9:1; 12:1; 16:1; 19:1; 21:1; 23:1; 26:1 (cf. Alden, p. 98). What follows is Job's speech, which responds to Eliphaz's first attempt to counsel him. It is part reply to Eliphaz, part ongoing complaint, and part prayer to God Himself.

ii. Weighed on the Scales (v. 2)

Far from confessing some hidden iniquity, Job tells his friends that they cannot comprehend the weight of his "grief/vexation" and "calamity/misery." With vivid and emphatic language, he longs for his pain to be measured on the scales.

iii. Weightier Than the Sand of the Seas (v. 3)

Sandbags can be used as weights. Picture the "sand of the seas"—and yet, Job says his grief and calamity would be "heavier." The incalculable weight of his vexation and distress provoked him to speak as he did in chapter three, longing for death. The term "rash" could be translated as "wild" or "impulsive"—or possibly "swallow," as the KJV does. The Jewish Bible reads: "That is why I spoke recklessly." Job claims that his "reckless" song of death in chapter three was due not to some hidden sin that warranted his calamity, but rather to the overwhelming weight of his frustration and misery

iv. Wounded by the arrows of God (v. 4)

Here, Job attributes his pain to "the arrows of the Almighty" and speaks of the "poison" from God's arrows." He is certain that God is sovereign over his pain. This perspective is, at least in part, shared by God Himself, as noted in 2:3:

The LORD said to Satan, "Have you considered My servant Job? For there is not one like him on the earth, a blameless and upright man, fearing God and turning away from evil. And he still holds fast his integrity, although you incited Me against him to ruin him without cause."

However, Job did not know that God was actually pleased with him and would eventually deepen Job's understanding of and relationship with Him—immensely. For now, Job perceived God as being "arrayed" in battle "against" him.

v. Do I not have a reason to cry out? (v. 5)

The expected answer to these rhetorical questions is "no." Job was not crying for death without reason. Donkeys and oxen only complain when they are dissatisfied. Job was not satisfied with his vexation and misery. Essentially, he says, "Do I not have a reason to cry out?"

vi. Perhaps voicing my complaint will make these things easier to swallow (vv. 6-7)

The vocabulary of verse six has been debated. "The certain words are 'Is ... eaten without salt, or is there taste'" (Alden, p. 99). The rest are used only here or are so extremely rare that it is difficult to determine their exact meaning. However, the overall gist is clear. In verse six, the expected answer is "no." Thus, in verse seven, Job states, "I refuse to touch them; they are like loathsome food to me." The implication is that either what God had served him, he couldn't swallow—it made him sick—or what Eliphaz had said, Job couldn't swallow—it made him sick. And Job refused to accept either without voicing his complaint.

Verses 1-7 combine to form Job's defense for speaking recklessly: My misery is immense; do I not have the right to complain? I won't accept my circumstances or your comfort without complaint to season it a bit. I've spoken rashly because of the greatness of my torment and trial.

2. I long for God to answer my prayer for death (6:8-10)

   a. My constant longing is for death (vv. 8-9)

In verse eight, Job passionately expresses his longing—his desire and prayer before God. Verse nine reveals that his prayer request and longing have not changed since the poem in chapter three. The terms "crush" and "cut me off" are metaphors for death. Like Moses (Num. 11:15) and Elijah (1 Kgs 19:4) before him, Job asked to die (cf. Alden, p. 100). My constant longing is for death. Yet, despite this longing, Job also expressed his faith.

   b. My comfort and concern is my faith (v. 10)

Job found some "comfort" in the fact that he had "not denied the words of the Holy One"—thus he longed to die. He yearned for death, yet he still trusted in the promises of God—the "Holy One," who is without fault, stain, or moral blemish. He did not reject or deny God's testimony of His own absolute purity and perfection. However, Job's comfort seems to be his concern here. If he did not die soon, he feared that his strength might not endure—as verses 11-13 confirm. He says, "I long for God to answer my prayer for death." Why?

3. My spiritual strength and hope are failing (vv. 11-13)

   a. How can I go on? (v. 11)

Job's "strength" to "wait" out this apparent spiritual abandonment was diminishing from his perspective. His hope flickered as he asked, "And what is my end, that I should endure?" How can I go on?

b. *Am I not just flesh and bones? (v. 12)*

Job was made of flesh and bones, not "bronze" and "stones". He felt he lacked the strength to stand firm or press on. The previous verses' references to "wait," "my end," and "endure" indicate that enduring in hope was the issue. Job essentially expressed: "I want God to answer my prayer to die, because I don't have the strength to go on."

c. *Where is my help? (v. 13)*

The word translated "deliverance" by the NASB in this verse is more often translated "sound wisdom" or "success." The essence of Job's questions here is that he no longer knew where to turn for help and wisdom. God had apparently abandoned him. How can I go on? Am I not flesh and bones? Where is my help? My spiritual strength and hope are failing (6:11-13). Next, Job shifts back to rebuking Eliphaz instead of continuing his prayerful contemplations.

4. A loyal friend is faithful, but you are like a dried-up river in summer [false hope and a great disappointment] (6:14-21)
   a. *A faithful friend should strengthen one's fear of the Almighty (v. 14)*

The word "despairing" is related to the term for "melting." Job's faith seemed to be melting away because of the physical and spiritual misery he was experiencing. He thus hoped for "kindness from his friend." "Kindness" is the Hebrew term *chesed*—loyal love, tender mercies, covenant faithfulness—perhaps the Old Testament equivalent of the New Testament's revelation of grace." In the Book of Job, it is used only here.

In referencing his "friend," Job evidently spoke of Eliphaz, though the plural will be used in verse 21. Eliphaz had not been loyal in love, tender in mercy, or full of lovingkindness toward Job—though he likely would have protested otherwise. The reason a "friend" should show steadfast love is so that the man melting in despair "does not forsake the fear of the Almighty."

Alternatively, as some English versions render the Hebrew, Job may have been accusing Eliphaz of forsaking his "fear of the Almighty" by the way he had judged Job. The ESV reads: "He who withholds kindness from a friend forsakes the fear of the Almighty." The New Living Translation states: "One should be kind to a fainting friend, but you accuse me without any fear of the Almighty." Either by example or in practice, Job's friend had not truly been faithful—to God or to him. A faithful friend should strengthen one's fear of the Almighty. Eliphaz had not. Job next poetically illustrates what his friend had really offered, instead of faithfulness and love.

b. *You have offered false hope (vv. 15-21)*
  i. The picture of a dried-up river in summer (vv. 15-18)

Verse 15 establishes the point: "But my brothers are as undependable as intermittent streams, as the streams that overflow" (NIV). Note that Job considered Eliphaz as speaking for all three of his "brothers." "Wadis" are small desert "streams" that run with melting snow but soon dry up in the heat of summer. Eventually, these wadis "go up into nothing and perish" (v. 18). Job uses the imagery of a dried-up river in summer to describe his friends. He then alludes to his own disappointment as follows.

  ii. The picture of disappointed travelers (vv. 19-20)

The "caravans" and "travelers" from the Arabian Peninsula looked in vain for refreshment and strength in these dry riverbeds. The Jewish Bible states: "They are disappointed in their hopes; when they reach the place, they stand aghast." Job felt like these travelers—searching for encouragement, strength, and refreshment from his friends, but receiving none.

iii. The picture directly applied (v. 21)

"And now you have become nothing" (KJV). Like the dried-up rivers, they were nothing—of no help and essentially useless; even worse than useless, because of the false hope they offered. Job suggests that they responded to him out of fear rather than love. They saw a man who was emaciated, disfigured, devastated—and seemingly damned by God. They wanted no part of that damnation. As the summer sun shone, they dried up. Job's friends offered false hope and were ultimately a bitter disappointment.

5. I haven't asked you to "help me" (6:22-23)

   a. I haven't asked you to help me financially (v. 22)

Job wasn't looking for a handout. The term for "bribe" can also refer to a "present." The NLT paraphrases: "Have I ever asked you for a gift? Have I begged for anything of yours for myself?"

   b. I haven't asked you to deliver me (v. 23)

Job had not asked his friends to save him or buy him back from his enemies. He simply desired kindness—love that believes all things, hopes all things, endures all things, and does not end when expectations aren't met. Instead, he could see through Eliphaz's words of supposed help. They did not believe him; could not endure seeing him in his state; and failed to offer him kindness. Thus, Job reminds them: I haven't asked you to "help me"—financially or otherwise.

6. You speak beautifully, but show me my sin [other than perhaps the frustrated words of a desperate man] (6:24-30)

   a. Show me my sin (v. 24)

Eliphaz had never specifically identified any sin of which Job was guilty; he merely insinuated that Job must have committed iniquity to be facing the calamity he now endured. Here, Job calls upon all his friends (plural) to "teach" him and "show" him how he has "gone astray."

b. *What does your argument prove? (v. 25)*

The word "painful" could also be rendered "forceful." "How forceful is your straight talk"—or perhaps, "How grievous is your straightforward speech." Eliphaz used "forceful" and "painful" words, but Job asks: "But what does your reproof, reprove?" Eliphaz had failed to help Job identify the supposed sin that led to his desperate condition.

c. *Are you so heartless that you would condemn me for words spoken in desperation? (vv. 26-27)*

The poetic nature of the Hebrew here has resulted in different translations. The Holman Christian Standard Bible states: "Do you think that you can disprove my words or that a despairing man's words are mere wind?" The ESV translates it as: "Do you think that you can reprove words, when the speech of a despairing man is wind?" The New Living Translation offers another possibility: "Do you think your words are convincing when you disregard my cry of desperation?" Given verse 27, the idea of disregarding the desperate cry may be the best interpretation.

Job seems to employ sarcasm and exaggerated rhetoric to make his point. The implication is that if you dismiss what I say or condemn me for expressing frustration, then you would even cast lots for orphans and barter over your friend. In other words, you are heartless, cruel, calculating, and lacking compassion. They had assumed the worst about him, and he could just as easily assume the same about their treatment of him. After rebuking his friends with hyperbole, Job swings back to defend his integrity.

d. *Look at me; I'm telling you the truth; have mercy on me (vv. 28-30)*

Alden notes: "Job softened the tone of his criticism between v. 27 and v. 28. Whether he noticed on their faces the agony of rebuke or whether he caught himself being unduly bitter, we do not know. It is a pleasant shift" (Alden, p. 105). It is possible that Job's friends had difficulty looking at him. "Now be so good as to face me; I will not lie to your face" (TNK). More literally: "And now, please, look upon me. Even to your face do I lie?" (YLT).

Job was asking his friends to stop judging him unjustly because his "righteousness" was at stake. "Stop assuming my guilt, for I have done no wrong" (NLT). The Bible in Basic English is helpful here: "Let your minds be changed, and do not have an evil opinion of me; yes, be changed, for my righteousness is still in me."

Job pleaded with his friends, asking if he had truly spoken anything "unjust" or "wicked." The word "calamities" was used in verse two and bookends the first half of Job's speech. The reference to his "palate" speaks to his ability to taste or discern whether he was the source of his own misery due to sin. "At the conclusion of the first half of his first response, Job saw a deadlock. By strong innuendo Eliphaz explained his suffering based on God's strict laws of retribution. Job, on the other hand, maintained his integrity, something he would do to the end" (Alden, p. 106).

In verses 24-30, Job essentially says: "You speak beautifully, but show me my sin [other than perhaps the frustrated words of a desperate man]." In chapter seven, he begins to reflect further on his misery.

7. My days are like an endless cycle of futility; my flesh is rotting; my future is hopeless—I will voice my anguish (7:1-11)

   a. *My futility is experienced day after day (vv. 1-3a)*

In verses 1-3a, Job's questions illustrate the futility of life. While this is a universal experience, Job perceives it acutely in his current circumstances. Each day feels like an endless cycle of futility, day after day. Notably, Job spoke of "months of vanity" in verse 3a. His suffering may have lasted less than two years; otherwise, he might have said "years." Nevertheless, "months" of continual pain, itching, and running sores would have seemed endless.

   b. *My futility is experienced night after night (vv. 3b-4)*

In verses 3b-4, Job contrasts his situation with that of a slave who finds shade and a hired man who receives his wage. When Job tries to rest, he cannot sleep. He asks, "When shall I arise?" but the night drags on as he tosses and turns "until dawn." While all men face life's futility, most find some relief in sleep, but Job is deprived of this solace. His insomnia compounds his exhaustion and despair. However, verses 13-15 reveal that when he finally does manage to sleep, things get worse.

   c. *My flesh is rotting (v. 5)*

One writer translates this verse as: "My flesh wears maggots as clothes; my skin is caked with dirt; it's scabby and festering" (Andersen, p. 135). The New Living Translation adds, "My body is covered with maggots and scabs. My skin breaks open, oozing with pus." Maggots typically thrive on decay, and Job essentially states, "My flesh is rotting."

   d. *My future is hopeless (vv. 6-10)*
      i. Soon the thread will run out (v. 6)

Though Job's days and nights drag on in futility, he senses that his time is swiftly coming to an end. He uses the imagery of a thread running out, as the Bible in Basic English states: "My days go quicker than the cloth-worker's thread, and come to an end without hope."

   ii. Soon the breath will be gone (v. 7)

Job may be slipping into prayer in verses 7-10, though this is uncertain since "God" is not mentioned in the Hebrew text. From Job's perspective, the end is near—a mere "breath" away. Consequently, he feels that his "eye will not again see good." His hope has vanished.

   iii. Soon the eyes will not see (v. 8)

Job may be suggesting that God will no longer scrutinize him to torment him, or perhaps that his friends will no longer "behold" him because he will "not be." In either case, Job's words convey a profound hopelessness for the future. It is essential to remember that he was suffering tremendously, expressing the erratic emotions of a sick and seemingly dying man.

   iv. Soon the cloud will dissipate (v. 9)

Later, Job will affirm the resurrection (Job 19:26-27). However, here he speaks poetically from man's perspective: people do not return from the grave. Just as a cloud disappears and does not reappear, Job expresses his feelings of hopelessness once again.

   v. Soon the house will be empty (v. 10)

Job would "not return again to his house." Soon the house will be empty—another expression of death in the near future. In summary, my future is hopeless.

   vi. So, I will not restrain my mouth (v. 11)

Since Job had only a short time left and apparently no hope for a bright future, he decided to hold nothing back. He would bear witness to the truth as he saw it and speak honestly—though he would later confess that he was speaking ignorantly (42:3-6). In this moment, Job was giving full vent "in the anguish of [his] spirit" as he complained "in the bitterness of [his] soul." Essentially, he said, "I only have a short time left, and I will not sugarcoat it." His subsequent prayer is without guile, even if it lacks adequate knowledge of God's inscrutable wisdom.

8. Who am I, O God? And what have I done that You have singled me out? (7:12-21)

   a. *Am I an unruly monster that You must constrain me? (v. 12)*

The "sea" and the "sea monster" are sometimes portrayed in Scripture as enemies of God—even satanically inspired enemies (Ps. 74:13; (Is. 27:1; Ezek. 32:2-3). Job thus cries out to God: "Am I your enemy that You must constantly keep a handle on me?" "Am I an unruly [demonic] monster that You must constrain me?" Unknowingly, Job has touched on the reality we see in chapters 1-2. The enemy of God was at work, and God was dealing with him, but in a manner that is inscrutable apart from divine revelation. Not perceiving the unseen realm, Job viewed himself as pitiful, dying, and hopeless. In God's eyes, however, Job was a testament to what it means to trust God.

Even here, in his agony, Job clings to faith by speaking honestly to God. His healthy, wealthy, and well-meaning friends were, no doubt, offended by Job's bluntness and boldness—especially in prayer. It is significant to note, however, that to my knowledge, not one word of prayer is ever recorded in the book as having been uttered by Job's three friends. For Job, who appeared to bear every mark of being abandoned by God, to call out to God—even in this way—was an act of sheer faith.

b. Leave me alone, I am nothing (vv. 13-19)

  i. You terrorize me at night (vv. 13-14)

Job believed God to be sovereign even over his dreams. He tells God, "If I try to find some measure of relief and rest in sleep, You terrorize me at night through dreams and visions." Was he having nightmares, or was he referring to Eliphaz's counsel that came via a dream? Probably the former, but whichever the case, the implied prayer is, "O God, why won't You leave me alone [i.e., allow me to rest]?"

  ii. You have made death preferable to pain (v. 15)

Job would choose strangulation over life; death over literally "my bones." It may be that Job's bones ached so badly that death was the only relief he could envision.

  iii. Leave me alone, for my days are but a breath (v. 16)

Most English translations render the first phrase here as "I loathe it; I will not live forever." The New Living Translation offers a good paraphrase: "I hate my life and don't want to go on living." The word "breath" is the same term often translated "meaningless" or "vanity" in the Book of Ecclesiastes.

Job prayed to God: "Leave me alone, for my days are meaningless."

  iv. What is man that You are concerned about him? (vv. 17-18)

In verses 17-18, the phrasing closely resembles that of Psalm 8, yet the context differs significantly. Psalm 8:4 states: "What is man that You take thought of him, and the son of man that You care for him?" In contrast, Job asks, "What is man, that you make so much of him, and that you set your heart on him?" (ESV). The Psalmist expresses awe at such divine grace and condescension and grace. Job is agitated at such apparent divine consternation and grim scrutiny—

"You inspect him every morning, and put him to the test every moment" (CSB).

   v. Leave me alone (v. 19)

Under normal circumstances, a believer finds comfort in God's watchful care. But Job, feeling cursed and condemned, wonders when God, in His displeasure, will ever look away—even just long enough for Job to swallow. The net effect of his plea is a desperate "Leave me alone, God."

c. *How have I sinned? What have I done to You? Why do You not pardon my transgression?" (vv. 20-21)*

While Job did not claim to be sinless, as verse 21 confirms, he is bewildered as to how he had sinned to deserve such devastation. "He was willing to repent of anything, but he had no idea what the offense was" (Alden, p. 113). So, Job asked God—frankly, but by asking, he demonstrated his faith.

In verse 21, Job reveals his belief that God is gracious, compassionate, and forgiving. This is why he was so confounded, so agitated in spirit and bitter in complaint. He had evidently sought God's forgiveness for any hidden sin, and yet he did not seem to be forgiven—at least, the evidence of his suffering suggests otherwise. Job's entire life was built on the conviction that God graciously forgives penitent sinners. Yet, it seemed that God was not extending forgiveness. Job asks why He wouldn't "pardon [his] transgression and take away [his] iniquity" before his death, fearing it may soon be too late. His circumstances and the judgments of his friends led him to question if he had sinned grievously. Job's deepest prayer and desire was to be right with God and reconciled to God before it was too late. As Andersen observes:

> If he seems defiant, it is the daring of faith. All Job has known about God he still believes. But God's inexplicable ways have his mind perplexed to [the] breaking-point. Job is in the right;

but he does not know that God is watching with silent compassion and admiration until the test is fully done and it is time to state His approval publicly (Jb. 42:8) (Andersen, p. 139).

Application

As we might expect from a man tormented both bodily and spiritually, Job's speech fluctuates wildly in emotion at times.

What can we learn from Job's painful defense and prayer? As the psalmist wrote in Psalm 62:8: "Pour out your heart to God." A believer can and must cry out to God in times of devastation and feelings of abandonment. Even in terror, anguish, or bitterness, we must cry out in faith.

- Abraham cried to the LORD after ten years of unfulfilled promises in Genesis 15:2-3: "What will You give me, since I am childless? Since You have given me no offspring?"

- Jacob, terrified of reuniting with Esau, pleaded with God—wrestled with God—for grace, and emerged triumphant, though he would walk with a limp (Gen. 32:24-32).

- Moses prayed in his distress: "O Lord ... why did You ever send me? Ever since I came to Pharaoh to speak in Your name, he has done harm to this people, and You have not delivered Your people at all" (Ex. 5:22-23). Later, he cried:

Why have You been so hard on Your servant? And why have I not found favor in Your sight, that You have laid the burden of all this people on me? Was it I who conceived all this people? Was it I who brought them forth ... I alone am not able to carry all this people, because it is too burdensome for me. So if You are going to deal thus with me, please kill me at once, if I have found favor in Your sight, and do not let me see my wretchedness (Num. 11:11-15).

- Hannah poured out her heart to God so fervently in 1 Samuel 1:12-18 that Eli the High Priest thought she was drunk, as her lips moved but no sound came out. Eli rebuked her, but God heard her.

- David cried out, "How long, O LORD? Will You forget me forever? How long will You hide Your face from me? How long shall I take counsel in my soul, sorrow in my heart all the day? How long will my enemy be exalted over me? Consider and answer me, O LORD my God; enlighten my eyes, or I will sleep the sleep of death" (Ps. 13:1-3).

- Asaph wrote in Psalm 77: "My soul refused to be comforted ... I'm so troubled that I cannot speak ... Will the Lord reject forever? And will He never be favorable again? Has His lovingkindness ceased forever? Has His promise come to an end forever? Has God forgotten to be gracious, or has He in anger withdrawn His compassion? Then I said, "It is my grief, that the right hand of the Most High has changed" (Ps. 77).

- The prophet Habakkuk prayed, "How long, O LORD, will I call for help, and You will not hear? I cry out to You, "'Violence!' Yet You do not save" (Hab. 1:2). When he received an answer that only deepened his confusion, he prayed, "Your eyes are too pure to approve evil, and You cannot look on wickedness. Why do You look with favor on those who deal treacherously? Why are You silent when the wicked swallow up those more righteous than they?" (Hab. 1:13).

- Jeremiah, like Job, cursed the day of his birth in Jeremiah 20:14-18. Just before that, he said: "O LORD, You have deceived me and I was deceived; You have overcome me and prevailed. I have become a laughingstock all day long; Everyone mocks me" (Jer. 20:7).

- In Lamentations 5:20-22, we read: "Why do You forget us forever? Why do You forsake us so long? Restore us to You, O LORD, that we may be restored; renew our days as of old, unless You have utterly rejected us and are exceedingly angry with us."

- Jesus, "In the days of His flesh, He offered up both prayers and supplications with loud crying and tears to the One able to save Him from death (Heb. 5:7)." Luke 22:44 adds, "And being in agony He was praying very fervently; and His sweat became like drops of blood, falling down upon the ground." In Mark 14:34, just before He prayed, Jesus admitted that He was "deeply grieved to the point of death."

When all hope seems lost, prayer is an act of faith. James 5:11 reminds us that Job endured, but how did he endure? Through honesty and prayer. Job later admitted that he spoke without adequate knowledge about God, His wisdom, and His sovereign ways. Yet, God vindicated Job's essential "rightness" before Him (42:8). Why? Because Job clung to the belief that God was his only hope. He desired God to reveal Himself and speak to His beleaguered servant. And in grace, God did so at the proper time. However, His revelation was not what Job expected. But gloriously, it satisfied Job's deepest longing, and he needed no explanation or no other vindication. His relationship with God remained intact.

How Jesus, in His humanity and days on earth, must have learned from the Book of Job! He, too—indeed even more so—was the innocent sufferer, vindicating God's glory and showcasing a believer's genuine faith. Jesus learned not to speak in ignorance. He appropriately cried out in faith, "My God, My God, why have You forsaken Me?" (Matt. 27:46).

Yet, 1 Peter 1:23 states: "While being reviled, He did not revile in return; while suffering, He uttered no threats, but kept entrusting Himself to Him who judges righteously."

Can we not learn these same lessons? Pray in faith, express ourselves with utter honesty, and entrust ourselves to the One who makes all things right—in His time.

Bildad [the religious traditionalist]— Job, Repent!
Job 8:1-22

The Book of Job can be seen as God's preface to Proverbs. While proverbial wisdom is helpful, it takes wisdom to apply. What may be theologically true as a proposition—may not actually apply to certain situations. What may be theologically accurate as a concept might not directly apply to specific situations the way we assume it does. Both Bildad and Job learned this lesson the hard way. Job received pious platitudes that were misapplied to his circumstances, and Bildad later discovered that he had not spoken what was right about God—and only through Job's intercession would he be restored.

In Job 8, we will explore four movements in the text that reveal Bildad's straightforward argument: ruin comes to those who forget God; therefore, Job ought to repent.

C. Bildad [the religious traditionalist]—Job, repent! (8:1-22)
  1. You're a windbag, Job—shut up! (8:1-2)

   This is the first recorded response from Bildad the Shuhite, and he gets straight to the point. Unlike Eliphaz, who was more gracious and subtle, Bildad starts with a blunt rhetorical question: "How long will you say these things?" The implied message is clear—"Shut up; stop talking already!"

His next line is even more graphic: "And the words of your mouth be a mighty wind?" The New Living Translation captures this imagery vividly, though perhaps with some exaggeration: "You sound like a blustering wind." "A man like Bildad has no stomach for the sort of dubious spiritual battle in which Job is embroiled. To him Job's complex ruminations are nothing but a load of double-talk and he tells him so outright" (Mason, p. 106).

Essentially, Bildad is saying, "Shut up, you windbag!" Verse three reveals the source of his irritation: he interprets Job's trials and now his words defending his own integrity, as a challenge to God's character. No doubt, Bildad believed he was defending God's righteousness. Thus, he asserts God's justice.

2. God is just—we must assume your family sinned and you've sinned; repent and be restored! (8:3-7)

   a. God is just (v. 3)

Bildad uses the term "pervert" twice here, referring to the twisting of something. He equates "justice" and "judgment" with "right/righteousness." The obvious answer to his rhetorical question is "no"—God does not twist judgment, nor does the Almighty distort righteousness. Bildad is correct; God is just. In fact, God later challenges Job about his understanding of divine justice in 40:8: "Will you really annul My judgment? Will you condemn Me that you may be right?" God addresses Job's words and attitudes, not misinterpreting Job's calamities. However, Bildad makes inappropriate conclusions about Job's misfortunes based on Bildad's own rigid view of retribution and reward, rather than a relationship grounded in grace through faith.

b. God dealt justly with your children (v. 4)

We can affirm in the abstract that God dealt justly—even regarding Job's children. But we cannot assume that he punished them for their sin. Yet this is the very assumption that Bildad makes here. The "if ... then" clause implies that Bildad suspected they had sinned. The Holman Christian Standard Bible reads: "Since your children sinned against Him, He gave them over to their rebellion." In other words, Bildad coldly states: "You know, God is just—therefore your children must have gotten just what they deserved." However, there is no indication in 1:19 that sin—other than Satan's hatred for God and His servant Job—had anything to do with their deaths.

Like any good counselor, however, Bildad offers hope for Job in verses 5-7. The problem is that he misdiagnosed the problem, based on faulty reasoning about God's justice, so his hope actually calls Job to sacrifice his integrity rather than maintain it by trusting God.

c. God will deal compassionately and restore you if you seek Him (vv. 5-7)
   i. If you seek God and beg for His compassion (v. 5)

"If you yourself would seek God and beg the compassion of the Almighty"—is left without the "then" until the middle of verse six: "surely now He would rouse Himself for you ..." Bildad's counsel is to "seek God" and "supplicate the Almighty." Pray and ask for mercy. The word "compassion" could be rendered "grace." However, Bildad's theology of grace suggests it is something one can merit by getting one's life right, as verse six indicates.

   ii. If you are clean and upright (v. 6a)

"If clean and upright you are ... then God will restore you." "Significantly, Bildad makes the cardinal blunder of thinking that one must be pure before he can approach God.

Jesus exposed the folly of this when He taught, 'It is not the healthy who need a doctor, but the sick' (Matt. 9:12)" (Mason, p. 108). The obvious implication is that Bildad believes Job to be "impure" and "crooked"—morally and spiritually. He assumes Job needs to seek God and beg for mercy and be clean and upright spiritually. Notably, the word "upright" is used in 1:1, 8; 2:3 to describe Job.

   iii. Then He will bless you abundantly (vv. 6b-7)

Again, the New Living Translation captures the essence of Bildad's message to Job: "And if you are pure and live with integrity, he will surely rise up and restore your happy home." But Job was blameless and upright, holding fast to his integrity, fearing the Lord and turning away from evil (2:3). Bildad did not think so, thus he continued.

"Then, even if your beginnings were modest, your final days will be full of prosperity" (CSB). The ESV translates: "And though your beginning was small, your latter days will be very great." Ironically, Bildad would be right about this (Job 42:10-17). Verses 5-7 combine to teach Job: God will deal compassionately and restore you if you seek Him [and clean your life up]. Thus, Bildad shifts from—You're a windbag, Job—shut up!; to God is just—we must assume your family sinned and you've sinned; repent and be restored! Next, he appeals to the wisdom of the ages.

3. Wisdom from past generations teaches us—judgment comes to those who forget God (8:8-19)

   a. The past generations confirm what I'm about to say (vv. 8-10)

Whereas Eliphaz appealed to his experience (4:8, 12ff), Bildad draws on the wisdom of "past generations" and "things searched out by their fathers." Bildad's authority is rooted in religious tradition. He argues that ancient wisdom, transmitted through generations, is certainly more valuable than the fleeting thoughts of one or two individuals.

Given the fleeting nature of life and the limited understanding of any single person, Bildad contends that we are ill-equipped to unravel the mysteries of life or the things of God. This perspective echoes the beliefs of the Catholic and Eastern Orthodox traditions, which assert that truth cannot be properly interpreted apart from their tradition. Sometimes even Bible church members and Southern Baptists appeal to how their daddy taught them, or how things have always been done. Many refuse to entertain the idea that tradition could be incorrect or even contrary to God Himself.

"While former generations have passed away, their accumulated wisdom remains, and to that old wisdom Bildad made his appeal" (Alden, p. 119). After establishing the authority of earlier sages as greater than his own, Bildad presents their wisdom in poetic form.

b. *The prosperity of the godless is fragile, and is soon destroyed (vv. 11-19)*
  i. The papyrus soon dries out and withers (vv. 11-12)

In verses 11-12, Bildad uses imagery that can be interpreted in two ways, either of which is possible. He may be illustrating that Job once flourished but is now cut off from blessings because, according to verse 13, he has forgotten God. Alternatively, he could be warning Job that he will not survive unless he heeds the wisdom of tradition—seek God and set your life right. Regardless of the interpretation, the papyrus plant symbolizes fragility. Its prosperity and life depend on water, its vital source. Without adequate water, it will dry up and wither, and Job is at risk of facing a similar fate.

  ii. So are the paths of all who forget God (v. 13)

If we consider the second interpretation of the reed metaphor, Bildad may be implying: "Your life is precarious. You are like a fragile reed in need of the water of the sages from past generations. If you reject my counsel on repentance, you will dry up and wither. You will "forget God" and your hope as a hypocrite will be obliterated." If we accept the first interpretation, Bildad suggests: "You have been cut off from the source of life because you have forgotten God. Your hope, and your once-flourishing life, are destroyed due to your hypocrisy." In either case, it is evident that Bildad implies Job has forgotten God, and as a result, his hope is akin to that of the "godless," which is fading away. The KJV translates "godless" as "hypocrite."

Bildad's words were sharp and cutting. He employs two additional illustrations from nature to depict the fragility of a hypocrite's confidence and prosperity.

> iii. Those who forget God experience a fragile prosperity and confidence, but are soon destroyed and forgotten (vv. 14-19)

The first illustration compares their confidence to a spider's web (vv. 14-15). The New Living Translation vividly states, "Their confidence hangs by a thread. They are leaning on a spider's web." The vibrant life of papyrus is short-lived. Though the spider may trust in its web, it does not last long. It may feel secure, but that web "does not stand" and "does not endure."

The second illustration describes a plant that is uprooted and forgotten (vv. 16-19). In verses 16-17, Bildad speaks of a "lush" plant thriving in the sunlight, spreading out over the garden. However, "His roots wrap around a rock pile." The plant has put its trust in something that cannot sustain it, as it "grasps a house of stones." These words are utterly misplaced when directed at Job, whose trust was solely in God. Yet, at that moment, God seemed silent and had apparently abandoned him. Bildad's words fit perfectly into Satan's diabolical scheme to destroy Job and defame God.

Verses 18-19 depict the plant as uprooted and disowned by its support system. Others may prosper (v. 19), but Job does not. The New Living Translation further clarifies verses 16-19: "The godless seem like a lush plant growing in the sunshine, its branches spreading across the garden. Its roots grow down through a pile of stones; it takes hold on a bed of rocks. But when it is uprooted, it's as though it never existed! That's the end of its life, and others spring up from the earth to replace it." The only "joy" the godless experience is brief prosperity, which eventually fades as the water is cut off, the spider web collapses, and the plant is uprooted. Such is their happiness—it dries up, collapses, and is uprooted.

In verses 20-22, the exhortation to repent becomes more explicit.

4. Repent and you will be lifted up (8:20-22)
   a. God will not reject integrity (v. 20)

In an ironic twist, Bildad speaks truth: "Behold, God will not reject integrity." The "integrity" is used to describe Job in 1:1, 8, and 2:3, where it is translated as "blameless." God will not refuse those who are blameless before Him, and Job was indeed such a man. However, Bildad's insinuation is that since God apparently had rejected Job, he must be blameworthy and lacking in integrity. Thus, Bildad shifts from his intended encouragement to warning and rebuke with the next phrase.

From Bildad's perspective, Job lacked divine support; God apparently was not with him. Why? It is certainly true that God does not "hold the hand of evildoers". But in regard to Job, this is another temptation to confusion and despair. Recall the less well-intentioned crowd that mocked Jesus with similar reasoning: "He trusts in God; let God rescue Him now, if He delights in Him" (Matt. 27:43; cf. Andersen, p. 142-43). Indeed, God delighted in His Son, even though Jesus cried out, "My God, My God, why have You forsaken Me?"

In this instance, Bildad makes a true statement about God but misapplies its implications to Job.

b. God will restore your blessings—if you repent (vv. 21-22a)

Bildad's counsel is succinctly offered in verses 5-6: seek God, beg for grace, clean up your life, and live uprightly—in a word, repent. He promises renewed blessings as the only possible consequence of following his advice. Instead of his current weeping and cries of pain, God would fill Job's "mouth with laughter" and his "lips with [joyful] shouting."

Notably, the idea of the righteous man's enemies being "clothed with shame" appears in Psalm 35:26; 109:29; 132:18. In the Psalms, this serves as a prayer for God to fulfill His promises regarding the Davidic covenant. "Here it is from the mouth of Bildad, an ancient Edomite who theology is not affirmed by Scripture" (Alden, p. 122-23). Context is crucial. In chapter 42, Bildad will find himself rebuked by God Himself for not speaking what is right about Him.

c. God will destroy the wicked (v. 22b)

Job had concluded his speech in 7:21 with a cry of desperation. If forgiveness and grace were not the way to God, then he would "not be"—he would die without hope. Here, Bildad ends with the same phrase in Hebrew: "And the tent of the wicked will be no longer." The wicked will die without hope, implying that Job needed to turn from wickedness before he was destroyed. However, Job was not wicked. He was forgiven and actually honored by God, though none of the men recognized this at that time. As Alden notes: "Job thought he would perish without vindication just like the wicked, even though he was, in fact, 'blameless.' Bildad thought Job would perish because he was among the wicked. Both were wrong" (Alden, p. 123).

Application

Reviewing Bildad's first contribution, he says: You're a windbag, Job—shut up! (8:1-2); God is just—we must assume your family sinned, and you've sinned; repent and be restored! (8:3-7); Wisdom from past generations teaches us—judgment comes to those who forget God (8:8-19); Repent and you will be lifted up (8:20-22).

What should we learn from this chapter? We know from the Book of Proverbs that wisdom principles and maxims are valuable and necessary. However, we must be careful and extremely discerning in how we apply them—especially to others.

Proverbs 25:11-12 states: "Like apples of gold in settings of silver is a word spoken in right circumstances. Like an earring of gold and an ornament of fine gold is a wise reprover to a listening ear." Additionally, Proverbs 15:23 says: "A man has joy in an apt answer, and how delightful is a timely word!" However, Bildad's words brought no delight to Job—not because Job was wicked or unwilling to turn from sin, but because Bildad's traditional wisdom did not apply to Job's situation. In fact, Bildad "seems to think of faith as a way of getting out from under one's cross, rather than of taking it up" (Mason, p. 110). "If Bildad were right and Job were to take his solution, Satan would have won his case. Job, in admitting guilt and accepting that his suffering is a consequence of his guilt, would thus make prosperity his ultimate goal and his religion nothing more than the means to that end" (Jackson, David R. Crying Out for Vindication. P&R, p. 82).

We must be cautious when applying God's Word to our lives and the lives of others. We cannot always understand the reasons behind circumstances. Believers are called to counsel one another, as stated in Romans 15:14. Yet, as James reminds us, "... everyone must be quick to hear, slow to speak and slow to anger." While we may not completely misapply true words like Bildad did—at least not as drastically—many of us may still reflect his lack of compassion, driven by a self-righteous zeal for truth.

May God grant us mercy—and mercy those to whom we minister. Let us learn from Job to cling to faith, even when others are calling us toward a prosperity gospel. Embrace the cross, die to self, and wait for the One who can vindicate genuine trust.

Job—I Need an Umpire! God, What's Going On?
Job 9:1-10:22

The Scriptures call us to sincerity and honesty in our relationship with God and with one another. However, these Scriptures were also given to us to provide hope. Job did not have the Book of Job, but we do. It teaches us that we can endure in faith, even in the face of terrible trials, because God is ultimately trustworthy, wise, and compassionate.

In Job 9-10, we will explore seven movements in Job's speech that urge us to cling to the fear of the Lord, by going to God—even with our speculations, doubts, fears, anger, etc.—without ultimately giving up the faith in search of lesser relief from our suffering.

D. Job—I need an Umpire! God, what's going on? (9:1-10:22)
   1. How can a man be vindicated before God? (9:1-20)
      a. *I know that God is just—but how can a man be vindicated before God? (vv. 1-2)*

Job acknowledged the truth that Bildad clearly asserted in chapter eight—namely, that God is just (8:3) and that He does not reject a man of integrity nor give a hand to evildoers (8:20). However, Job was perplexed about how one could be proved "right with God." He knew he was a man of integrity, yet everyone—including Job—believed that the marks of God's curse were upon him. "Yes, I know all this is true in principle. But how can a person be declared innocent in God's sight?" (NLT). Yes, I know that the godless perish—but how can a godly man be vindicated before God if he is evidently falsely accused? No doubt, his three friends would have pointed to temporal blessings. But Job knew otherwise.

"[He] also knew that other things were true that Bildad had not included. Job knew of exceptions to the friends' generalizations" (Alden, p. 124). In fact, he was the exception most prominent in his thoughts. The phrases "right with God" or "vindicated before God" led Job to consider what it would be like to argue his case—to prove his innocence before God.

b. *If one wanted a legal hearing with Him—how would that go? (vv. 3-20)*
   i. A man would have no answer (v. 3)

The term "dispute" implies a legal action—a "lawsuit," if you will. As the New Living Translation puts it: "If someone wanted to take God to court, would it be possible to answer him even once in a thousand times?" (NLT). Job is contemplating this idea but recognizes that there would be no way to successfully prosecute the case—regardless of effort—"a thousand times"—no evidence or argument could prevail. In verses 4-10, Job further explains why one would not stand a chance in challenging God in court.

   ii. God is too skillful and too strong—who can safely argue with Him? (vv. 4-10)
      aa. The point stated (v. 4)

God is too wise and strong to lose any case a man might bring against Him. Interestingly, when Job did have an audience with God, and the opportunity to "stiffen his neck" before Him, as suggested in 40:3-5, Job could not answer—but he was not harmed. Instead, his encounter with God brought revelation and hope. Job's assertion here, however, is that God is too skillful and too strong to argue against safely. He illustrates this point in verses 5-10.

  bb. The point illustrated (vv. 5-10)

In Hebrew, a nearly identical statement was made by Eliphaz in 5:9 (cf. Elihu's comment in 37:5).

Ironically, Job and his counselors—including Elihu at the end—substantially agree on God's transcendence, power, and wisdom. In fact, God Himself will later make a similar point in His speech more beautifully and dramatically. However, Job (at least it seems, while he is in the midst of the emotional valley) and his friends are not trusting in God's character; instead, they are making theological arguments to justify their presuppositions about why Job is suffering. Theology must be applied with genuine trust to be truly understood. Job's assertion here is that God is so far beyond man in strength and wisdom that attempting to subpoena Him to prove one's innocence seems absurd.

  iii. God is beyond comprehension (v. 11)

In verse 11, Job essentially states: "If God were to meet me in court, how could I even know He was there?" He is beyond comprehension—invisible, hidden. There is likely a sense of frustration in Job's words. Eliphaz had encountered a spirit and heard its message, but if God were to pass by, Job would not perceive Him. God is beyond comprehension.

   iv. God is sovereign and thus who can question Him? (vv. 12-13)
      aa. His sovereignty is unquestionable (v. 12)

In verse 12, it is clear that even if a man disagrees with God's actions or believes God is acting inappropriately, His sovereignty remains unquestionable.

      bb. His sovereignty extends even over evil (v. 13)

If a man were to take God to court to demand that He "turn back His anger," God would not comply. In fact, God is sovereign even over the "helpers of Rahab." "Rahab" refers to the mythical sea monster, a symbol of evil (Isaiah 51:9), later associated with Egypt and its monsters that reside the Nile.

Has Job unwittingly touched on the spiritual realm again? Perhaps, yet even if he was considering God's sovereignty over the demonic realm, this realization does not bring him comfort at this moment. His point is this: if one were to take God to court, how would that process unfold? A man could not even present his case. God is too wise and strong; He is beyond comprehension and, therefore, beyond questioning.

   v. How could I then answer Him? (v. 14)

If even "the monsters of the sea are crushed beneath his feet" (NLT v. 13), then how could Job possibly respond to such immense power, wisdom, and sovereignty? This truth is reiterated in chapters 40 and 42. However, at this moment, Job is not contemplating trusting in God's power, wisdom, and sovereignty; instead, he imagines subpoenaing God to vindicate his own innocence.

His thoughts about a court date with God are filled with theology but seem to lack the type of trust that might issue in comfort. However, the prayer at the end of this chapter and throughout chapter 10 reveals that he was not completely void of faith. Here, Job asks—how could I then answer Him—if He is so beyond me?

vi. How could I ask for mercy—when I'm seeking vindication? (v. 15)

If Job could somehow compel God to testify in court, even though he believes himself "right" regarding his innocence, he would struggle to make his case—because the divine witness would also be the Judge. As a Judge who is all-powerful, sovereign, and incomprehensible, the only reasonable response would be to beg for mercy. However, Job is not seeking mercy for a crime; he is innocent. As Reitman notes, "A defendant begging mercy of his judge amounts to admitting guilt; hence, my own mouth would condemn me (9:20a). Thus, Job cannot logically plead for both justice and mercy at the same time" (Reitman, p. 89).

vii. How could I believe He was even really listening to my case? (vv. 16-18)
  aa. The point stated (v. 16)

Bildad had urged Job to seek God and beg for mercy from the Almighty (8:5). Yet, Job reflects that if he could get a hearing with God, his current circumstances lead him to believe God would ignore him.

  bb. The picture of divine indifference (vv. 17-18)

The term "tempest" or "storm" may allude to the death of Job's children and God's sovereignty over that event. Job's body is covered with "wounds," and he has faced one tragedy after another. From his perspective, God would "not allow [him] to get his breath". Rather he was saturated with "bitterness."

The apparent evidence led Job to believe that if he could somehow get God to appear in court, God would be indifferent or even hostile to his case.

> viii. How can I maintain my righteousness before Him? (vv. 19-20)
>> aa. He is too strong for me to make my case before Him (v. 19a)

If it is a matter of strength, Job recognizes that he lacks the "power" to win a court case against God. "Behold, He is the strong one!"

>> bb. He is the Judge, so how can I cross-examine Him? (v. 19b)

From a human perspective, God is above the Law—as He is the Judge. Will the defendant cross-examine the Judge? Again, God will make this point in a way that will ultimately bring Job consolation. But here, Job's distress does not quite grasp the grace that can be found in God's wisdom, justice, sovereignty, and transcendence. He only sees the futility of trying to question God.

>> cc. You can't win a case against the One who will Judge the case. He would hold anything I would say against me (v. 20)

Here, Job insists he is "righteous," and though his friends disagree, we know he is correct. The term "guiltless" is the same as "blameless" in God's assessment of Job in 1:1, 8; 2:3. However, Job is afraid that if God were called into court and he tried to testify, he would be overwhelmed by God's presence, causing his "mouth" to "condemn" him. He feels that God would "declare [him] guilty." Anything he says can and will be held against him.

Verses 1-20 reflect Job's elaborate musings on the question posed in 9:2—"But how can a man be vindicated before God?" Job argues that even if he could call God into court to question Him and clear his name, he would ultimately lose—not due to his own guilt, but because of God's terrifying transcendent glory and his own inability to testify clearly in His presence.

Next, in order to challenge the simplistic reward-retribution theology of Bildad and Eliphaz, Job begins to introduce the reality of injustice in a world governed by God's sovereignty.

2. Let's consider God's justice in this world (9:21-24)
   a. *It may cost me my life—but I plainly declare: I am guiltless (v. 21)*

As God confirmed in 1:8 and 2:3, Job is "guiltless/blameless," and Job here states this plainly. He adds, "I do not know my soul; I reject my life." The Christian Standard Bible translates this as, "Though I am blameless, I no longer care about myself; I renounce my life." Job is determined to declare the truth even if it costs him his life, which he currently values little. In verses 22-24, he reflects on the supposed advantages of being "blameless" or "guiltless."

   b. *Further—in God's sovereignty, He destroys the guiltless and the wicked (vv. 22-24)*

The term "destroys" is more literally "puts an end to." There is "one" end for both the "blameless" and the "wicked." Job points out to his prosperity-minded friends that God appoints death as the "end" of life for both the righteous and the wicked.

Verse 23 illustrates this further: "If death comes suddenly through disease, He makes sport of the fate of those who have done no wrong," according to the Bible in Basic English. Job, though using provocative language, simply points out that the "innocent" sometimes die of the plague. Since God is sovereign, the death of the innocent can certainly seem to "mock" the value of being innocent.

In verse 24, Job laments the injustices present in a fallen world and questions who is sovereign over these matters if not God. Our protagonist struggles profoundly with his faith; however, *he is not asserting these thoughts as facts but rather questioning the conventional wisdom that his friends offer as a way out.* Reality does not completely align with a theology of reward and retribution, as there are clear injustices and inequities in the world. Undoubtedly, God must be sovereign over them, or He ceases to be God.

So how do we understand these issues? Job begins by contemplating how a man can be justified before God. Believing himself to be blameless yet suffering from injustice and tragedy, Job urges his friends to reconsider their simplistic theology. He provocatively challenges them to reflect on God's justice in the world.

In verses 25-31, Job returns to his thoughts about appearing in court before God while lamenting the apparent futility of doing what is right.

3. Righteousness seems futile (9:25-31)

   a. *My time is running out—and there is no court date in sight (vv. 25-26)*

Job compares his days to a "runner," "boats," and "an eagle," each illustrating the concept of speed. His days are fleeting, and he perceives no goodness in them. One moment, he longs for death; the next, he mourns the brevity of his existence. Such are the emotions of one who is severely tested both physically and emotionally.

   b. *If I dropped my case—You would still hold me guilty (vv. 27-31)*

Job expresses that even if he were to drop his "complaint" and put on a happy face—he was afraid that more "pains" would come. He is convinced that God would not "acquit" him. Even if Job attempted to move on, he feels as if his relationship with God were severed. He still felt as if God held him guilty (it is possible to see the second-person singular pronoun "you" to refer to Bildad, but one would expect the plural to refer to his friends).

If he is deemed guilty as his friends had asserted or if he were held guilty before God, it would be meaningless and empty to "move on." He elaborates on the apparent futility of seeking vindication with God in verses 30-31. No matter how hard he might try to be right with God and clean in His sight, Job felt as though God was still condemning him.

Notably, in verses 28 and 31, Job addresses God directly in prayer, expressing that it seems useless and futile to strive for righteousness before Him. It seems Job, too, has misinterpreted his circumstances. He speaks in ignorance (42:3), *yet he is still reaching out to God.* This interaction embodies a key aspect of persevering in faith—especially when faith feels absent. Even when voicing complaints about the seeming futility of trying to be right with God, it is an expression of faith—be it ever so fragile—to tell God about it.

4. If only there were a mediator (9:32-35)
   a. *The difference between a man and God makes vindication seem impossible (v. 32)*

Here, Job acknowledges that his rhetorical approach to a lawsuit is merely fantasy, as God is not a man before whom Job could defend himself in a court of law. The vast difference between man and God renders such a scenario impossible.

b. *The desire for mediator/arbiter expressed (v. 33)*

Job expresses a longing for an umpire who could mediate between him and God, someone who could "lay his hand upon us both." He yearns for binding arbitration, where an impartial third party could facilitate reconciliation rather than simply render a judgment on who is right. As Andersen notes, "The Hebrew ... does not mean a judge, who merely decides who is in the right; he is a mediator who settles the quarrel by reconciliation, a negotiator who brings both parties together, by laying his hand upon us both as a common friend" (Andersen, p. 151). Though Christ is no doubt foreshadowed in the idea, it is reconciliation that Job is longing for—not strictly forgiveness.

c. *The desire for God's discipline and dread to be removed (v. 34)*

Job envisions a mediator who could negotiate a reconciliation in which God's "rod" would be lifted, allowing him to be free from the "dread" of God. Job believes that if he were not so terrified of God's sovereign hand, he could present his case without fear, as confirmed in verse 35.

d. *The direct communication that would occur if a mediator were found (v. 35)*

If such an arbiter were found, he could "speak and not fear" God. However, as the Christian Standard Bible puts it, "But that is not the case; I am on my own."

In chapter 10, Job turns almost exclusively to prayer.

5. **God—why do You oppress me when You know I'm not wicked? (10:1-7)**

   a. *I will give full vent to my complaint, whatever the consequences (v. 1)*

Much like his earlier declaration in 7:11, Job insists that he will hold nothing back. He would speak honestly, even if he later acknowledges that he spoke ignorantly. In chapter six he spoke largely in view of his friends and their counsel. Here he turns directly to God. "My soul is disgusted with living; I will complain without restraint; I will speak out of the bitterness of my soul."

   b. *Why do You contend with me? (v. 2)*

Initially, Job asks God not to condemn him and then seeks clarity on why God is contending with him. Job was asking for something that he already had. God had not condemned him. In fact, God had previously commended Job before the angelic host as a man who feared Him. However, Job was unaware of this. Like his friends, he has misinterpreted his circumstances and calamities. Even though he is mistaken about God's motives and his situation, in faith Job continues to bring his pain to God, persevering amid great suffering.

c. *Is it right for You to oppress me and approve the schemes of the wicked? (v. 3)*

In verse 3, Job sees himself as the work of God's "hands," a creature under His sovereign care. Yet he feels wronged and rejected, questioning if God somehow smiles upon the "schemes of the wicked."

d. *Are You not all-knowing? (vv. 4-6)*

In verses 4-6, Job reflects on the limitations of his friends, who can only "see as a man sees." They had lived only a few years compared to eternity. But God does not have "eyes of flesh" or live His "years as the days of a mortal" that He needed to somehow find proof of Job's sin.

Job and God knew the truth about his integrity. Here, Job somewhat facetiously asks if God has to investigate because He is not omniscient and eternal. However, verse seven reveals the essence of Job's prayer-complaint: "You know I'm not guilty—yet there is no deliverance from Your hand."

Job was perplexed and pained because he was convinced that God *is* all-knowing. God knew that he was "indeed not wicked." Furthermore, since God is sovereign, there was no deliverance from His power, except by God Himself. Job did not perceive himself as rescued, even though both God and he knew he was "not guilty."

Again, it must not be overlooked that Job is talking to God—even in his pain, questions, and feelings of rejection. And he will continue to do so.

Job 9:1-10:22

6. God—did You create me to destroy me? (10:8-17ab)

   a. *The question posed (vv. 8-9)*

Job questions why, if God "fashioned" him "round about" and "made [him] as clay," it seems He did so just to "destroy" him and "turn [him] into dust." Job asks, "God—did You create me to destroy me?" This may allude to the creation account in Genesis 1-3.

   b. *The creation of Job pictured (vv. 10-12)*
      i. Conception (v. 10)

The reference to "milk" turning into "cheese" illustrates conception in his mother's womb. Job's own "embryonic development" is portrayed as liquid—i.e., "milk"—transforming into a solid—"cheese."

   ii. Clothed in skin, flesh—knit with bones and sinews (v. 11)

Soon, the tiny baby, under God's sovereign and creative care, is clothed "with skin and flesh" and knit "together with bones and sinews." Alden comments, "This verse impinges on the abortion debate because it suggests that from the point of conception Job was a person for whom God cared" (Alden, p. 137). In verse 12, Job shifts from the development of his own body in his mother's womb to the theological implications of his fetal development and beyond.

   iii. Created and cared for by God (v. 12)

Here, Job acknowledges that God was the source of his life. He also uses the term *"chesed"*—steadfast love. God had produced life and shown love in regard to Job and had providentially cared for him. God is the Author of life, steadfast love, and providential care. However, in verses 13-17, this embattled believer reveals the spiritual battle he was wrestling with...

c. The concealed plan of God to destroy Job (vv. 13-17ab)

i. Job's speculation assumed (v. 13)

Job knew that God was omniscient, knowing the end from the beginning. Why, then, had God granted Job life and lovingkindness while concealing in His heart the plan to destroy his health, his wealth, and his family? Job speculated that he was the object of God's wrath and that he was created and sustained for such a fate. In reality, however, Job was the object of God's favor, despite suffering horribly.

ii. Job's guilt would be punished (v. 14)

Job assumed that God's plan included divine judgment for any "sin" he might commit. And in the next verse, he confirms that such a situation would be just.

However, even Job's righteousness could not bring relief from this divine plan to bring him low.

iii. Job's righteousness challenged (vv. 15-16)

If Job was "wicked", then "woe to me!" he says. But even if he is righteous, he feels he cannot lift his head. Job knew he was righteous—that is, not perfect, but as right with God as any sinner who trusted in the grace of God could be. Yet he was "sated with disgrace and conscious of [his] misery." He suffers as if he were wicked, and this suffering appears to be part of God's plan. Job struggles to maintain confidence in his innocence, otherwise he felt that God would "hunt [him] like a lion" and unleash divine power against him.

iv. Job's counselors/accusers (v. 17ab)

Job states, "You renew Your witnesses against me and increase Your anger toward me." This may be an allusion to Job's friends, who seem to be part of God's plan to harm the very one He created and sustained with life and lovingkindness.

In verses 1-7, Job prays: God—why do You oppress me when You know I'm not wicked? Then in verses 8-17ab, he asks: did You create me to destroy me?

7. God—leave me alone so that I may have some peace before I die! (vv. 17c-22)

   a. God—I still wish I had died in the womb (vv. 17c-19)

Job expresses his anguish with a phrase similar to "Changes and warfare are upon me." In verse 18a, he echoes his earlier question from verses 8-9—why did You create me? He laments, "Why then have You brought me out of the womb? Would that I had died and no eye had seen me! I should have been as though I had not been, carried from the womb to the tomb."

Job's desire had not changed from his original death wish expressed in chapter three (see especially 3:11). He continues to wish he had died in the womb.

   b. God—withdraw from me that I may have some peace before I die (v. 20-22)

As in 7:16 and 19, Job asks God to leave him alone and allow him a moment of peace before death. In verses 21-22, he seems to have lost the more positive perspective on the rest that death would bring, which he expressed in 3:13-22. Amid his turmoil and pain—and his faltering faith—Job appears to have for the moment lost sight of the peace of life after death. Here he depicts it to be "the land of darkness and deep shadow, the land of utter gloom as darkness itself... the land of no return." Even the strongest believers can struggle with hopelessness and despair in the face of death.

Application

Yes, those who fear God are blessed by God. But those blessings may not always be manifested in the ways people expect. Pain and injustice exist in the world, even for the righteous who fear God. Believers may struggle mightily to trust and fear God, wrestling with hopelessness, anger, resentment, fear, and doubts about His justice. Yet, through it all, they bring their anger, their resentment, their fears, and their doubts to God. Genuine believers may contemplate the injustices they have suffered and may find themselves blind to the very truths they know intellectually about God, possibly holding these truths against Him for a time.

For a while, Job found God's wisdom, power, sovereignty, and omniscience to be a source of bitterness rather than comfort. Later, God would reveal these very same attributes to Job in a way that left him needing no further explanation or vindication. For now, it is important to remember that those who fear God should turn to Him in prayer, even when they are overcome with anger, resentment, disillusionment, and pain.

Though perhaps Job's exact wording and apparent attitude may not serve as a model for us, his perseverance in faith should inspire us, as indicated in James 5:11. Only God has the ability to vindicate us. We must wait on Him, even if we find ourselves speculating, pontificating, or speaking in ignorance.

As mentioned in our introduction, Job did not have the Book of Job. We can learn from the Book of Job what Job did not know at the time: that God is doing something good, far beyond our understanding, and we can trust Him. As noted in several previous chapters, Jesus, the innocent sufferer *par excellence*, learned this lesson. While being falsely accused and reviled, He uttered no threats. While feeling abandoned by God, He continued to entrust Himself to the One who judges righteously.

Zophar—Job, Repent, God is Incomprehensibly Great and Wise!
Job—I Also Can Speak Eloquently about God's Greatness, but I'm Ridiculed and the Wicked Prosper!
Job 11:1-13:3

Mike Mason writes: "If our gospel is not one that, like Job's, will stand up to the prolonged test of having absolutely no circumstantial evidence of worldly success, then it is a gospel of straw. It is a gospel founded on appearances, not on the cross of Christ" (Mason, p. 146).

Christ trusted His Father's Word when everyone else believed He was a failure—cursed by God. Saving faith cannot ultimately be destroyed because it is a God-given conviction of the heart based on truth, which will endure until the end, believing that God is ultimately trustworthy and good—only in Him is wisdom and life. But the testing of such faith can be incredibly challenging. Job discovered this in ways most of us cannot even imagine. Job's testing, however, has benefited countless believers through its inspired record.

In this lesson, we will unpack Zophar's first speech and Job's first response to Zophar. This exchange illustrates that knowledge *about* God does not necessarily provide help to those struggling with their faith amid difficulty. Not until we are satisfied with trusting the wisdom and power of God will peace prevail. We should persevere in seeking God until He brings us to that place.

E. Zophar [the fire and brimstone preacher]— Job, repent; God is incomprehensibly great and wise! (11:1-20)

1. I must answer a fool as his folly deserves, lest he be wise in his own eyes (11:1-3)

a. Your multitude of words cannot go unanswered (vv. 1-2)

Of Job's three friends, Zophar only responds to Job twice (here and in 20:1), while Eliphaz and Bildad speak three times. Zophar opens by questioning whether a multitude of words should go unanswered, suggesting that a talkative man cannot be acquitted. He expresses his need to respond to Job.

Two proverbs come to mind regarding Zophar's reasoning here. Proverbs 26:5 states, "Answer a fool as his folly deserves, that he not be wise in his own eyes." No doubt, Zophar wanted to humble Job. Perhaps he had even convinced himself that it was in Job's best interest. Proverbs 10:19 also declares, "When there are many words, transgression is unavoidable, but he who restrains his lips is wise" (cf. Prov. 12:23; 15:2; 17:27-28; Eccl. 5:3). Zophar evidently felt compelled to speak due to Job's "multitude of words." However, in doing so, Zophar failed to restrain his own lips in wisdom. Job will point this out in 13:5.

Essentially, Zophar justified his decision to speak by claiming, "A man of talk should not be vindicated merely because he complains the loudest." While there is some proverbial wisdom in Zophar's assertion, the tone and substance of his argument reveal that he has misjudged Job. He believed that Job's problem was hidden sin that went far beyond the words of a man frustrated by his suffering and his friends.

b. Your boasts and scoffing deserve a rebuke (v. 3)

The Christian Standard Bible offers a literal yet vivid translation: "Should your babbling put others to silence, so that you can keep on ridiculing with no one to humiliate you?" It is unclear whether Zophar believed Job was boasting against and mocking God or his two friends. Regardless, Zophar evidently feels compelled to "answer a fool as his folly deserves, lest he be wise in his own eyes."

Mike Mason's comments on Zophar's speech are well stated:

> Zophar has obviously been chomping at the bit for a chance to put in his two cents' worth, and right off the bat he shows himself to be the sort of fellow who shoots first and asks questions later. In his criticism of Job he is not just blunt but insulting, calling his friend a scoffer and a windbag (v. 4) and broadly accusing him of arrogant self-righteousness (v. 4). Clearly the discussion is heating up. It may be in Zophar's nature to be caustic and abrupt, or it may just be that things have reached such an impasse that all the friends are now prepared to level direct accusations at Job. In any case, from this point on the dialogue assumes more the character of a full-blown argument than a civil discussion. Mudslinging becomes the order of the day, and Zophar's openly scornful attitude certainly contributes to this. It is worth noting, however, that none of Job's friends is a mere two-dimensional strawman. All are complex characters in their own right, with lively and interesting minds. Granted, Zophar is probably the least sophisticated of the three, the one who wastes the least breath on tact and diplomacy. Yet this very trait can be both a strength and a weakness, and it may even have been Zophar's rough-and-ready [bluntness] that drew him to Job as a friend in the first place. For is not Job this way too? Like many people, Zophar is probably as genuinely likable a person in good times as he is nasty in bad (Mason, p. 131).

2. You're getting less than you deserve (11:4-6)

a. You claim to be innocent before God (v. 4)

"For you have said, 'My teaching is pure, and I am innocent in your eyes'"—The pronoun "your" is singular, evidently referencing Job's claim before God. Although Job had not said these exact words, Zophar may have been paraphrasing the essence of Job's complaint—and perhaps most specifically, Job's public complaint to God in 10:7: "According to Your knowledge, I am indeed not guilty, yet there is no deliverance from Your hand." Or perhaps 6:10: "But it is still my consolation, and I rejoice in unsparing pain, that I have not denied the words of the Holy One."

Zophar understood Job to be claiming that his "doctrine" or "beliefs" were pure and that he was "clean" in the eyes of God. Even if paraphrased, it is a fairly accurate representation of Job's claims. Yet, Zophar interpreted them as rebellious and careless words, rather than honest expressions from a man who truly feared God but was greatly suffering and feeling abandoned in his relationship with Him. Job never claimed to be perfectly sinless (Job 7:21). But he did claim that there was no breach of faith or hidden wickedness that would render him guilty before God and men.

b. You would be surprised if God were to speak concerning you (vv. 5-6ab)

Previously, he had accused Job of being a "man of lips," but now he expresses a desire for God to open His lips against Job, implying that God would not engage in empty talk or mockery as Zophar believed Job had. Instead, He would "declare ... the hidden things of wisdom." In chapters 38-41, God did indeed declare to Job the secret things of wisdom—that God is incomparably wise and powerful and thus is unquestionably trustworthy. But here, Zophar has in mind a devastating rebuke of Job.

It seems Zophar is more focused on Job's humiliation than on Job's well-being. In 6:8, Job wished for death. Here, Zophar uses the same expression, "would that" or "if only," in saying how he wished God would humiliate and surprise Job with a true assessment of Job's purity.

For sound wisdom has two sides—This somewhat obscure statement seems to convey that there are "two sides" to every story. Job had boldly proclaimed his side—his alleged innocence. But Zophar yearns for God's perspective to be revealed. Unbeknownst to Zophar, after God speaks, he and his friends, Eliphaz and Bildad, will seek Job's intercession on their behalf (42:7-9).

c. *You need to know that you're getting less than you deserve (v. 6c)*

The New Living Translation interprets this as: "Listen! God is doubtless punishing you far less than you deserve!" But more literally, Zophar is saying, "Know that God has chosen to overlook some of your sin" (cf. HCSB). Like much of what his two friends have said, Zophar's words may contain some abstract truth but are woefully misapplied to Job's situation. Job is suffering not for his sin but for his faith.

Yes, if God were to mark iniquities who could stand? But there is forgiveness with God that He may be feared (Ps. 130:3-4). No one in this life receives the full consequences of their sins. However, this perspective does not truly benefit Job unless one assumes he is suffering for his sin, which he was not. As Mason states:

> The characteristic sin of evangelicals is this bull-in-a-china-shop approach to the consciences of other people. How often have we met buttonholers like Zophar in the church foyer? More to the point: how often have we been like him ourselves? The prime danger of fundamentalism is that a good firm grip on fundamental doctrines can be accompanied by a fundamental lack of respect (to say nothing of love) for other people.

Orthodox theology is a good servant but a poor master, if our faith is not "faith expressing itself through love" (Gal. 5:6) (Mason, p. 132).

Later, the Apostle Paul warned Timothy about those who desired to teach God's Word but did not truly understand what they were saying or the issues they confidently asserted (1 Tim. 1:7). He reminded Timothy: "But the goal of our instruction is love from a pure heart and a good conscience and a sincere faith" (1 Tim. 1:5). Zophar made bold assertions but failed to grasp the glory of God he was discussing. He was, in essence, a noisy gong and a clanging cymbal (1 Cor. 13:1).

The clear implication of Zophar's words is that Job was suffering due to his sin and actually deserves even worse.

3. Do you really think you can comprehend the depths of God's greatness and wisdom? (11:7-12)
   a. *God's wisdom is beyond you (vv. 7-9)*
      i. You can't discover the deep things of God (v. 7)

Zophar continues by trying to convince Job that he could not claim to have "pure doctrine" or "innocence" before God if he truly understood God's greatness and wisdom. Zophar asks: "Can you solve the mysteries of God? Can you discover everything about the Almighty?" (NLT). In chapters 38-41, God will ask Job similar questions—not to humiliate Job and win an argument, but to strengthen Job's faith and cause him to endure in trusting God's wisdom and power. Here, however, Zophar's questions imply that Job can't really know God well enough to assert his innocence.

   ii. You can't ascend to the heavens or plumb the depths of Sheol (v. 8)

Only God knows how wise and wonderful He is. Again, a beautiful bit of theology—yet totally misapplied in order to shame a righteous man, who is bewildered by his suffering.

iii. You can't measure it by earth or sea (v. 9)

Here, Zophar asserts that God's wisdom is beyond Job's comprehension. No doubt this is true as God Himself will confirm later. But this truth in the abstract, spoken by another finite creature in the context of hostility does not really help Job spiritually.

b. God's ways are beyond you (vv. 10-12)
   i. You must understand that He does what He pleases (v. 10)

Zophar uses legal terminology to suggest that God is free to bring judgment as He pleases. As the NIV reads: "If He comes along and confines you in prison and convenes a court, who can oppose Him?"

Zophar then connects this legal language to divine sovereignty and God's knowledge of those who sin.

   ii. You must understand that He sees your sin (v. 11)

Zophar says, "God knows empty men; and He sees wickedness, will He not discern it?" Implication being—you must understand that He sees your sin.

   iii. You must understand that you are an empty-headed, stubborn fool (v. 12)

The Jewish Bible offers a literal translation of Zophar's sarcastic remark: "A hollow man will get understanding, When a wild ass is born a man." The language indicts Job as an empty-headed, stubborn fool. McKenna's reminder is helpful here:

> Zophar falls victim to his own verbiage. His agitation ignites verbal violence that flares up and becomes a careless curse. Not only does he denounce Job as an "empty-headed ass," but in contemporary language he declares that wisdom will elude Job "till hell freezes over."

Somewhere in the process, Job's pitiful condition has been forgotten, and his anguished cry has been ignored. Zophar is consumed by his own anger and personifies the quip, "With friends like you, who needs enemies?" Pity the sufferer who is comforted by the likes of Zophar (McKenna, p. 103).

Zophar's counsel to Job is clear—God's wisdom is beyond you, and His ways are beyond you, you are stubborn, empty-headed fool. Do you really think you can comprehend the depths of God's greatness and wisdom? (11:7-12). Then, like Eliphaz and Bildad before him, Zophar calls for repentance with the promise of blessing.

4. Repent and be blessed—don't and you will die (11:13-20)
   a. If you repent you will be blessed (vv. 13-19)
      i. If you will seek God and pray to Him (v. 13)

A literal rendering would be: "If you yourself would prepare your heart and spread out your palms to Him." The pronoun is emphatic. Zophar urges Job to personally and urgently seek God in his heart and plead with Him in prayer. While seeking God and asking for His grace is a good thing—Zophar believed Job needed to repent of hidden sin.

   ii. If you will put away iniquity and sin (v. 14)

This may refer to no longer tolerating sin within his family, and thus perhaps a backhanded remark about his children. Zophar is clearly calling Job to turn away from iniquity and sin. The blessings of doing so are detailed in verses 15-19.

   iii. Then you will not be afraid (v. 15)

According to Zophar, if Job repented, he "could lift up [his] face without defect and [he] would be firm and not fear." Job had said he could not lift his head (10:15) and was "afraid" of all his pains (9:28). He lamented, "For what I fear comes upon me, and what I dread befalls me" (3:25), and he suffered fearful nightmares (7:13-14). But Zophar claims that if Job turns from sin, sorrow and fear will be reversed.

    iv. Then you will forget your trouble (v. 16)

If Job would repent, Zophar promised that his friend would "forget" these awful days, and remember them as water under the bridge, so to speak.

    v. Then you will experience brighter days (v. 17)

Job contemplated the "darkness" of death because of his pain and suffering (3:4-5; 10:21-22). But Zophar promised that if he repented, he would experience brighter days.

    vi. Then you will experience rest and security (vv. 18-19a)

In 3:26, Job states: "... I am not at rest, but turmoil comes." In 7:6, he mourned that his days were quickly coming to an end "without hope." In chapter six, Job felt that his faith—though still there—was failing. But here Zophar promises that his faith and hope would be renewed.

    vii. Then you will experience prosperity (v. 19b)

Little did Zophar know that soon he would indeed seek Job's favor. But here he promises prosperity and influence to Job if he repents. Sadly, verses 15-19 describe Job "as he used to be, before the malice of ... Satan moved the Lord to put his character to the test." Neither Zophar nor Job understood that Job's testing was proof of his privileged relationship with God (Andersen, p. 158-59).

b. If you don't repent, you will die without hope (v. 20)

Finally, Zophar ends his altar call with the dire consequences of Job's refusal to repent—blindness, captivity, and hopelessness in death. These are in some sense descriptive of Job's current assessment of his own situation. Thus,

Zophar believes that both Job's current and future states hang on his repentance from sin.

However, as we've noted repeatedly, Job did not have some hidden sin from which to repent. He was a blameless and upright man, fearing God and turning away from evil. But he was suffering immensely and felt completely abandoned by God.

Job's response to Zophar is detailed in chapters 12-14.

F. Job—God is indeed incomprehensibly great and wise; thanks for the help; but I'm ridiculed and wicked prosper! (12:1-14:22)

   1. Tell me something I don't already know—Oh wise ones (12:1-3)

      a. *What would the world do without your wisdom? (vv. 1-2)*

   Job was not above sarcasm either. Here he tells all three of his friends, using the plural pronoun, "You people really know everything, don't you? And when you die, wisdom will die with you!" (NLT). What would the world do without your wisdom?

      b. *What have you said that I don't already know? (v. 3)*

   The Jewish Bible states: "But I, like you, have a mind, And am not less than you. Who does not know such things?" Job's friends spoke in proverbial wisdom that was widely recognized. He was aware of the same general truths. Yes, God is great and beyond full comprehension—thank you! Job begins with sarcasm, "Tell me something I don't already know—Oh wise ones." Next, he attempts to help them understand the enigmas and inequities of life in a fallen world, where not every God-fearing person is blessed with prosperity, and not every wicked person suffers in this life.

2. I am ridiculed and the wicked prosper (12:4-6)
a. I am a laughingstock for trusting God (v. 4)

Job used the term "joke" or "laughingstock" twice in this verse. In days gone by, Job "called on God and He answered him". "The verb 'called' is a participle and describes Job's former close relationship with God, who would answer when Job prayed. This is what he missed the most (Job 13:22; 23:5; 30:20-21; 31:35)" (Alden, p. 150).

But now, people laughed, claiming that God "answered him" with judgment. Job believed he was "just and blameless," and so did God, though Job did not know it. But now, he felt the ridicule of others who were convinced that his "just and blameless" reputation was merely a façade. Job was making the point: I am a laughingstock for trusting God.

b. I am held in contempt by you who are at ease (v. 5)

The Jewish Bible reads: "In the thought of the complacent there is contempt for calamity; It is ready for those whose foot slips."

> No matter how wise and good a person may have been in the past, when misfortune strikes we tend to see it as exposing the victim's hidden foibles. If a man has a heart attack, then perhaps he was working too hard [or not eating right]. If our neighbor goes bankrupt, then probably he had it coming to him. Whatever our theology might be, in any tragedy there is just something in our finite minds that gravitates immediately toward the theory of human causes. Job's purpose in chapter 12 is to expose the utter godlessness of such thinking (Mason, p. 141).

Job asserts that he is truly a blameless and upright man who seeks God. Yet he is perceived as a joke and one who is under God's judgment. The righteous do not always prosper, contrary to the neatly compartmentalized reward-retribution theology (cf. 7:11-19).

c. *I declare that the wicked do prosper (v. 6)*

The third line of this verse is perhaps better translated: "[Those] who carry their god in their hands" (NET). Job's point is clear: "Oppressors" sometimes do "prosper," and "those who provoke God are secure." Job calls on God in faith, yet there seems to be no answer. Those who hold their god in their hands appear to prosper. As the Bible in Basic English puts it: "There is wealth in the tents of those who make destruction, and those by whom God is moved to wrath are safe; even those whose god is their strength." *I am ridiculed while the wicked prosper* (12:4-6).

3. Nature recognizes God's sovereignty—and so should you (12:7-12)

   a. *Ask the animals to teach you [Remember, I'm a donkey] (vv. 7-8)*

In verses 7-8, it is notable that the pronouns are singular. Job may have been quoting a well-known song or poem. His point seems to be that animals and nature can teach individuals something. In this context, he is likely pointing out that creation demonstrates God's sovereignty over it. See Zophar's assessment of Job in 11:12.

   b. *All creation knows that God is sovereign and does as He pleases (vv. 9-10)*

It is particularly interesting that the name Yahweh is used only here in the large poetic section of Job (chapters 4-37). The One true and living God is sovereign over all creation, and all creation knows it. So should Job's friends. In verse 10, he states that the LORD controls who lives and dies. Man does not manipulate God by his righteousness or through some coerced repentance.

Notably, Job makes a point here, but he is also contemplating the implications of God's sovereignty concerning his own life. As Alden writes: "Here Job only spoke it, but he would existentially embrace it when God spoke it to him in chaps. 38-41" (Alden, p. 151). Nebuchadnezzar would hear Daniel say essentially the same thing in Daniel 4:17, 25, but it was not until Nebuchadnezzar embraced it by faith that it brought him peace (Dan. 4:34-35, 37).

c. Are you listening and trying to understand what I'm saying? (v. 11)

Job may have been commenting on the unpleasant and undigestible arguments of his friends (cf. 6:6). However, this question seems better understood as a rebuke of their unwillingness to hear his argument and consider whether he is speaking the truth. Are you listening and trying to understand what I'm saying?

d. Age should bring wisdom [but you have proved otherwise] (v. 12)

The Hebrew allows for this to be translated as a question: "Is wisdom in the aged, And understanding in the long-lived?" (TNK). Nature recognizes God's sovereignty—and so should you (12:7-12).

Next, Job matches his friends and exceeds them in eloquence when speaking of God's greatness. His emphasis is on God's sovereignty, which helps him cope with the reality that sometimes the wicked prosper while the righteous suffer.

4. I too can speak eloquently of God's infinite power, wisdom and sovereignty (12:13-25)

   a. God is the source of wisdom, strength, counsel, and understanding (v. 13)

Job affirms that God possesses "wisdom and power." God's wisdom and might will be the central message *to* Job in chapters 38-41, but at this point, Job has not yet grasped the implications and comfort that it brings. Clearly, Job's point in verse 13 is that God—not man—is the source of wisdom, strength, counsel, and understanding. He then highlights God's sovereignty.

b. *God is the sovereign Whom no one can withstand (vv. 14-25)*
   i. He is sovereign over circumstances, which cannot be reversed (v. 14)

In His inscrutable wisdom and power, God's sovereign actions are irreversible. Man's deeds of contrition and contrived repentance cannot change what God has done.

   ii. He is sovereign over the weather (v. 15)

"The weather and the rain in particular are also within the parameters of God's rule" (Alden, p. 153). God is sovereign over the weather. Does not drought affect even the righteous?

   iii. He is sovereign over the deceived and the deceiver (v. 16)

Deception is prevalent in this world, yet God is the source of "sound wisdom." The weak are "misled," but "strength" belongs to Him. Is He not sovereign over both the deceived and the deceiver? Everything is not as simplistic as you make it out to be.

   iv. He is sovereign over making fools of the wise (v. 17)

The wisdom and power of God can overturn the wisdom of the wise men of this world. Even the best counselors and most discerning judges can be wrong at times. God is sovereign over this as well. Everything is not as neatly packaged as you present it, Job says.

   v. He is sovereign over the decisions of kings (v. 18)

Is there not ample evidence that sometimes the seemingly irreversible decisions of "kings" are reversed? Those shackled by a king can be freed, and vice versa.

vi. He is sovereign over who is honored and dishonored (v. 19)

Here, Job raises the question: Are there not instances where those who are honored ultimately find themselves destitute? "Job knows from personal experience that the Lord 'overthrows men long established.' This is exactly what has happened to him" (Mason, p. 145).

vii. He is sovereign over advisers (v. 20)

Sometimes wise counselors give poor advice. "And God is sovereign over that too," he asserts. Perhaps Job did not fully grasp the implications of this statement, or he may have found comfort in the truth he proclaimed.

viii. He is sovereign over the mighty (v. 21)

Sometimes the privileged and the strong are sovereignly humiliated and made weak. There are many examples of this phenomenon. As Job has said, "The LORD gives and the LORD takes away" (1:21).

ix. He is sovereign over mysteries (v. 22)

Sometimes things that men believe will never be revealed, are revealed. God alone is the One who does this; He is sovereign over mysteries.

x. He is sovereign over the rise and fall of nations (v. 23)

God is the One who "makes nations great, then destroys them... enlarges [them], then leads them away." See Acts 17:26.

xi. He is sovereign over the bad decisions of the rulers of the earth (vv. 24-25)

Job observes that, realistically, world leaders in his time (and ours) "grope in darkness with no light." They make poor decisions, leaving the world to wander in darkness. Yet God remains in control.

In verses 14-25, Job eloquently articulates God's greatness, emphasizing His control over what many would consider "improbable events." God is not limited to a simplistic reward-retribution mindset; He is sovereign over the unexpected. Job was grappling with these thoughts, seeking help and hope amid what felt like abandonment by God. His friends only accused him and urged him to repent. Job wanted them to see—perhaps even out of love, for their own good—that things cannot always be neatly explained. God does as He pleases—even when it contradicts conventional human wisdom, including proverbial wisdom that is true in general, but not universally. Job summarizes his thoughts up to this point in 13:1-3.

5. I understand these things—therefore, I want a hearing with Him (13:1-3)

   a. *I have witnessed the inscrutable wisdom and unrivaled sovereignty of God (v. 1)*

Job asserts that he has experienced the enigmas and improbable occurrences that arise in a fallen world. He discerns that, despite God's sovereignty, He "does the unusual and often operates in ways directly opposite of what is expected" (Alden, p. 156). Job has witnessed the inscrutable wisdom and unrivaled sovereignty of God.

   b. *I know what you know about God's wisdom and power (v. 2)*

As he stated in 12:3, Job reaffirms that he "also" understands the proverbial wisdom espoused by his friends. He is in no way "inferior" to them. Job knows what they know about God's wisdom and power. In verse 3, however, Job returns to the subject that preoccupied his thoughts before Zophar spoke.

   c. *I still want to speak to and argue my case with God (v. 3)*

Human counselors had left Job convinced that only God could help him. The pronoun, "I" is emphatic. He personally wanted to speak with the One who possessed the "almighty" power he has described in the previous chapter. Job believes that in communicating with God, he will receive a more attentive response than from his friends. "He felt quite sure that God's explanation of the matter would be different from the interpretation" of his counselors (Alden, p. 156). And frankly he spoke rightly about this (see 42:7). As Andersen notes:

> [Job] is conceding that [he and his counselors] have much common theological ground. But this is not enough for Job. He has still to find out how these truths apply to himself. This requires direct dealing with God. While 'argue my case' has primary reference to the settlement of a legal dispute, the use of the same root in Isaiah 1:18 (where 'let us reason together' is God's offer) includes the desire, not to win the suit, but to reconcile the offended party by sorting out the misunderstanding. Job is willing to confess to any sins that may be proved against him (13:23), but so far neither his memory nor his friends have done this. His own vindication and God's will go hand in hand, but what he needs more is understanding of the ways of God through rational discussion. So far, the friends have failed to supply the needed explanation (4-12). It must come from God (Andersen, p. 164).

Application

Once more, Job's faith clung to the truth that only God held the answer to the perceived breach in their relationship. Only God could strengthen Job's faith and restore their relationship, as he understood it. Job tenaciously clung to this faith—though later he would confess that he had spoken without knowledge. So we too, when challenged in our faith beyond, it would seem, its limits, we must seek an audience with God for hope and help. We must not turn to easy answers or contrived repentance. Instead, we must hold fast to God and seek His guidance when faced with overwhelming enigmas and apparent contradictions to conventional wisdom. Continue to seek God, regardless of how desperate or alone you may feel.

Jesus' teachings in Luke 11:5-13 and 18:1-8 emphasize the importance of persistence in seeking God for help in overcoming temptation and attaining justice. Most people give up too soon, failing to persist until they receive answers. Job's friends settled on an explanation that satisfied them well enough, but Job found it theologically inadequate. He kept seeking God—boldly and persistently. This perseverance is how believers are called to endure the most severe trials. And gloriously, God's sovereign grace guarantees the final outcome. As the Apostle Paul wrote, "For I am confident of this very thing, that He who began a good work in you will perfect it until the day of Christ Jesus" (Phil. 1:6; cf. 1 Thes. 5:23-24; 1 Pet. 5:10).

Job—Oh to Die and Live Again
Job 13:4-14:22

Although we are only about a third of the way into the Book of Job, one wonders if God didn't intend for us to become overwhelmed and exhausted by the constant dialogue, arguing, and human reasoning—begging for both silence from men and revelation from God.

Not until God speaks in chapters 38 to 42 will there be diving revelation that transcends human misinterpretations, misapplications and presuppositions about suffering and blessing. But even these exhausting human speeches are inspired by the Holy Spirit and beneficial when understood in their proper context.

In Job 13:4-14:22, we see six movements in Job's speech, which reveal a man clinging to hope while grappling with despair. Job's continued responses should inspire us to hold onto hope in the midst of apparent hopelessness and encourage us to minister more compassionately to other believers when they are battling despair in this life.

F. Job—God is indeed incomprehensibly great and wise; thanks for the help; but I'm ridiculed and the wicked prosper! (12:1-14:22)

2. You are worthless counselors, who distort the truth in the name of God (13:4-12)

a. You misrepresent the truth and mistreat your patients (v. 4)

In 13:3, Job states, "I would speak to the Almighty, and I desire to argue with God." This implies he believed himself to be speaking honest words from a place of integrity. Here in 13:4, in stark contrast to his own honesty before God and his friends, Job declares: "But you put a false face on things" (BBE) or "whitewash with lies" (ESV)—and "As physicians, you are worthless quacks" (NLT). You misrepresent the truth and mistreat your patients.

b. You ought to stay quiet and actually listen to my argument (vv. 5-6)

The Christian Standard Bible here reads: "If only you would shut up and let that be your wisdom!" Job's words echo the sentiments of Proverbs 17:28: "Even a fool, when he keeps silent, is considered wise; when he closes his lips, he is considered prudent." In verse six, both "argument" and "contentions" are legal terms (Alden, p. 157). Job was asking them to genuinely listen to his case. It appears from the rest of the book that they did not heed Job's request here.

In verses 7-11, Job accuses his friends of misrepresenting God's justice.

c. You cannot win favor with God by misrepresenting justice to make Him look better (vv. 7-11)

i. Will you misrepresent justice for God's sake? (vv. 7-8)

The New Living Translation captures the essence of verse seven well: "Are you defending God with lies? Do you make your dishonest arguments for his sake?" Not only did his friends presume to speak for God, but Job also charges them with making wicked and treacherous arguments on His behalf. In verse eight, Job accuses his friends of attempting to win God's favor (lift the face of God) by condemning him—claiming to be on God's side in the battle against Job.

    ii. Will it be well with you when He examines you? (v. 9)

Job's rebuke here is not merely an accusation; it is a warning rooted in love. He could have simply said, "Leave me alone," but he didn't. Why? Undoubtedly, he cared for these men and "took their friendship seriously" (Mason, p. 151). If they were not honestly dealing with the suffering of a righteous man who fears God, but were rather accusing Job to avoid experiencing the same affliction, "will it be well when [God] examines" them? Can they deceive God into being favorable to them? Clearly not! Job was cautioning his friends that honesty is more valuable than prosperity. God knows the truth and recognizes that they were not being entirely honest in their arguments or their assessment of Job.

    iii. Will not He reprove you? (vv. 10-11)

Job believed that God would indeed rebuke the half-truths and erroneous arguments of his friends. This proved to be true in 42:7-9, where God, in His terrifying majesty, declared: "My wrath is kindled against you ... because you have not spoken of Me what is right as My servant Job has ..."

You cannot win favor with God by misrepresenting justice to make Him look better (vv. 7-11). In verse 12, Job returns to the point he made in verse four.

d. You offer worthless advice (v. 12)

As Job sat in "ashes" and scraped himself with a potsherd (2:8), he demonstrated the ugliness and barrenness of burnt ashes, as well as the fragility of broken clay pottery. These were as helpful to him as—perhaps even more than—his friends' theological musings.

3. It may cost my life, but I will maintain my righteousness (13:13-19)

   a. *Be quiet so I can speak—then I will face the consequences (v. 13)*

This marks the second time in this speech that Job urges his friends to "be silent" (cf. v. 5). They will be dismayed before God because of their dishonest arguments, but Job is prepared to "speak" and face the consequences—"let come on me what may"—because he was speaking with integrity.

   b. *Why would I speak like this if I were not innocent? (v. 14)*

Job was convinced of his innocence before God. He wanted his friends to be quiet because they would have to answer to God for their half-truths spoken on His behalf. But Job would "speak" and let the chips fall where they may. Verses 15-19, however convey a greater confidence than mere personal integrity.

   c. *My hope is in God—no matter the consequences—this will be my salvation; a godless man has no such hope (vv. 15-19)*
      i. *My hope issues in the confidence to argue my ways (v. 15)*

This famous verse has sparked heated debate regarding the best way to translate it. Most English versions render the Hebrew as a statement of faith and hope in the midst of Job's tumultuous speeches.

It is possible to interpret Job's statement as a declaration of hopeless defiance: "Truly, he will put an end to me; I have no hope; but I will not give way in argument before him" (BBE). The New Living Translation takes what seems to be a mediating position: "God might kill me, but I have no other hope. I am going to argue my case with him."

The question arises: Is Job's hope placed in his argument, or in God's eventual vindication of him? Considering verse 16, it seems best to align with the majority of English translations: "Though He slay me, yet will I trust him" (KJV). Job asserts, "My hope issues in the confidence to argue my ways." Job's friends were essentially calling him to find hope in his own repentance. Job remained steadfast in his hope in God's vindication. In fact, his hope was in God's salvation.

> ii. My salvation is in Him—such is not the confidence of the godless (v. 16)

Job emphasizes that "salvation" is found in God, which allows him to argue before Him. Such confidence is unavailable to the godless. Satan, adverse circumstances, and half-truths hold no sway over the person who waits for God, knowing that deliverance lies solely in Him. Abraham experienced the freedom of faith in the midst of the greatest trial when God asked him to sacrifice Isaac, his beloved son. Jesus too found His hope and salvation in God—even in the face of death.

> iii. My case is prepared—listen carefully; I will be vindicated (vv. 17-18)

As in verses 6 and 13, Job calls his friends to "listen" to him. His declaration in verse 18 that he would be "vindicated" may have irritated one of his as yet unnamed audience members, as revealed in 32:2. The young man, Elihu, was angry that Job justified himself before God (32:2; cf. 27:5, 6). However, Job may simply have been asserting that God would ultimately vindicate his faith before these men, which is precisely what the LORD does in 42:7-9.

> iv. My mouth will be silent and I will die if someone can successfully prosecute the charges against me (v. 19)

Eventually, Job would indeed become "silent," but he would not "die" (40:3-5; 42:1-6). At this moment, he was saying that no one could successfully "indict" him, successfully prosecute charges against him. If they could, he would willingly remain silent and accept his fate. This is a declaration of innocence, set against the accusations from his friends.

In verses 13-19, Job says—It may cost my life, but I will maintain my righteousness. He then directs his case directly to the Lord.

4. God—please show me my sin; why am I treated like Your enemy? (13:20-27)

   a. *You must enable our relationship (vv. 20-22)*

      i. Only You can change the reality that I'm terrified of You (vv. 20-21)

The pronouns in 13:20-14:22 are singular, and along with the content of Job's words, indicate that Job is praying to God rather than addressing his friends. In a sense, Job has been avoiding an audience with God, stating that if God would remove his terror, he would not "hide" from God's face.

Job was affirming to God that only He could change the reality that Job was terrified of Him, due to his current circumstances. If God were to remove His "dread," then Job would have the confidence to present his case before Him.

      ii. Only You can open the avenues of our communication (v. 22)

Job was telling God that he was willing to meet, but he acknowledged that only God could facilitate that communication. "His frustration was that God said nothing, leaving him to stagger and rage in doubt and despair" (Alden, p. 164). Job was telling God that he was eager to work on their relationship, but God remained silent. Thus, he prayed, "You must enable our relationship. You must reveal why our relationship seems broken" (vv. 23-24).

b. How have I sinned? (v. 23)

Job wanted to deal with his "iniquities and sins," to repent, if only God would "make known" his "rebellion." Otherwise, Job felt lost in the dark. He believed he had conducted himself as a righteous man—not in sinless perfection, but as a believer who walked with God by faith, confessing his sin and offering the appropriate sacrifices by faith (we can assume this based on 1:5, 8; 20-22; 2:3, 10). Could it be, though, that Job was beginning to wonder if perhaps his friends were right, but he just didn't know his sin? Whatever his exact motive, he was asking God for an official indictment.

c. Why is our relationship broken? (v. 24)

In verse 20, Job expressed that out of terror, he was, in some way, hiding from God. Here he asks, "Why do You hide Your face...?" Psalm 13:1 reads: "How long, O LORD? Will You forget me forever? How long will You hide Your face from me?" In Psalm 11:7, the psalmist says: "For the LORD is righteous; He loves righteousness; the upright will behold His face."

Job felt as though God considered him an "enemy." How have I sinned? Why is our relationship broken? Yet, God does not respond to His suffering child. Perhaps the God of love remained silent because He wanted Job and his friends to be completely exhausted by their own theological speculations.

d. You must see what you've done to me (vv. 25-27)
  i. I am frail and at your mercy (v. 25)

By using the imagery of "a driven leaf" and "dry chaff," Job illustrated his own frailty and insignificance. Why would God even take the time to allow this to happen to him—or, in Hebrew thought, do this to him?

ii. I am suffering bitterly (v. 26)

Job reasoned that perhaps he was now suffering for "the iniquities" of his "youth"—sins long since passed. If God did bring a charge, would it be from years gone by?

iii. I am a prisoner to your sovereignty (v. 27)

Job here tells the LORD that he feels like a prisoner, bound by divine sovereignty. He calls on God to restore their relationship. In verses 20-27, he pleads: God, please show me my sin; why am I treated like Your enemy? Next, he prays about the bitterness of life and death.

5. Life is hard, and then you die! What else is there? (13:28-14:12)

   a. *The brevity of life (13:28-14:6)*
      i. Man wears out (v. 28)

Here, Job reflects on his wretched condition. He feels himself wearing out and decaying. In the previous verse, he stated, "I am a prisoner to your sovereignty." Now, he describes himself as rotting away in that prison.

   ii. Man is short-lived and full of turmoil (v. 1)

Job is rotting and wearing out, but everyone's life is "short-lived and full of turmoil." Life is not as neatly packaged as Eliphaz, Bildad, and Zophar have claimed. Everyone experiences turmoil.

   iii. He is like a flower or a shadow (v. 2)

Job uses two word-pictures to communicate the brevity of life. It is here one moment and gone the next. In verses 3-6, he returns to the ultimate sovereign over these matters.

iv. You are sovereign over this (vv. 3-6)
  aa. You are the Judge (v. 3)

One who is wearing out, short-lived and full of turmoil, and here today and gone tomorrow, is under the scrutiny of the divine Judge. What does that mean for man?

  bb. Man is depraved (v. 4)

Job clearly understands that man cannot make himself "clean" or sinless. God, You are the Judge, and man is depraved. His final statement, "not one," may also be a call of faith—"Is there not One?" That is, are You not able, O God? (see Andersen, p. 171).

  cc. You are Sovereign (v. 5)

Job acknowledges that God controls man's lifespan. He is absolutely sovereign over the days, months, and limits of men's lives.

  dd. You are Master (v. 6)

Here, Job prays to God as the Master, asking Him to look away so His slave can rest. He uses vivid language to depict the brevity of life. Man's life is short. God is Judge. Man is a sinner. God is sovereign and Master. Thus, Job asks that He allow His hired man to get some rest in their brief and bitter life.

b. *The finality of death (vv. 7-12)*
  i. A tree that is cut off can grow back (vv. 7-9)

Job notes that "there is hope for a tree", in that even when it is "cut down," it can "sprout again." A tree that is cut off can grow back, but it is not the same for man. We have only one life.

ii. A man does not grow back, or have a new start after he dies (vv. 10-12)

Job asserts that when one dies, they truly die (v. 10). "People are not like trees that grow back after they are cut down. They are like the water that disappears in a dry gulch" (Alden, p. 166). In verse 12, Job speaks of the finality of death from an earthly perspective, declaring that "in the present world order no evidence exists that a person may return to life" (Hartley, Job, 234; quoted by Alden, p. 168).

Job is reflecting on the brevity of life and the finality of death under God's sovereignty. There is no escape and no second chance at life once death arrives. A tree can start over, but man cannot. In summary: Life is hard and then you die! What else is there? (13:28-14:12). But in contemplating death and its seeming finality, his faith momentarily grasps a glimmer of hope in verses 13-17. In fact, these verses may serve as the centerpiece of his poem and thoughts at this point.

6. Oh to die and live again—I will wait for it (14:13-17)

a. Job's honest longing for the refuge of the grave (v. 13)

Job takes a somewhat surprising turn—though perhaps not for someone enduring his emotional and physical torments—by praying that God would grant him refuge in the grave, "until Your wrath returns to You, that You would set a limit for me and remember me!" The New Living Translation expresses it this way: "I wish you would hide me in the grave and forget me there until your anger has passed. But mark your calendar to think of me again!"

It seems as if Job begins to merge his longing for death with a flicker of hope. In the grave, he could be shielded from his current torments under God's sovereign watch, yet he holds onto some hope that God would set a limit on the grave and "remember" him. This longing is articulated more clearly in verses 14-17, where he expresses a hopeful and honest desire for refuge of the grave.

b. Job's hopeful longing for the resurrection from the grave (vv. 14-17)
   i. I will wait for my change (v. 14)

Here, Job dares to contemplate the possibility that death is not the hopeless end. He uses many of the same words he previously employed to express hopelessness, but now in a context of hope. It is as if he is daring to suggest that there might be another perspective rather than the finality of death.

The word "wait" was also used in 13:15, where it was translated as "I will *hope* in Him." Here, he states that throughout his struggles in this life, he would "wait in hope" until his "change comes." With this statement, Job was holding onto hope for something beyond what appears to be the finality of death. The term "change" is often associated with a "change" of clothes (Gen. 45:22; Judges 14:12-13, 19; 2 Kings 5:5, 22, 23). The Apostle Paul later adopts this imagery for the resurrection in 1 Corinthians 15:53-54. Job has been contemplating the human perspective, but here he suddenly entertains the possibility that death might serve as a refuge, a place to wait in hope for his new garments.

   ii. You will call, and I will answer You (v. 15)

Here now Job uses a term he had previously employed negatively in 13:22. In that instance, he told God that it was up to Him to enable their relationship. Now, he expresses hope that perhaps from the grave, God "will call" and Job "will answer." In 10:8-13, Job had called on God to remember the care with which He had fashioned him. Here, he holds onto the hope that God would "yearn for" His handiwork. If there is a resurrection, Job could wait in hope, praying that God would call and care for him.

iii. You will pay attention to my steps, but not my sin (v. 16)

The word "now" can refer to the time when the previous verse is fulfilled. That is why many English translations render it as "then." "Surely then you will count my steps but not keep track of my sin" (NIV). In 13:27, from an earthly perspective, God seemed to be carefully scrutinizing Job's actions to hold him guilty. But at the time of the resurrection, Job held out hope that God would "count" his "steps" in the sense of preserving and caring for him—not like a hunter tracking his prey, but like a father watching over his child (Alden, p. 169). As well, in the resurrection, God would not "observe" Job's sin. In fact, Job asserted that God would eliminate it.

iv. You will put an end to my sin (v. 17)

If we had only the first phrase, "My transgression is sealed up in a pouch," we might wonder if it suggests that Job's sins could be held against him. However, the second phrase clarifies Job's thought: "You would plaster over my iniquity." The term "wrap up" shares the same root used in 13:4, where Job accuses his friends of plastering over the truth with their lies and half-truths.

Job hopes for a day when his sins are no longer accessible or recalled. In 11:14, Zophar suggested that Job needed to put his iniquity far away from him. Yet here, Job yearns for the day when God will dispose of and remove the stain of his sins.

In verses 18-22, he returns to the harsh realities of life that he faces. By faith, he can see glimpses of hope, but in front of him in this life, he faced what seemed to be the inevitable erosion of any earthly hope. Pain, loss, and emotions have a way of making us vacillate in our perspective.

7. But in this life, there is nothing but hopelessness and the inevitable pain of death (14:18-22)
   a. *The inevitable illustrated (vv. 18-19a)*
      i. Mountains wither (v. 18)

Even mountains inevitably erode. Rockslides and erosion gradually change the landscape. In this life, one cannot stop the inevitable.

   ii. Stones wear away (v. 19ab)

The "torrents" of storms alter the landscape and forever change its appearance. Similarly, Job's life had been irrevocably changed. He may contemplate hope after the grave, but he faced the realities of a life here on earth forever altered—inevitably wearing away under the torrent of his painful circumstances. These two figures illustrate the inevitable in this life.

   b. *The inevitable declared (vv. 19c-22)*
      i. Hope in this life is inevitably destroyed (v. 19c)

Just as mountains inevitably erode and the landscape is washed away, God causes man's expectations to perish. Every man faces death, and his earthly hopes and dreams are ultimately destroyed. Verses 20-22 confirm this idea.

   ii. Death is the inevitable end of this life (vv. 20-22)
      aa. At death, a man departs and decays (v. 20)

As the landscape changes, so too does a man's appearance under God's sovereign rule—over a lifetime and then in death. At death, a man departs and decays—like the mountains and rocks.

   bb. At death, a man does not know his legacy on earth (v. 21)

Job waxes philosophical as he contemplates the separation death brings—from family and the future—though at this time, he had no family except for his wife. This is reminiscent of the thoughts found in Ecclesiastes 2:18-19 and 9:5. Ultimately, at death, a man does not know his legacy on earth.

> cc. At death, a man does not know the pain of others—only his own (v. 22)

Death and its pain tend to be the all-consuming focus of a dying person. This is what Job was facing in this life, before his hope of resurrection. Thus, he concludes with a dose of earthly realism. While he clung to the hope of dying and living again, in this earthly life he experienced nothing but hopelessness and the inevitable agony of death (14:18-22).

Application

The righteous man, who ultimately persevered in faith, experienced profound spiritual and emotional highs and lows during his suffering. We should remember this before we offer hollow platitudes and superficial wisdom (13:12). Perhaps true wisdom calls us to silence, urging us to refrain from commenting on matters we do not fully understand. Honesty and prayer may hold more value than abstract theology and pious judgments. While theology is important, biblical love encompasses grace and mercy, even toward one's enemies, let alone a suffering friend with whom one may disagree. As Mason provocatively notes:

> ... as long as Job's theology failed to line up with that of his friends', their hearts would remain fundamentally closed to him. How many Christians are like this, making soundness of doctrine their yardstick for measuring out mercy? Does our compassion suddenly run dry once others make it crystal-clear that they do not buy our brand of theology? Do we realize that if God had followed this policy in regard to the human race, there would be no gospel? (Mason, p. 150).

We can see the tenacious character of Job's persevering faith. He was willing to wrestle and fight for his relationship with God, which felt entirely lost. Rather than cursing God and dying, Job pleaded with God to meet with him and reveal his sins.

Job's prayers and refusal to abandon his faith can help sustain us during times when we feel forsaken by God and pressured by others to seek answers elsewhere—be it through charismatic healings, deliverances, holistic diets, self-discipline, or psychological techniques disguised in Christian language. Ultimately, God alone must provide answers, and His answer is in His name—I am! I am enough!

Job will find this out, after human counsel exhausts him and everyone else. God *is* the answer, not our repentance, although Job does experience a genuine change in his perspective (see commentary on 42:6) upon recognizing God's trustworthiness.

The Book of Job urges us to engage honestly with God, confront our pain and hopelessness, and ultimately seek help from Him. After all is said and done—and there is nothing more that man can say—God will be enough.

Eliphaz's Second Speech—Who Do You Think You Are, Job?
Job 15:1-35

From a young age, even Jesus Himself had to learn to navigate the challenges posed by well-meaning people (and sometimes those who were not so well-meaning) who felt compelled to correct, question, or challenge Him. At age 12, having been about His Father's business in the Temple, Jesus' mother asked Him, "Son, why have You treated us this way? Behold, Your father and I have been anxiously looking for You" (Luke 2:46). John the Baptist initially hesitated to baptize Jesus and questioned Him about it. Throughout His ministry, both friends and foes alike misunderstood Him. Peter challenged Him regarding His prophecy of crucifixion and resurrection in Matthew 16. The religious leaders accused Him of blasphemy and ultimately condemned Him to death. In response, Jesus answered truthfully and appropriately to the various questions, concerns, and accusations, but He never allowed Himself to become embroiled in prolonged arguments. Rather, He entrusted Himself to God alone. He was truly free, not needing to prove Himself to others, but living solely for the will of God.

In contrast, we often find ourselves drawn into debates that compel us to defend our viewpoints rather than promote faith in God. If friends and foes alike argued with the sinless Son of God, we too will face conflicts. In Job 15, we enter into the middle of an argument between friends. Good intentions have fallen prey to pride. Job is still seeking help in God, albeit with great difficulty, while his friends have perhaps lost perspective. They have begun to insult and speak condescendingly to their devastated friend.

In Job 15, Eliphaz's second speech presents three main points that, through negative example, call us to humility and greater theological honesty in our ministry to others. Our study of the Book of Job continues, this time focusing on Eliphaz's second attempt to counsel Job.

G. Eliphaz—Who do you think you are Job? (15:1-35)
1. Job, you're a fool whose own words prove the wickedness of your heart (15:1-6)

   a. *Does a wise man belch hot air—and argue with vain and unprofitable words? (vv. 1-3)*

      i. Eliphaz's second answer (v. 1)

As in 4:1, "Eliphaz the Temanite answered" Job (cf. 2:11; 22:1; 42:7). This time, he abandoned his earlier, more polite approach (cf. 4:2-6).

   ii. Eliphaz's vulgar analogy—you excrete hot air from your belly (v. 2)

In 6:26, Job had said, "Do you intend to reprove my words, when the words of one in despair belong to the wind?" And then Bildad, in 8:2, asked, "How long will you say these things, and the words of your mouth be a mighty wind?" Here, Eliphaz dismisses Job's insight as mere "wind," implying that Job's "belly" was full of the east wind—suggesting that hot air is coming out of him. Does a wise man belch out such nonsense? From this analogy, Eliphaz then turns to a direct assessment of Job's argument.

iii. Eliphaz's assessment of Job's argument—you use vain and unprofitable words (v. 3)

Eliphaz was clearly stating that Job's reproof was of no use, and his speech was of no value.

Taking verses 2-3 together, Job's dear friend and leader of his three companions—a self-proclaimed defender of wisdom and a self-appointed counselor to Job—essentially states, "Your speeches have been as valuable as a giant belch."

> How often do Christian acts of mercy that began in a spirit of genuine love and compassion end up going sour as the element of judgment enters in? Real suffering is such an ugly business, such a messy and draining and thankless and long, drawn-out affair that all the soundest theology in the world, powered by the most heartfelt sympathy and the loftiest motives and all the grandest resources, simply crumbles to dust in the face of it. Therefore, the Apostle Peter warns, "If anyone serves, he should do it with the strength that God provides" (1 Peter 4:11). Any charitable venture that does not find its source in the tireless energy and the inexhaustible compassion of the Lord Himself is doomed to failure. Only the Holy Spirit has a strong enough stomach to take on the extremities of suffering (Mason, p. 179).

Ironically, in attempting to illustrate that Job's speech is unhelpful, Eliphaz asks: Does a wise man belch hot air and argue with vain and unprofitable words? The irony continues with his next statement.

b. *Your words do away with the pursuit of proper worship—and thus they reveal your guilt (vv. 4-6)*
   i. You distract from the fear of God, and proper perspective of God (v. 4)

The pronoun is emphatic: "Moreover, you yourself frustrate fear [the proper respect and reverence God deserves] and you distract from a proper contemplation of God." Eliphaz claims that Job's argument was disrespectful toward God and detracted from a proper view of Him. Convinced of this, Eliphaz felt compelled to rebuke his suffering friend, justifying it as love for both God and Job. Job's manner of speaking seemed to confirm Eliphaz's suspicion that he was guilty of some grievous sin, as the following verses indicate.

ii. You testify to your own guilt by the way you speak (vv. 5-6)

Eliphaz believed that Job's sin was the tutor for his bold arguments before God—seeking to be vindicated before God in some heavenly court. The phrase "you choose the language of the crafty" may allude to the Serpent in Genesis 3. Eliphaz used the same word in 5:12, warning that God frustrates the plotting of the shrewd. In verse 6, Eliphaz emphasizes that it is not he who condemns Job; rather, it is Job's own words and lips that testify against him. You testify to your own guilt by the way you speak. In verses 1-6, Eliphaz declares: Job, you're a fool whose own words prove the wickedness of your heart.

2. Who do you think you are to reject God's wisdom through us? (15:7-16)

   a. *Are you somehow wiser than everyone else in the world? (vv. 7-10)*

      i. Have you lived longer than any other person ever? (v. 7)

Eliphaz implies that Job is acting as if he possesses more insight than everyone else. Thus, he unleashes a barrage of rhetorical questions intended to shame Job into silence. Did you pre-exist the creation of the "hills," or were you the first Adam to be born? The parallelism might even suggest the idea of a pre-existent man—are you the Adam who existed before creation?

This could be seen as the Old Testament equivalent of asking, "Who do you think you are, God?" Eliphaz poses the question: "Have you lived longer than any other person ever?

ii. Is wisdom limited to you? (v. 8)

In 12:3, Job stated, "But I have intelligence as well as you; I am not inferior to you. And who does not know such things as these?" In 13:2, he reiterated, "What you know, I also know; I am not inferior to you." Job was telling his friends that their advice was common knowledge but insufficient to help him in his trial. He sought answers directly from God. In doing so, Job made, to his friends' minds, shocking and provocative statements. They assumed he was proud and arrogant.

iii. What do you know that we do not know? (v. 9)

Similar to Job's assertions in 12:3 and 13:2, Eliphaz claims that he and his friends were just as wise as Job. In fact, in verse 10, he implies they are actually wiser than Job.

iv. We are older and wiser than you (v. 10)

Some translations suggest that the aged and experienced stood with Eliphaz, Bildad, and Zophar. However, it is also possible that one of these men was actually "older" than Job's "father." His point is clear: the wisdom of the "aged" supports our claims—we are older and wiser than you.

Yet, age does not guarantee wisdom. As the psalmist wrote in Psalm 119:99-100: "I have more insight than all my teachers, for Your testimonies are my meditation. I understand more than the aged, because I have observed Your precepts." This possibility evidently did not occur to Eliphaz. Therefore, he asks Job: Are you somehow wiser than everyone else in the world?

b. *Is God's wisdom [as spoken through us] not enough for you? (vv. 11-13)*
   i. Are not our words of consolation adequate to minister to you? (v. 11)

Since God had not spoken directly to Job at this point, it seems likely that Eliphaz was referencing his initial speech.

He may have "spoken gently" then, but now the gloves are off. Perhaps 5:17-26 illustrates the gentlest and most consoling words offered to Job, yet they are framed within the context of reward-retribution theology and contingent upon Job's repentance for whatever he may have done to warrant divine discipline.

> ii. Why do you turn to anger and speak such foolishness? (vv. 12-13)

According to Eliphaz, Job's "heart" (v. 12) led him to utter shocking "words" (v. 13). His "eyes" flashed with anger, and his spirit seemed to be turned "against God." Eliphaz asks, "Why?" Why are you allowing your emotions to control you? This is a curious question from someone who has described Job's situation using imagery of excretions of wind. However, as Alden notes, "We could answer the question: Job could not reconcile his innocence and his suffering with the simplistic theology of retribution. He saw no reason for his misery, yet everyone believed that it must have been caused by sin" (Alden, p. 174).

Eliphaz, Bildad, and Zophar, however, thought they were offering helpful counsel—repent, seek God, and be restored. Is God's wisdom, [as spoken through us] not enough for you? In verses 14-16, Eliphaz challenges Job's claim of innocence.

> c. How can you claim to be righteous in light of the doctrine of depravity? (vv. 14-16)
> i. Men are born sinners (v. 14)

Eliphaz's point is that men are born sinners and therefore cannot be perfectly pure or righteous. Here, he refers back to the revelation given by the mysterious spirit, as he recounted in 4:12-19. As we discussed in those verses, Eliphaz wants to convince Job that his claims of righteousness and innocence overlook God's infinite holiness.

ii. God is holier than you could ever imagine; therefore how could a man be pure in His sight? (vv. 15-16)

Again, Eliphaz overstates his case. Yes, God is infinitely purer than His holy ones—evidently referring to angels, as indicated by the parallel mention of "heavens" in the next phrase. But this does not mean that He does not trust them. In Genesis 3, God entrusted two angels with guarding the entrance to the Garden after the fall. In Genesis 18, He trusted the rescue of Lot to two angelic servants. We could add that He trusted His heavenly messengers to deliver revelation to Daniel (Dan. 8:16; 9:20-27) and to Mary, who would bear Jesus (Luke 1:19, 26). Angels announced Christ's birth to shepherds (Luke 2:8-14) and proclaimed His resurrection (Matt. 28:2ff; Mark 16:5; Luke 24:4). God also sent an angel to strengthen His own Son after His wilderness temptation (Matt. 4:11) and in the Garden of Gethsemane (Luke 22:43). Eliphaz overstated the transcendence and holiness of God, *to the exclusion of the grace, the tender mercies, and the condescension of God.*

Job's zealous friend continued his argument. If even angels cannot be truly pure before God, "how much less pure is a corrupt and sinful person with a thirst for wickedness!" (NLT). Was he speaking generally of mankind or specifically about Job? One wonders. But his point is clear: man is a sinner, and God is holier than one could ever imagine. While these statements are true as theological propositions, to conclude that Job could not be "right" with God misapplies these truths.

Job understood God's holiness and man's depravity, but he held out hope that there is "One" who could cleanse man— God Himself (cf. 14:4). He believed that one could be "righteous" before God through genuine faith, not personal achievement. He had not broken faith. He was right with God, but everyone around him, except God, the angels, and us as readers of the Book of Job, believed he was wicked at heart, because of the suffering he was enduring, as evidenced by Eliphaz's words.

3. Wisdom tells us that the wicked suffer, even if they seem to prosper for a time—therefore repent of your vain hope (15:17-35)

   a. *I will speak wisdom confirmed by men of old (vv. 17-19)*

As Job has repeatedly called his friends to "listen" (13:6, 17), Eliphaz now calls Job to "listen" to the wisdom he has "seen." This wisdom consists, in verse 18, of "what wise men have told, and have not concealed," as they gained knowledge from their "fathers." Eliphaz's wisdom was tried by tradition and supported by "wise men" of old.

To whom alone the land was given, and no alien passed among them—This somewhat obscure reference was meant to bolster Eliphaz's claim to wisdom that follows. But its exact reference is more difficult to define. Was he referencing Abraham, Isaac, and Jacob, "to whom alone the land was given"? Or, perhaps as a Temanite, he was referring to Esau and his sons? Regardless of the specific reference, he claims that the poem on wisdom that follows is pure, untainted by corrupt teachings or "alien" wisdom. The rest of the chapter contains the essence of the wisdom, as he proclaims in eloquent language the same theology he and his friends have already espoused.

   b. *The wicked inevitably suffer for their sins (vv. 20-35)*
      i. The wicked is tormented now because of his rebellion against God (vv. 20-26)
      aa. He is tormented by fear (vv. 20-22)

"Writhes in pain" is also used in the context of childbirth elsewhere (Job 39:1; Ps. 51:7; Prov. 8:24-25). The second half of verse 20 affirms the belief that "the ruthless also suffer torment for a preset period of time." The NLT reads: "The wicked writhe in pain throughout their lives. Years of trouble are stored up for the ruthless." Verses 21-22 clarify that it is the expectation of judgment that torments them now: "The sound of terror rings in their ears, and even on good days they fear the attack of the destroyer. They dare not go out into the darkness for fear they will be murdered" (NLT). The wicked may appear to prosper, but they live in fear—the fear of retribution, the "destroyer," the "darkness," and the "sword".

> bb. He is tormented by the reality that today is all he has, because he is an enemy of God (vv. 23-25)

He is constantly trying to get more, because "a day of darkness is at his hand" (v. 23). He is constantly having to prepare himself for attack, "distress and anguish terrify him" (v. 24). Why? Verse 25 states: "Because he shakes his fist at God and is arrogant against the Almighty" (author's paraphrase; cf. NLT). He is tormented by fear; he is tormented by the reality that today is all he has.

> cc. He is too stubborn to repent—rather he continues to fight God (v. 26)

The wicked man stubbornly, defiantly, and foolishly "rushes headlong" at God with his "shields." These "shields" may represent the stubborn arguments that Job continues to employ—in Eliphaz's opinion. The wicked are tormented now because of their rebellion against God. They live in fear, face the impending doom that today is all they have, and are too stubborn to repent—trusting instead in their own defenses while launching an offensive charge against God. This is the torment and idiocy of the wicked in their current state. But as you would expect, Eliphaz connects it to his theology of retribution in this life.

> ii. The wicked will inevitably suffer for their sins (vv. 27-35)
>> aa. He may have enjoyed the prosperity of the wicked for a time (v. 27)

In ancient times, and in some cultures today, prosperity is evidenced by being well-fed. Yes, the wicked man may prosper for a time—"he has covered his face with his fat and made his thighs heavy with flesh." However, ...

    bb. He will not escape temporal devastation (vv. 28-30)

- His wealth will not endure (vv. 28-29)

Eliphaz seems to predict that the wicked, despite their temporary prosperity, will eventually live like squatters—in "desolate cities, in houses no one would inhabit, which are destined to become ruins." One wonders if the dump where Job sat resembled this description.

Because the second phrase declares that that his wealth will not endure, it is best to render the first phrase: "He will no longer be rich" (NIV). The last phrase, "and his grain will not bend down to the ground," is obscure in the original text. It could refer to crop failure or a loss of influence in the land, as many English versions interpret: "nor will his possessions spread over the land" (NIV). As Job sat there destitute, Eliphaz boldly declared that the wicked man's wealth will not endure.

- He will not escape the darkness (v. 30)

What the wicked man fears, according to verses 22-23, will overtake him. "He will not escape from the darkness." "Shoots" most likely refers to his crops but could also be a poetic allusion to his children. The wicked man will perish by the breath of God's mouth. He will not escape temporal devastation.

    cc. He must repent of his false trust and self-deception—or suffer an untimely death (vv. 31-35)

- Repent of your empty hope (v. 31)

This may be a veiled reference to Job's claims of hope in God in 13:15, and vindication and resurrection in 14:13-17. The wicked man ought not to deceive himself; his hopes are "empty"—worthless, vain, and unreal. Repent of your empty hope.

- Or emptiness and an early death will be your reward (vv. 31c-33)

When your hope or trust is truly in nothing, your reward will also be nothing. Emptiness will be the reward of the one who deceives himself into thinking that God will vindicate his trust in Him. How demonic is such a thought, even if expressed in exquisite poetry.

Verses 32-33 convey that the wicked ultimately face an untimely death. His branch will not green; his vine will not produce wine; his beauty will fail like the flower from the olive tree.

Verses 34-35 are particularly devastating once the poetic allusion is understood.

- The godless have no children and lose all their wealth because they are pregnant with iniquity (vv. 34-35)

Job had wished his own mother had been "barren" on his birthday (3:7), but it was he and his wife who were childless. Eliphaz states that this is the fate of the godless. As well, "fire consumes the tents of the corrupt."

In 1:16, the "fire" of God fell from heaven, consuming Job's sheep and servants. In verse 35, the imagery is one of conception and pregnancy. The wicked "conceive" trouble, give birth to evil, and their belly forms deception. The godless bear no children (no fruit of the womb) and lose all their wealth because they are pregnant with iniquity. What might that imply about Job's tragedies?

Eliphaz warns: Repent of your empty hope, or emptiness and an early death will be your reward.

Application

What can we learn from this agonizing chapter and Eliphaz's argument? Witnessing Eliphaz's courtesy devolve into vulgarity and the insinuation of "you're getting what you deserve" should call us to humility and, if necessary, silence. How often have we engaged in arguments not to bless others (even if we momentarily convince ourselves that is our motive) but because we are offended that they do not share our perspective? Many of us may be guilty of the very thing we seek to convict others of. Eliphaz attempted to convince Job that his arguments were useless and of no value, when in fact, his own arguments were such. He was personally offended that Job rejected his wisdom, so he repeated it with greater forcefulness and less tact. His final poem about the wicked receiving their due seems to overlook Job's honest assessment that this is not always true in life, thereby disregarding reality.

Eliphaz overstated his theological position to emphasize a point, ultimately conveying demonic wisdom rather than life-giving truth. Furthermore, there is no indication that Eliphaz sought divine wisdom for himself or on behalf of his friend; instead, he relied on an experience in chapters 4-5, and here on the traditional wisdom passed down from the wise men of old. In contrast, Job, though perhaps not as winsomely (from the human perspective) as one might hope at times, consistently turned to God with his grief.

God's Word alone can give hope and strengthen faith, appropriately ministering conviction, reproof, correction, and training in righteousness (2 Tim. 3:16-17). Eliphaz delivered half-truths, experiences, and tradition. We must be honest in counseling others. We do not always have every answer, but we should continue to trust and pray for suffering brothers and sisters, urging them to look to the Word of God and to rely on the One who can grant them comfort in their pain.

Job—God is My Attacker & My Advocate
Job 16:1-17:16

Psalm 27:1 reads, "The LORD is my light and my salvation; whom shall I fear? The LORD is the defense of my life; whom shall I dread?" However, what if you truly grasped God's sovereignty over all things, and you suddenly (in one day) experienced the loss of all your wealth and all ten of your children? Shortly thereafter, you were afflicted with a debilitating and torturous illness. Would you not be tempted to view God as your Attacker?

Many who profess belief in Him turn away under such pressure. Yet, those who genuinely fear the Lord will persevere—sometimes haltingly and with great difficulty—navigating the painful tension of feeling that God is both their Attacker and, paradoxically, their only hope; their Advocate. These are the struggles that Job faced, and his friends could not understand.

In Job 16-17, we will explore five sections that reveal Job's exasperation, prayer, and hope mingled together in yet another exhausting speech. These chapters urge us to seek hope and strength from God alone amid devastation and pain.

H. Job—God has attacked me, yet He alone is my witness that I am innocent (16:1-17:16)
1. You are sorry comforters (16:1-5)
a. Why do you keep repeating yourselves? (vv. 1-3)
   i. I've heard your troublesome counsel before (vv. 1-2)

Essentially, Job is saying, "I've heard this all before—you're not helping." The word translated as "sorry" has been used multiple times by Eliphaz to describe Job's current state (cf. 4:8; 5:6, 7; 15:35; cf. Zophar's use in 11:16). Eliphaz's last word to Job in 15:35 noted that the wicked conceive "mischief"—the same Hebrew term. Here, Job uses the word to describe his friends as mischievous or "troublesome comforters."

   ii. When will you stop talking? (v. 3)

In 8:2, Bildad had asked Job, "How long will you say these things, and the words of your mouth be a mighty wind?" And in 15:2, Eliphaz asked, "Should a wise man answer with windy knowledge and fill himself with the east wind?" Job here accuses his friends of the same, questioning when their "windy words" will cease. In 6:26, Job had likened his own speech about death to "words of wind": "Do you intend to reprove my words, When the words of one in despair belong to the wind?" Here, in 16:3, he asks, "What plagues you that you answer?" implying, "I have an excuse; what's yours?"

b. If the tables were turned, I could talk like you—or I could strengthen and comfort (vv. 4-5)
   i. If I were in your place (and you in mine), I too could be condescending and judgmental (v. 4)

The shaking of the head is a gesture of disdain and reproach (Ps. 22:7; 109:25; Lam. 2:15; Matt. 27:39; cf. Alden, p. 182). The King James rendering is both literal and vivid: "I also could speak as ye do: if your soul were in my soul's stead, I could heap up words against you, and shake mine head at you." Job is saying, "If I were in your place (and you in mine), I too could be condescending and judgmental."

ii. Or I could strengthen and comfort you (v. 5)

The phrase translated "solace of my lips" is more literally "quivering of lip." Job's quivering lips would "withhold." It is not explicitly stated what his quivering lip would withhold, but most translations interpret it as holding back even more "pain" or "grief." If the tables were turned, I could speak like you—or I could choose to strengthen and comfort.

In verses 1-5, Job tells his friends, "You are sorry comforters". But the mention of his own moving lips reminds him that, in his current condition, whether he speaks or remains silent, he feels like the victim of an attack. Strikingly, in verses 6-17, he intermittently prays and yet graphically proclaims:

2. God has attacked me though I am innocent (16:6-17)

   a. *Whether I speak or I hold back, I find no relief from my pain (v. 6)*

Enough of contemplating what he would do if the tables were turned; Job quickly considers reality. There is nothing he can do to ease his own pain. Speaking does not alleviate the pain, and if he refrains from speaking, he literally asks: "How will I walk?" or "How will it go?" Either way, he finds no relief. Why? Verse seven begins with a statement and shifts to prayer:

   b. *God, You have worn me out and wrecked my family (v. 7)*

Job proclaims, "Surely now He has worn me out." The same root in a different syntactical form is translated as "impatient" in 4:2, 5. From Job's perspective at this time, God was the cause of his exhaustion, weariness, and impatience.

But rather than continue speaking about God, Job turns to Him directly: "You have laid waste all my company"—the pronoun is singular, referencing God directly. "You have ravaged all my household." God, You have worn me out and wrecked my family.

c. You have emaciated my body (v. 8)

The Geneva Bible reads: "And Thou hast made me full of wrinkles." The Jewish Bible ends the verse with: "My gauntness serves as a witness, And testifies against me." Speaking directly to God, Job says—I have proof of your enmity. God, You have emaciated my body.

In verse nine, he turns back to third person to describe his feelings of God to those around him.

d. He has become my adversary (v. 9)

The King James again is graphic: "He teareth me in his wrath, who hateth me: he gnasheth upon me with his teeth; mine enemy sharpeneth his eyes upon me." Here Job, though using pronouns, seems to explicitly call God his "adversary" as he honestly expresses his current perspective (unless he somehow jarringly is speaking of a previously unnamed enemy). Yet, in verses 18-21, he acknowledges that God alone is his hope.

In verse 10, Job uses the third person plural pronouns—"they"—possibly referring to the Chaldeans and Sabeans, but more likely to his friends, or perhaps more generally to everyone else. "People jeer and laugh at me. They slap my cheek in contempt. A mob gathers against me" (NLT). This language almost echoes that of Jesus (Psalm 22:7-8; Matthew 27:39-43). Job recognized that, in God's sovereignty, he was being mocked, shamed, and opposed. As he states explicitly in verse 11: "God hands me over to an evil man, Thrusts me into the clutches of the wicked" (TNK).

e. God has declared war on me (vv. 12-14)

In 1:3, the narrator designates Job as "the greatest of all the men of the east." Here, Job asserts that God has "shattered" him; "seized" him by the "neck and shaken [him] to pieces." In verse 12, Job depicts himself as broken, choked, and marked for execution by God. In verse 13, God's arrows strike their target, splitting Job's "kidneys open" and pouring his "gall on the ground." A literal rendering of verse 14 would be: "He bursts upon me with burst in the face of burst" (Alden, p. 185). God is pictured in verse 14 as an unrelenting "warrior."

This language may shock our sensibilities, but we must remember Yahweh's own words to Satan in 2:3: "The LORD said to Satan: "Have you considered My servant Job? For there is no one like him on the earth, a blameless and upright man fearing God and turning away from evil. And he still holds fast his integrity, although *you incited Me against him to ruin him without cause*" (emphasis added).

Job did not know of the heavenly challenge that was taking place. He only knew what he had experienced. And from his perspective God had declared war on him. What was his response?

f. I have humbled myself and mourned—though I am innocent and my prayer is pure (vv. 15-17)

Jacob mourned the loss of Joseph with "sackcloth" in Genesis 37:34. Job had not turned to attack God—but rather mourned. The phrase "And thrust my horn in the dust" signifies humbling oneself. He did not rely on human strength or pride. Job's face bore the marks of "weeping" and sleeplessness. He mourned, and humbled himself, and wept, and could not sleep, even though there was no violence in his hands and his prayer was pure.

In summary, verses 6-16 capture Job's perspective on his current situation. His friends were sorry comforters—calling him to repent and be restored. Instead, Job maintained: God has attacked me, though I am innocent. However, swinging the pendulum to a seemingly unreconcilably paradox, Job continues in verses 18-21 to proclaim his faith.

3. Yet God [or a Heavenly Mediator who is a companion of God's] is my only Advocate and hope (16:18-21)

   a. I don't want my case to be forgotten, even if I die (v. 18)

This may be a poetic way of calling for vindication before death, or it may convey his desire that his case not be forgotten, even after he dies. According to Genesis 4:10, Abel's blood cried out to God from the ground, and God did not allow such injustice to go unheard, even after Abel's death. In verses 19-21, Job's hope seems to soar to new heights.

   b. Yet even now my Witness and Advocate is in heaven (vv. 19-21)
      i. Job's confidence—my Witness is in heaven and my Advocate on high (v. 19)

Job's language suggests a personal reawakening, be it ever so brief. "Even now, behold, in the heavens is One who testifies" to my innocence. He cried out that even if he dies, he longs for vindication and holds onto hope that "even now" he has a "witness" to his innocence. This witness is "in heaven". If only Job knew how true that was!

The word "advocate" is a rare word used only here in the Scriptures. It is parallel to "witness". Some argue that Job hoped for a witness other than God; however, the phrases "in heaven" and "on high" seem to confirm that Job's ultimate hope rested on someone in "heaven" who still knew the truth of Job's integrity and would one day testify on his behalf. Additionally, the possible allusion to the blood crying out from the ground suggests that Job recognized God as the one who heard and vindicated Abel's plea for justice. Job's confidence remained in God, even though it seemed He had turned against His servant. Another clue to Job's hope is found in verse 20, where he looks to God as his only recourse.

ii. Job's case—my friends scoff; God is my only recourse (v. 20)

The Hebrew here is challenging, and various translations exist. However, the latter part of the verse is clear: "My eye drips to God." Job is crying out to God as his only hope—perhaps through a Mediator. The first half of the verse is debated. The NET Bible and NIV suggest an advocate or mediator: "My intercessor is my friend as my eyes pour out tears to God." Even if the traditional rendering, "My friends are my scoffers; My eye weeps to God" is more accurate, it is evident that Job still sees "God" as his sole hope. This conviction drives him to express his desire in verse 21.

iii. Job's desire—that a man might plead with God as with his neighbor (v. 21)

Was Job actually identifying his heavenly witness as "a man" who could somehow approach "God" as a "friend" or "companion/neighbor"? Did Job perhaps grasp the promise of Genesis 3:15—a figure born of woman who possessed the character, power, and attributes of God Himself? In Isaiah 2:4 and 11:4, the Messiah will "render a decision"—same root as "plead." Job's confidence lies in a heavenly witness; only God can vindicate his case, and his desire is for an Advocate—one equal with God—who can arbitrate on his behalf.

In this moment, Job has clarity of faith and hope.

Yet as one might expect from a man who has lost ten children, all his possessions, and is suffering immensely from physical disease, his emotions and thoughts can quickly plummet. But we often see glimmers of genuine faith in him as he still clings to God in prayer—even if he expresses himself to God with language that might make those of us who are not experiencing his pain blush.

In 16:22-17:5, Job once again contemplates his current situation and turns to prayer.

4. God—defend me from these mockers (16:22-17:5)

   a. *The cemetery is not far off (16:22-17:1)*

In chapter seven, Job seemed to indicate that his time was coming quickly to an end. Here, he uses the expression "a few years" to poetically convey that his years are numbered and soon enough he would "go the way of no return"—referring to the grave. The next verse seems to confirm this idea: My spirit is broken, my days are extinguished, the grave is ready for me. "Grave" is plural and clearly refers to a graveyard or cemetery. "My breath/spirit is corrupt, my days are running out, the cemetery awaits me."

   b. *The contempt of mockers is upon me (v. 2)*

This may allude to Eliphaz, Bildad, and Zophar, as Job used the verb form of this word in 13:9—translated "deceive"—to describe their counsel. Job stands on the brink of death, surrounded by mockers, forced to watch as they ridicule him. Who can he turn to for help?

   c. *God—only You can ultimately prove my innocence (vv. 3-5)*

   i. Only You can verify my innocence (v. 3)

The words used here are also found in Proverbs (6:1; 11:15; 17:18; 22:26) concerning underwriting or cosigning for a debt. They refer to providing proof or verification that something is true—in this case, Job's claims of innocence. Using second person singular pronouns, Job is telling God that only He can verify his claims of innocence. Job still holds that God alone is his hope, and he expresses this to Him.

   ii. But You have kept their heart from understanding (v. 4)

Job believed God was sovereign over even the lack of insight his friends had in discerning his situation—"For You have hidden their heart from insight." However, in the second part of verse four and into verse five, Job believed they were culpable and that God would "not exalt" them.

iii. Yet they are in danger of judgment (v. 5)

Using a proverbial saying, Job warns his friends that their position may have lasting ramifications—even for their own families. One cannot adhere to a man-centered, reward-retribution theology without devastating others—especially one's own family.

In 16:22–17:5, Job prays: God—defend me from these mockers. The cemetery is not far off; the contempt of mockers is upon me; and God—only You can ultimately prove my innocence (yet You do not approve of their mocking and bad practical theology).

In verses 6-16, Job once more contemplates the realities of his present condition. However, he remains resolute in his belief that he is innocent, and that somehow, this truth will be revealed.

5. The righteous will hold to his way, though mockers may mock, and all hope seems gone (17:6-16)

   a. In God's sovereignty, I am held in contempt (vv. 6-8)

   i. I am a byword and the object of scorn (v. 6)

Job asserts that God has sovereignly "placed" him as a "proverb of the people." In other words, Job's name has become synonymous with ridicule and the perception of being forsaken by God. The word translated as "spit" is rare, but it appears to convey open contempt and a sense of shame or disgust.

   ii. I am grieved and diseased (v. 7)

Taken literally, this could mean that Job is losing his sight and experiencing weight loss. The phrase "because of grief" emphasizes the physical effects of his sorrow.

iii. I should be defended by the upright (v. 8)

The Hebrew here is difficult. Job could be using bitter irony to describe his situation—his "upright" friends are "appalled" by him, and claiming to be "innocent," they turn against him. Or more likely, he is expressing that he should be defended by the upright rather than attacked.

Verses 6-8 combine to say— "In God's sovereignty, I am held in contempt." But this would not deter Job from persevering in hope of final vindication by God.

b. *Nevertheless, the righteous will hold his way and grow stronger—though mockers may continue to mock, and all hope seems gone (vv. 9-16)*

  i. The righteous will hold his way and grow ever stronger (v. 9)

As Andersen writes: "There is hardly a place in the book of Job concerning which commentators are in wider disagreement than this statement" (Andersen, p. 185). Some believe Job's ultimate repentance reflects a stubborn self-righteousness (cf. Barrick, William D., "Messianic Implications in Elihu's 'Mediator Speech' (Job 33:23-28)," pp. 4-6—though Barrick does not specifically reference this verse). Others argue that Job is speaking from a place of great faith.

It seems to me that, in light of James' positive summary of Job's perseverance in James 5:11 and his discussion on testing leading to endurance and maturity in James 1:2-4, Job is not being sinfully obstinate here but rather tenacious in faith. The righteous will hold to his way and grow ever stronger. But admittedly, there may be a mixture of both, as there is at least a hint of sarcasm in verse 10.

  ii. Take another shot at me, for I do not find a wise man among you (v. 10)

The Hebrew here contains a strong disjunctive particle (Alden, p. 192), contrasting this statement with the previous verse. While I will grow stronger, you need to take a different approach. The New Living Translation captures the sarcasm well: "As for all of you, come back with a better argument, though I still won't find a wise man among you."

> iii. My life and hopes are torn apart, and they keep trying to tell me that everything will be fine if I repent (v. 11-12)

Here, Job contemplates his life from a human perspective. Everything he loved and lived for is long gone; his hopes and dreams have been "torn apart." In verse 12, he juxtaposes the almost comical counsel of his friends in view of his current situation. They turn night into day, claiming 'the light is near' in the presence of darkness. In stark contrast to Job's living nightmare, his friends promise that everything would be fixed if he would just repent.

> iv. Even if I long for death, I will not give up my hope of God's vindication (vv. 13-16)

Job employs poetic imagery to discuss the grave. If he found a place to live and rest in the grave—and the pit and the worm were his closest family—would he still have hope?

Some may question, if you die, where then is your "hope"? *Will it go down with me to Sheol? Shall we together go down into the dust?* —The familial references in verses 13-14, combined with verse 16's implication that Job's hope would accompany him to the grave, reinforce the point: even if I long for death, I will not give up my hope of God's vindication.

Application

In chapters 16-17, we observe five movements in Job's speech: 1) You are sorry comforters (16:1-5); 2) God has attacked me though I am innocent (16:6-16); 3) yet God—or a Heavenly Mediator who is a companion of God—is my only Advocate and hope (16:17-21); 4) God, defend me from these mockers (16:22-17:5); 5) The righteous will hold to his way, though mockers may mock, and all hope seems gone (17:6-16).

A persistent challenge in the Book of Job is discerning whether the counsel offered by the characters is sound advice, or a godly perspective at any given moment, often expressed in obscure poetry. The cumulative effect of this over approximately 35 chapters can leave one hesitant to endorse any single statement as a source of counsel or strength—though not necessarily impossible. This may be intentional.

By the time the reader reaches chapter 38, with God's Self-revelation, there arises a deep yearning for something undeniably trustworthy. We find this in God Himself—and His Self-revelation. He alone is faithful, wise, and Almighty. He alone is trustworthy. This is the one truth that Job seems to grasp, which eludes his friends.

Job may struggle and doubt and be angry—but in the end he kept seeking God as his only hope. And in the end, God revealed Himself as faithful and trustworthy—no matter the loss, the questions, or the pain. Before God's Word made these truths clearer to Job, the suffering servant wrestled with the unresolved tension: God has attacked me, yet He alone is my witness to my innocence. Job persevered by the grace of God, with a dogged pursuit of the Lord Who was silent for a time. As James says, Job found that the Lord is full of compassion and merciful in the end. So shall we.

Bildad—Let Me Tell You Again! Job—I Am Rejected, But Not Forever
Job 18:1-19:29

As we reflect on the story of Job, we are privy to a reality that Job and his friends were not. In chapters 1-2, Job is revealed to be honored by God, serving as a trophy of grace before the angelic realm. His sufferings, though horrific, serve as a testament to God's inherent trustworthiness. However, Job was unaware of the satanic challenge to God's glory; he only knew the pain and horror of death, loss, and illness. Meanwhile, Job's friends perceived only devastation and the apparent absence of any divine protection.

In chapter three, Job cried out for death. By chapter four, his friends began to try to "help" Job by essentially calling him to repent and get his life right with God. Job, however, believed he was—or at least had been—right with God. Thus, chapters 4-31 capture the ongoing poetic argument between Job and his three friends. We resume our study in the middle of this argument, with Bildad's second lecture and Job's proclamation of both pain and hope.

In Job 18-19, we will examine two speeches that illustrate how genuine saving faith clings to the promised hope of future redemption, regardless of the human or demonic assaults aimed at undermining one's trust in God's grace and ultimate vindication.

Job 18:1-19:29

I. Bildad—Let me tell you again! (18:1-21)

1. Stop talking and start thinking (18:1-4)

a. How long before you stop talking and show some sense? (vv. 1-2)

This is Bildad's second recorded speech. As in 8:1, "Bildad the Shuhite" responded to his friend, Job (see also 25:1).

The NIV captures the essence of Bildad's first statement in this second attempt to counsel Job: "When will you end these speeches? Be sensible, and then we can talk." This not only insults Job, implying that he was not being sensible, but it also serves as a command. Darby translates the second phrase as: "Be intelligent, and then we will speak." *How long before you stop talking and show some sense?*

b. Why do you regard us as stupid animals, rather than wise counselors? (v. 3)

In 17:10, Job had remarked that he did not find a wise man among them. Here, Bildad asks Job why he views them like stupid animals. Perhaps this is because they refused to truly listen to him or show any real compassion for his suffering. However, Bildad did not wait for an answer; he merely wishes to make his point sarcastically—that Job should recognize their wisdom.

c. You're destroying yourself in anger (v. 4a)

The Hebrew translated more literally is: "He who tears his soul in his anger" (Alden, p. 194). In 16:9, Job had stated that God's anger had "torn" him—using the same term Bildad employs here. Perhaps he is suggesting that it is not God who is ripping Job apart, but rather Job's own anger. There may be some element of truth to this, yet Bildad's foundation for addressing Job is flawed. He believed Job to be essentially wicked rather than a righteous man (1:1, 8; 2:3) striving to hang on to faith.

d. *Do you expect the world to be turned upside down for you? (v. 4b)*

Bildad questions whether Job expects God to overturn the natural order simply because of his anger. The underlying assumption may be that God has established the universe such that the wicked suffer—and that Job somehow wants God's laws of reward and retribution to be suspended for him.

In summary, Bildad's message in verses 1-4 is: *Stop talking and start thinking.* The remainder of his speech focuses on the terror and desolation faced by the wicked—the implication being that Job ought to examine why he is experiencing such suffering.

2. The wicked live in terror and die desolate [so think about it, Job, why are you suffering?] (18:5-22)

   a. *The wicked man is terrorized (vv. 5-14)*

   i. In darkness (vv. 5-6)

The repetition of "light" in these verses, along with the ensuing darkness when light is extinguished, poetically illustrates the end of the wicked. It is a terrifying end. The implication is that Job's life is flickering, like a flame on the verge of being extinguished. Why? Because he is wicked and faces the terror of impending darkness.

   ii. In danger of stumbling and being captured (vv. 7-10)

The poetry of these verses refers to stumbling and capture. Six synonyms for "trap" are used in verses 8-10 (Alden, p. 196). In verse seven, the wicked man's steps become shortened or weakened, as he is tracked for certain capture. His capture results from his own actions—his schemes lead to his downfall. His own "feet" lead him into the trap and captivity as he walks on the net (v. 8). In verse nine, his "heel" is seized, and the "trap snaps shut." Verse ten states, "The rope ... lies hidden on the ground" (TNK); "and a trap for him on the path."

iii. In fear, failing health, and terror (vv. 11-14)

Verses 11-14 combine to speak of the terror that grips the wicked man. "Terrors frighten him on all sides and dog his every step" (v. 11; NET). "His strength is depleted; disaster lies ready for him to stumble" (v. 12; CSB). "Disease eats away at his skin; the first stages of death devour him gradually" (v. 13; CJB [The Complete Jewish Bible]). "He is dragged from the security of his tent and marched off to the king of terrors" (v. 14; NET).

The wicked man is terrorized—in darkness; in danger of being trapped; and in fear, failing health, and terror.

b. *The wicked man and his house perish (vv. 15-22)*
   i. No possessions (v. 15)

When judgment comes, everything is lost. Like Sodom and Gomorrah, "burning sulfur is scattered over his tent." Bildad tells Job, who has lost everything, that the wicked man has *no possessions*.

   ii. No hope (v. 16)

Like a tree whose roots are "dried below," he is dead. No branch above can be used to plant, either. The branches are withered or cut off. Such a tree has no life—*no hope* of recovery.

   iii. No honor (v. 17)

The reference to branches in verse 16, combined with the phrase "no name" and the direct statement in verse 19 of having no offspring, paints a picture of a man without children or legacy. Specifically, in verse 17, the wicked will receive no lasting honor. "Memory of him perishes from the earth, and he has no name abroad." Note the implications in regard to Job.

iv. No fellowship (v. 18)

Just as Cain was banished to be a vagrant and wanderer (Gen. 4:12), the wicked man is "driven from light into darkness, and chased from the inhabited world." Death is the ultimate fate of those driven from light to darkness and expelled from the world.

v. No offspring (v. 19)

As Darby translates this verse: "He hath neither son nor grandson among his people." As Job sat there childless, Bildad describes the wicked as having "no survivor where he used to live" (ESV).

In verse 20, Bildad does attribute something other than mere loss to the wicked. According to verse 20, the wicked man possesses one thing—infamy.

vi. Only infamy (v. 20)

From east to west, the wicked man serves as a warning. Shock and horror define the legacy of the wicked. As Job's three friends sat horrified by his appearance and circumstances, there could be no doubt to whom Bildad was referring.

vii. Such are the wicked, who do not know God (v. 21)

Alden's words serve as an appropriate summary: "The 'dwelling' and the 'place' of the ungodly is the grave, but the route by which they arrive is dreadful and disgusting. This 'evil man' of Bildad's description was emaciated, scared, and ignorant of God, a forgotten man. And these were supposed to be words of comfort?" (Alden, p. 198).

Bildad concludes—*Stop talking and start thinking; the wicked live in terror and die desolate [so think about it, Job, why are you suffering?]* In short: Bildad says: *Let me tell you again, Job!*

Chapter 19 records Job's response to these words of condemnation.

J. Job—I am rejected, but not forever (19:1-29)

1. You are against me without shame (19:1-6)

a. How long will you torment me with words? (vv. 1-3)

"And Job answered and said ..." (cf. 3:2; 6:1; 9:1; 12:1; 16:1; 19:1; 21:1; 23:1; 26:1).

While Bildad began by asking "How long" Job would continue to speak, Job now asks: "*How long* will you torment my soul and crush me with words?" The argument persists. While Bildad spoke of the torment of the wicked, Job highlights the torment caused by Bildad's words. From Job's perspective, Bildad's speech just added to his suffering.

"Ten times" may be a figure of speech, as there have only been five speeches from his friends. And the number of insinuations and insults have far exceeded "ten" in those speeches. The Jewish Bible reads: "Time and again you humiliate me. And are not ashamed to abuse me." *How long will you torment me with words?*

b. Even if I've mistakenly sinned, it's my error—not yours (v. 4)

The word for "erred" refers to unintentional sin in Numbers 15:22. Thus, some translations read "made a mistake." Job emphasizes that even if he is genuinely mistaken about whether or not he has sinned, it remains his concern before God—not theirs. While this may be debatable theologically (yes, sin affects more than just our own lives), Job was questioning why his friends were torturing him over something that has not directly affected their lives, their families, and their health.

c. If you seek to exalt yourselves and make my humiliation an argument against me—then know that God has bent me and gone to battle against me (vv. 5-6)

As the New Living Translation reads: "You think you're better than I am, using my humiliation as evidence of my sin." Job warns his self-righteous friend—not to assume he is superior simply because he is not suffering. Verse 6 emphasizes the sovereignty of God in suffering.

The term translated as "wronged" does not necessarily imply injustice, although it can (cf. 8:3; 34:12). Job literally stated: "Know then that God has *bent me* and surrounded me with His net." Job's suffering and circumstances arise from God's sovereignty, not from his own sin or because he is a greater sinner than Bildad or his other friends.

This verse marks a transition in Job's focus, shifting to God as his apparent adversary in verses 7-12.

2. God is against me (19:7-12)

   a. He does not answer my prayer for help (v. 7)

Here Job offers circumstantial evidence that God Himself is against him. The specific "violence" he refers to is not detailed; it could relate to his horrific circumstances or the accusations from his friends. Regardless, he cries out, "but there is no judgment." Essentially, Job asserts: *God does not answer my prayer for help.*

   b. He has considered me His enemy (vv. 8-12)
      i. No escape (v. 8)

Indeed, God had hedged him in, as confirmed in 1:10. However, Job perceives this as a trap with no escape rather than as ultimate protection. He could see no way of escape from the pain, suffering, and abuse he now endures. He expressed similar feelings in 3:23.

   ii. No honor (v. 9)

In 29:7-14, 20-21; and 30:1 Job described his humiliation. From chapters 1-2, we know Job was greatly honored by God before the angels. But here, from his limited perspective, Job felt as if God had stripped him of his honor.

   iii. No hope (v. 10)

In his current state, Job's hope could soar and plummet in a moment. In 7:6, 14:19, and elsewhere, he declares he has no hope. Yet in 13:14-15 and 14:13-17, he boldly proclaimed that he held out hope of vindication. Here, he uses language that describes his feelings of hopelessness.

   iv. No escape (v. 11-12)

Using poetic imagery, Job describes God as his "enemy," whose "armies come together" to build a ramp against him and "camp around" his tent. This conveys the idea of no escape from God's attack and His troops.

Thus, Job articulates his feelings that not only are his friends against him, but even God Himself is against him. He sees no escape, has no honor, possesses no hope, and, as an enemy of God living in a tent—faces no escape.

3. Have mercy—everyone has forsaken me (19:13-22)

  a. Everyone has forsaken me (vv. 13-19)
    i. Relatives and friends (vv. 13-14)

Though Job continues to reference his current perspective on God's dealings with him in verse 13, he shifts in verses 14-22 to focus on his relationships with people, asking his friends to show him pity rather than persecution.

God had separated Job from family and friends, leaving him forgotten and forsaken by relatives and close friends.

Everyone had forsaken him—relatives, friends, and even those he employed.

  ii. Servants (vv. 15-16)

Guests and maidservants treat Job as if he were a stranger, and he must beg his servant to answer him. Job felt that everyone had forsaken him—family, friends, guests, and servants.

  iii. Wife and brothers (v. 17)

Using the term "mouth" in verse 16, evidently led Job to remember his wife's response to his "breath." It was "repulsive" to her. As the ESV translates, "I am a stench to the children of my own mother." Job's siblings rejected him in disgust.

  iv. Children (v. 18)

Those who should show respect for their elders, "young children," scorn Job. When he rises, they jeer and scoff at him. The great man was now the brunt of children's scorn.

  v. Loved ones (v. 19)

The term "associates" can be translated as "closest friends." His closest friends detest him, and those he loves have "turned against" him.

In summary, Job feels abandoned by everyone. In verses 20-22, citing his failing health, he pleads for pity.

b. *Have mercy, O you my friends (vv. 20-22)*
  i. I'm wasting away—pity me, O you my friends (vv. 20-21)

Job, who is "skin and bones," has "escaped death by the skin of my teeth" (NLT), and he asks for pity from his friends. By stating, "For the hand of God has struck me," Job was not agreeing with his friends' retribution theology. Rather, he was acknowledging God's sovereignty in his suffering, asking his friends to show him pity rather than persecute him—as the next verse confirms.

> ii. Why do you persecute me, and are not satisfied with my current distress? (v. 22)

Was it not enough for them, that God had pursued Job with such suffering? Are Job's friends not "satisfied" with the pain he endures?

Job's response can be summarized in three parts thus far: *You have forsaken me* (vv. 1-6); *God has forsaken me* (v. 7-12); *Have mercy, O you my friends* (v. 13-22). Next, Job swings the pendulum from pleading for mercy to a dogged conviction of faith and hope, even it is perhaps mixed with a bit of anger over his friends' lack of compassion.

4. Write it down forever. Be careful my friends, my Redeemer lives and He will bring justice (19:23-29)

   a. Job's conviction and confession of faith/hope (vv. 23-27)

   i. Write it on my tombstone forever (vv. 23-24)

The following context indicates that Job longs for a permanent record of his faith and hope, one that would testify long after his death. Essentially, he says, "Write it on my tombstone forever." Indeed, Job's words would be "written ... inscribed in a book." The "iron stylus" and "rock" evoke images of an engraved monument. He urges—"Write it in stone." His stunning and stubborn confession is captured in verses 25-27.

> ii. I know my Redeemer lives, and in the end He will take His stand on the earth (v. 25)

"Now I myself know my Redeemer lives—and in the end he will rise on the earth." The phrase "stand upon the earth" literally translates to "rise above the dust." Although the specific identity of this "Redeemer" is not explicitly stated, Job goes on to express that he will "see God." It seems likely that he understood his Redeemer/Vindicator to be God

Himself, who alone knows the truth about Job's innocence. Did Job envision his Messiah rising from the dead to vindicate him? We cannot know for certain. It is clearer from our perspective on this side the Gospels and the Cross. However, Job certainly holds out hope for divine vindication.

It is important to remember that Job was angry and felt utterly abandoned. His confession of faith and hope here is a blend of genuine hope and a stubborn refusal to acquiesce to his friends' accusations. So he proclaims: *I know my Redeemer lives, and in the end He will take His stand on the earth.* He wanted his hope and conviction to be inscribed on his tombstone—my Redeemer lives and will rise up over the dust.

   iii. Even after I die—in my flesh, I will see God; oh how I long for it (vv. 26-27)

The Hebrew here is extremely difficult, but it is clear that Job believes he will "see God." Most English translations interpret the Hebrew syntax to suggest Job believed he would "behold God" while in the flesh, even after his skin had long since been destroyed. This implies a belief in resurrection.

Verse 27 is emphatic: "Whom I myself will behold, and my eyes will see and not another." Job believes he will personally look upon God. To have a living Redeemer and to see God personally is to trust in God's ultimate vindication. The Christian Standard Bible offers a helpful rendering: "I will see Him myself; my eyes will look at Him, and not as a stranger." When Job sees God, it will not be as a stranger, but as his Redeemer/Protector/Defender. And Job desires for this conviction of faith to be inscribed on his tombstone.

Literally, the phrase translates to "my kidney is overwhelmed in my bosom." The New Living captures the emotion well: "I am overwhelmed at the thought!" For a moment, Job is overtaken by the emotion of this thought. But the prospect of seeing God on that final day serves as a reminder to Job that there will be judgment for those who do not share the same hope in God's gracious salvation.

b. Job's caution to his accusers (vv. 28-29)
  i. If you condemn me for all of this (v. 28)

If Job's friends continue to hold onto their reward-retribution theology without genuine trust in God's grace, they are in grave danger. Should they persist in condemning Job—believing that a person's right standing with God depends on their own righteousness—they risk facing condemnation themselves.

  ii. Be afraid of being condemned yourselves (v. 29)

If Job's friends persist in their quest to find sin in him to justify their retribution theology, they should "fear the sword" themselves. God would vindicate Job, and they would be liable to "judgment." God evidently agreed with Job on this point, as seen in 42:7.

Application

In chapter 18, Bildad essentially restated his argument: the wicked live in terror and will be judged. In chapter 19, Job seeks pity from his friends, feeling forsaken by them, by God, and by everyone—listing all whom he could think of. Then, in a flash of both steadfast faith and stubborn rebuke, Job proclaimed his conviction that his Redeemer lives, and he would see God with his own eyes, in his own flesh—even after death. He warns his friends that their theology applied to him would indeed lead to judgment—not his, but theirs.

This is one of the rare chapters in the dialogue section of the book where Job does not pray. But we might view his words in 19:27 as an act of worship, reflecting his overwhelming emotion when contemplating his resurrection and Redeemer. Still, his enduring faith shines through. It may cry for mercy; it may express feelings of utter abandonment; but at its core, it holds the conviction that salvation is found in God alone, in a living Redeemer who rises above the dust. Man is not the source of salvation or vindication. Temporal blessings, as assessed by humans, do not measure one's salvation. Trust in God cannot be destroyed—by all the forces of hell or the folly of men.

Praise God!

Zophar—The Wicked Prosper Only for a Moment
Job—Face Reality!
Job 20:1-21:34

Throughout the earlier sections of the book, Job himself would often turn to prayer in the middle of his speeches, while his friends only talked to him about God. Although there was no direct prayer in Job's speech in chapter 19, he did declare his faith and alluded to worship (19:23-27).

However, in chapter 21, Job "confines his remarks to his friends and does not fall into either a soliloquy or a prayer" (Andersen, p. 197-98). As always, he speaks with stark honesty, reflecting his path of endurance in the face of relentless suffering. His faith refuses to dismiss or overlook the apparent contradictions of conventional wisdom in a fallen and unjust world.

It would seem that at least part of the purpose of the dialogue section of Job is meant to lead us to the inescapable conclusion that human reasoning does not lead to real comfort in the fear of the Lord. Only revelation from God can bring rest and strengthen faith.

In Job 20-21, two speeches illustrate that human reasoning does not lead to true wisdom and comfort in the fear of the Lord but instead results in strife and confusion.

Job 20:1-21:34

K. Zophar—The wicked prosper for only a moment, then they get what they deserve (20:1-29)

1. I must speak wisdom though you insult me (20:1-3)

a. I am concerned and thus compelled to answer (vv. 1-2)

This is Zophar's second and final speech (cf. 2:11; 11:1; 42:9). He evidently had nothing more to say after this, though his two friends would continue the debate for another cycle (Bildad's last speech only lasts six verses).

The NIV captures the thought well here: "My troubled thoughts prompt me to answer because I am greatly disturbed." Zophar was indeed inwardly agitated—no doubt convinced that he was concerned for Job. He essentially states: *"I am concerned and thus compelled to answer."* Next, he makes it clear that he also feels insulted.

b. I am insulted but will answer with insight (v. 3)

Here Zophar claims to respond to Job's insulting reproof with a "spirit of understanding." "I've had to endure your insults, but now my spirit [of insight] prompts me to reply" (NLT). *I must speak wisdom though you insult me.* Verses 4-29 reveal Zophar's supposed "insight" or "wisdom".

2. The wicked triumph only for a moment, then they get what they deserve (20:4-29)

a. The wicked may rejoice for a time, but their triumph is short (vv. 4-5)

In verse four, Zophar claims his wisdom is "from of old, from the establishment of man on the earth." We might say—from the beginning of time. Verse five simply states: "That the triumphing of the wicked is short, and the joy of the godless momentary." *The wicked may rejoice for a time, but their triumph is short.*

b. *The wicked may be exalted beyond measure, but he will soon come to an ignoble end (vv. 6-11)*

   i. Though he is momentarily exalted, he will be destroyed like his own dung (vv. 6-7)

Verse six poetically describes either the wicked man's pride or his stature in this world. Zophar claims that no matter how high a man may soar, he will suffer the same end "as his own excrement." His exaltation will be so brief that "Those who have seen him will say, 'Where is he?'" The wicked man who might be momentarily exalted will be shoveled into a hole and buried—then gone, leaving those who saw him to wonder where he is.

   ii. He will vanish like a vision or dream in the night (vv. 8-9)

Just as a "dream" or "vision in the night" quickly disappears, so does the wicked man's exaltation. He will fly away like a dream and be chased away like a nightmare, leaving his acquaintances and family behind. Verses 7-9 allude to the fact that wickedness will no longer be seen in this world, although, as verse six states, "his loftiness reaches the heavens and his head touches the clouds" for a time.

   iii. He will leave a legacy to his sons of having to pay restitution for his wickedness (v. 10)

The mention in verse nine of "his place" is expanded upon here in verse 10, with the reference to "his sons." In Zophar's theological system, the "sons" of the wicked "will beg from the poor, for they must give back their stolen riches" (NLT).

   iv. He will die and lie down in the dust—no matter how strong he was (v. 11)

The wicked man's strength will lie "down with him in the dust," along with his bones. No matter how strong he might have been for a short time, he will not escape the judgment of death.

The wicked may be exalted beyond measure, but he will soon come to an ignoble end. He will be buried like manure, fleeting like a bad dream, and his children will pay the price for his wickedness as he lies in the dust. But Zophar does not stop at emphasizing this ignoble end …

c. The wicked loves ill-gotten gain, but will not be able to enjoy the spoil (vv. 12-19)
   i. He savors his wicked ways (vv. 12-13)

The wicked man relishes the taste of "evil" and lets it melt in his mouth, "under his tongue" (cf. NLT). He savors his evil ways like a man tasting fine food or wine. But verses 14-16 highlight how fleeting this enjoyment truly is.

   ii. He is poisoned and sickened by them (vv. 14-16)

His savory food, his wicked ways, transform food in his "stomach" into poison, "the venom of cobras." His "riches" make him vomit. And "God will expel them from his belly." The wicked may savor his ways, but he will soon be poisoned and sickened by them. Notice in verse 15 that divine judgment is imminent. Verse 16 again employs the imagery of poison.

   iii. He cannot enjoy the wealth he has attained through his wickedness (vv. 17-19)

In contrast to the venom and poison mentioned in verse 17, there are "rivers flowing with honey and curds." Yet, the wicked man cannot enjoy his wealth. He neither holds on to it nor enjoys it—verse 18. The reason for this is stated in verse 19: "For he oppressed and abandoned the poor; he seized a house he did not build" (CSB). This marks the first specific transgression mentioned—oppression of the poor.

Verses 12-19 combine to poetically declare Zophar's retribution theology: *The wicked love ill-gotten gain but will not be able to enjoy the spoil.* In verses 20-29, he elaborates on their judgment.

d. *The wicked will be fully repaid for his wickedness (vv. 20-29)*
   i. He has no enduring satisfaction (vv. 20-21)

Isaiah 48:22 and 57:21 align with Zophar here, at least in principle—there is no rest for the wicked. Proverbs 8:11 clarifies that wealth and prosperity can mislead one into thinking he is protected from harm. Zophar, like Bildad and Eliphaz, demonstrates an understanding of proverbial wisdom, but misapplies it to Job's situation.

Zophar's point in verses 20-21 is that the wicked find no lasting satisfaction. As the *New Living Translation* states: "They were always greedy and never satisfied. Nothing remains of all the things they dreamed about. Nothing is left after they finish gorging themselves. Therefore, their prosperity will not endure."

   ii. He will be suddenly judged, in the midst of his success (vv. 22-23)

In verse 22, Zophar proclaims: "When he has all he wants, trouble will come; Misfortunes of all kinds will batter him" (TNK). Verse 23 paints the picture of the wicked attempting to fill his belly, only to face divine judgment "while he is eating." Thus, he will be suddenly judged amid his success.

   iii. He may run, but he will not be able to escape (vv. 24-25)

Through vivid imagery, Zophar pictures the wicked trying to escape from an "iron weapon" [spear?] and being pierced by a "bronze bow" [arrow]. The arrow is described as going all the way through him coming out his back. It has pierced his liver; he quickly must face a painful, terrifying death. *He may run, but he will not be able to escape.*

iv. He will lose his wealth, his health, and his family in the day of God's anger (vv. 26-28)

"Darkness" and "fire" will consume his treasures, devouring him and the "survivor in his tent." The "fire" that consumes will not be "fanned" by human hands. In verse 27, the wicked man lacks an advocate in heaven; instead, "the heavens will reveal his iniquity, and the earth will rise up against him." He will find no refuge. Finally, verse 28 states: "The possessions of his house will be carried away, dragged off in the day of God's wrath" (ESV).

v. He will be fully repaid by God (v. 29)

This is Zophar's final recorded statement in the Book of Job. There is no hint of hope or mercy. "God" is mentioned twice. "This is the reward that God gives the wicked. It is the inheritance decreed by God" (NLT). Andersen's comments are insightful here:

> Zophar has no compassion and his god has no mercy ... And Zophar is at heart as much a materialist as the wicked man he condemns. He sees the carrying off of 'possessions' (verse 28) as a judgment. The loss of fellowship with God, in this life or after it, does not strike him as a far worse fate. Yet it is precisely this loss that fills Job's mind with horror, and this need that arouses his most desperate longings (Andersen, p. 197).

So ends Zophar's attempts to "help" his dear friend Job. His message is clear: *The wicked prosper for only a moment, then they get what they deserve.* Chapter 21 records Job's response to Zophar's prosperity doctrine.

L. Job—face reality (21:1-34)
1. Consider my condition and what I've been through (21:1-6)
   a. *Since you are so concerned, let this be your comfort (vv. 1-3)*
      i. Listen to my words and let this be your comfort (vv. 1-2)

Zophar claimed to have listened to Job's reproach (20:3). However, here once more, Job implores his friends (using the plural) to "listen carefully" to what he has to say (13:5-6, 17). They could then, perhaps, be comforted, or else offer him some real "consolation." In fact, he may well have been implying that the best "consolation" they could offer is to listen to him.

   ii. Let me speak and then you can mock (v. 3)

Notably, Job uses a singular pronoun here, evidently addressing Zophar directly. "Bear with me, and I myself will speak; then after I speak, you may mock." With cutting irony, Job asks his friends to listen, so they can either find comfort or appropriately comfort him afterward. The implication seems to be—*Since you are so concerned, let this be your comfort.*

b. *Stop talking and look at me—how have I offended you? (vv. 4-6)*
   i. Is my rambling against man? (v. 4)

Job's "complaint," his troubled rambling, was not directed against man or to man. Rather, it was to God. And then Job asks, "And why should I not be impatient?" Job was not only suffering physically and emotionally from the losses and now the accusations; but he had also been pleading with God to reveal Himself, yet He did not seem to be answering Job's prayers. In essence, Job was telling his friends that his problem was one only God could resolve. They needed to stop offering their prosperity theology and be quiet, as the next verse makes explicit.

   ii. Is not my condition enough to make you shut up? (v. 5)

The word "astonished" is translated as "appalled" in 17:8. Ironically, Job would put *his* and over *his* own mouth when God revealed His astonishing wisdom and majesty at the end of the book (40:4). But for now, Job tells his sorry comforters: Isn't my appearance, my appalling condition, enough to make you shut up?

Building on the imagery of the terrors of the wicked, Job states in verse six that something indeed disturbs and horrifies him.

> iii. Contemplating the reality about the prosperity of the wicked makes me disturbed and horrified (v. 6)

The NIV reads: "When I think about this, I am terrified; trembling seizes my body." The implication is that Job is not reflecting on his own suffering; rather, as the following context clarifies, he is contemplating how the wicked live, grow old, and become powerful. Thus, he elaborates in verses 7-16 ...

2. Actually the wicked do prosper in spite of their rebellion against God (21:7-16)
   a. *My question is—Why do the wicked live, grow old, and become powerful? (v. 7)*

The term "continue" means to either advance in age or in position/prosperity. Either way, Job's question is, "Why do the wicked prosper?" In verses 8-15, he makes a series of observations about the wicked and their prosperity.

   b. *My observation is—The wicked do live long and prosper (vv. 8-15)*
      i. They see their children established (v. 8)

In modern vernacular: "[The wicked sometimes] live to see their children grow up and settle down, and they enjoy their grandchildren" (NLT). Job had lost his ten children. In 18:19, Bildad asserted that the wicked man would die childless. But Job here claims to have observed wicked individuals who witness their offspring prosper.

   ii. They are safe from fear (v. 9)

The wicked often experience temporal security and show no signs of the "rod of God upon them." There are no signs of divine disfavor or judgment. They find themselves free from fear.

   iii. They prosper materially (v. 10)

The imagery here is of material prosperity: "Their bull breeds and does not fail; Their cow calves and never miscarries" (TNK).

   iv. They have fun and enjoy their lives (vv. 11-12)

The focus shifts back to children, depicted like a "flock." These "little ones ... skip about ... sing to the timbrel and harp and rejoice at the sound of the flute." They are safe enough to let their children play, sing, and dance. The implication is that the wicked have fun and enjoy their lives, at least their children do.

   v. They don't suffer in life or death (v. 13)

The Jewish Bible reads: "They spend their days in happiness, And go down to Sheol in peace." In other words, they enjoy good times and do not endure a prolonged, painful death (apparently in contrast to Job's experience).

   vi. They reject God and yet they prosper (vv. 14-15)

In verse 14, Job acknowledges that these prosperous, secure, blessed people tell God to leave them alone. And like Pharaoh, verse 15 records their question: "Who is the Almighty, that we should serve Him". They believe there is no benefit in prayer. Job's point is clear—*they reject God, and yet they prosper. My question is—Why do the wicked live, grow old, and become powerful?* (v. 7); *My observation is— The wicked do live long and prosper* (vv. 8-15).

  c. *My perspective is—I still do not envy the wicked, and their prosperity did not come from their own hand (v. 16)*

Job here disassociates himself from the wicked man's perspective on God and their success. Their "good" did not originate from their own "hand." Somehow, inscrutably, God remains sovereign over their apparent success. And the godless thinking, "the counsel of the wicked," is far removed from Job. The *New Living* is once again insightful: "They think their prosperity is of their own doing, but I will have nothing to do with that kind of thinking" (NLT).

In verses 7-16, Job tells Zophar—*actually the wicked do prosper in spite of their rebellion against God*. In verses 17-26, he expands on the mysterious sovereignty that must somehow oversee these matters.

3. Some live and die in prosperity, some die bereft—God's wisdom is inscrutable (21:17-26)
   a. *Do the wicked always suffer in this life? (vv. 17-18)*

In these verses, Job questions the consistency of the divine retribution his friends, including Zophar, have suggested. His rhetorical questions indicate that Job does not perceive a consistent pattern in this life. In 18:5, Bildad claimed that the lamp of the wicked is extinguished. Job counters by asking, "How often does that really happen?" While Psalm 1:4 compares the wicked to "chaff" blown away by the wind, it speaks of future judgment. In this life, the situation is not always so clear. Therefore, Job asks: *Do the wicked always suffer in this life?*

   b. *Do wicked people care if after they die their sons must make restitution for their iniquity? (vv. 19-21)*
      i. A proverb asserted and challenged (v. 19)

Job appears to quote a proverb or summarize his friends' belief that the sons of wicked men will pay for their father's sins. Some today misinterpret Exodus 20:5-6, leading to the concept of the "sins of the generations." Jeremiah 31:29 reflects a later proverbial statement used in Israel: "... the fathers have eaten sour grapes, and the children's teeth are set on edge" (see also Ez. 18:2). But the prophet corrects this notion, stating, "But everyone will die for his own iniquity;

each man who eats the sour grapes, his teeth will be set on edge" (Jer. 31:30).

Here Job seems to reference this idea that somehow the children of the wicked will pay for the father's wickedness, and this should be a reason to repent. But Job retorts in 19b: "Let God repay him so that he may know it".

> ii. What does a wicked man care about his children suffering after he's gone? Let him drink of the wrath of the Almighty (vv. 20-21)

Job continues the thought from the latter part of verse 19, asking, "For what does he care for his household after him?" Job challenges his friends' belief in retribution, questioning—*do the wicked really suffer in this life? And do wicked people care if after they die their sons must make restitution for their iniquity?* Next Job implies that his counselors' water-tight theological system could not adequately deal with the inscrutable wisdom of a sovereign God.

> c. Do people have the ability to instruct God on how He deals with the wicked? (v. 22)

The following verses make it clear that Job is acknowledging God's sovereignty over how He chooses to govern the lives of men. The obvious answer is that no one can "teach God knowledge." He is all-knowing and perfect in wisdom. He "judges" even the "exalted ones"—the most powerful. Therefore, *do people have the ability to instruct God on how He deals with the wicked?*

> d. One dies in prosperity and another in pain—but both die (vv. 23-26)

One man dies with unblemished bones, wholly at ease and secure (v. 23). Verse 24 uses an obscure term that could be rendered: "His pails are full of milk." He is well-nourished and suffers no broken bones; they are healthy.

In contrast, verse 25 states that another "dies with a bitter soul, never even tasting good." Some die in prosperity, while others die in pain. And in verse 26, Job underscores their common fate—death. "Together they lie down in the dust, and worms cover them." God is sovereign in how He deals with people. Some enjoy health and wealth, while others face problems and pain. Yet, in an odd display of equality, both ultimately decompose in the grave, regardless of their health or suffering.

Verses 17-26 collectively illustrate that *some live and die in prosperity, some live and die in poverty—God's wisdom is inscrutable.* In verses 17-33, Job returns from contemplation to directly addressing his friends.

4. Face reality, friends, sinners don't always suffer in this life (21:27-33)
    a. *It is clear what you think—suffering identifies the wicked (vv. 27-28)*

In essence, Job states: "I know what you're thinking and the tactics you will employ against me." As we read verse 28, we must remember that Job was basically homeless. The *New Living* offers a helpful interpretative paraphrase: "You will tell me of rich and wicked people whose houses have vanished because of their sins." Job knew that his assertion that the wicked do prosper will prompt them to present hand-picked examples to support their point and implicate Job as wicked. So in verse 29, he preempts their arguments by inviting them to ask those who have been around.

    b. *But ask those who have seen the world if the wicked always suffer (vv. 29-33)*
        i. Recognize the testimony of those who have been around (v. 29)

If his friends would consider the testimony of those outside their own reward-retribution, prosperity circle, they would realize that most people do recognize the injustices that remain unavenged in this fallen world.

> ii. The wicked is kept from calamity [or perhaps he is reserved for judgment after death] (v. 30)

The NASB suggests that Job is asserting the wicked man's judgment is future—"the day of calamity ... the day of fury"—indicating divine judgment after death. This is possible, and it is certainly in keeping with the rest of Scripture. But such a statement on future, eschatological judgment might seem to be a bit out of place, given Job's argument that the wicked do not necessarily suffer as his friends have claimed. Many other English translations interpret the Hebrew as supporting Job's thesis: "Evil people are spared in times of calamity and are allowed to escape disaster" (NLT).

> iii. The wicked does not always get what he deserves (v. 31)

The wicked, often prosperous and powerful, are seldom confronted or held accountable for their actions. The rich get richer because no one confronts or repays his evil actions. The wicked does not always get what he deserves, as Job's friends seem to think.

> iv. In fact, he often gets a glorious funeral when he does die (vv. 32-33)

These verses describe a funeral. The plural term for "grave" suggests opulence (Alden, p. 227). A guard will be set over his tomb, and in verse 33, even "the clods of the valley will *sweetly* cover him." The last sentence in verse 33 may refer either to the inevitability of death or to a grand escort during the funeral procession.

Job asserts—*Face reality, friends, sinners don't always suffer in this life.* They even have an honorable burial. Verse 34 encapsulates Job's critique of their counsel thus far.

5. Your counsel has proven comfortless and false (21:34)

Reality does not align with Job's friends' theology of temporal retribution for wickedness. Thus, Job exclaims: "How can your empty clichés comfort me?" (NLT). Their "answers were unfaithful" to reality and the truth. *Your counsel has proven comfortless and false.*

Application

Zophar claimed that the wicked may triumph momentarily, but they always face temporal judgment for their wickedness. Job's response can be summarized in two words: Face reality!

Indeed, Scripture clearly declares that the wicked will ultimately face God's judgment (see for example 2 Thess. 1:5-10). However, it also reveals, as Job declared, that this judgment is not always evident in this life (Eccles. 4:1; 7:15-18; 8:12-9:3; 11:13-14 address this in some measure).

This section of Job teaches us not to gloss over the realities of life or deny the injustices and inscrutable realities that grieve and confuse us. It teaches us that it is unhelpful and actually unfaithful to pigeonhole God's wisdom into a theology of reward and retribution, where prosperity and adversity measure one's standing before Him.

Job was wrestling to somehow hold on to his faith when it was assaulted by not only circumstances and pain, but also friends who undermined his trust in a gracious God. He felt as though God was not holding onto him, though He was. Job's friends had turned God and religion into a transactional system. Do this, and you will receive that. Job believed that God was a Person with whom one had a relationship based on grace—a friendship. The communication seemed broken; Job was struggling to understand why and how to repair the relationship. He prayed. He cried. He expressed his feelings to God, openly and honestly. In doing so, he refused to reduce God to an abstract set of principles.

James 5:11 states that Job's endurance should serve as an example to suffering believers, ultimately pointing to God's mercy and compassion. Job persevered in the battle for his faith—questions, fears, anger, doubts, tears, earthly realism, and all. God was full of compassion and mercy. And He is now. He will extend the same compassion and mercy to us—questions, fears, anger, doubts, tears, and all.

Eliphaz—Repent and Be Saved
Job—I Can't Find God, but I Believe
Job 22:1-24:25

As I read through the Book of Job, I am confronted by my own sinful irritation with Job's reactions to his tragedies, his suffering, and the well-meaning advice from his friends. Initially, Job exhibits outstanding faith and conduct, but he later responds with a seemingly critical spirit, which I am tempted to find disappointing. His words can come across as demanding, arrogant, and rude. All the while I forget that he is a righteous man favored by the Lord. God delighted in Job, and therefore he was suffering.

Sadly, I sometimes fail to connect the biblical truths of Job with how I should view my circumstances and react when treated in ways I feel I don't deserve. The wisdom literature is meant to help us understand how to live in the fear of the LORD in a fallen world, while waiting for the promised King and His kingdom. Proverbs provides maxims on living skillfully, along with the blessings for adhering to wisdom and the consequences for ignoring it.

In contrast, the Book of Job serves as a preface of sorts to Proverbs, illustrating that there are exceptions to the expected outcomes of proverbial wisdom and blessing. Nevertheless, the fear of the Lord must remain central to life, whether we experience temporal blessings or suffer beyond what we can comprehend. Saving faith, which embodies the fear of the Lord, cannot be bought or sold through temporal blessings; it arises from a supernatural relationship with One who is utterly trustworthy—even when circumstances tempt us to doubt His goodness.

In Job chapters 22-24, two speeches highlight our longing for the clarity and fidelity of God's self-revelation amid human speculation regarding circumstances and suffering in this life.

M. Eliphaz—I've heard enough/Repent and Be Saved (22:1-30)

1. Your "righteousness" and "integrity" are of no concern to God (22:1-3)

   a. Man's power and wisdom are of no benefit to God (vv. 1-2)

This is Eliphaz the Temanite's final speech, his concluding attempt to counsel Job. As in 4:1, "Eliphaz the Temanite answered" Job (cf. 2:11; 4:1; 15:1; 42:7).

The pronoun, "himself," could be rendered "him"—referring to God. Eliphaz's clear inference is that *man's power and wisdom are of no benefit to God*. As the Apostle Paul stated to the Athenians in Acts 17:25: "nor is He served by human hands, as though He needed anything..." Eliphaz is asserting that God is transcendent and thus, man cannot dictate how God governs the universe, as Eliphaz believed Job was attempting to do. Once again, we see an orthodox truth in the abstract, misapplied to Job's situation.

Eliphaz believed not only that Job was trying to teach God wisdom, but also that Job was claiming to deserve something from God based on his claimed righteousness and innocence.

b. Man's righteousness or integrity is of no benefit to God (v. 3)

Here we see Eliphaz's doctrine of transcendence go beyond biblical revelation. He claims—via rhetorical question—that the Almighty does not take pleasure in the "righteous" standing of men and does not "gain" if one possesses "integrity." However, this is contradicted in chapters 1-2, where Yahweh evidently takes pleasure in Job's righteous standing before Him and highlights Job's integrity before Satan and the angelic realm. A believer's righteousness is indeed important to God; He shed the blood of His beloved Son to grant His chosen ones that righteousness.

In summary, verses 1-2 convey Eliphaz's message to Job: *Your "righteousness" and "integrity" are of no concern to God.* According to Eliphaz, Job's sin was significant because it warranted the tragedy he experienced—but Job's claim of "righteousness" and "integrity" did not concern the Almighty.

2. You are a despicably wicked man, Job—that's why you are suffering (22:4-11)

   a. Is it because of your reverence that you are suffering? (v. 4)

   All of the men had a mistaken interpretation of Job's circumstances, viewing Job's current suffering as evidence of God's judgment against him. Yet we know Job's suffering was due to God's pleasure in Job's faith—his fear of Yahweh that made him right with God and issued in integrity. But Eliphaz's question is clear: Is it because of your fear that God "rebukes you" and "enters into judgment with you?" (cf. TNK on the last phrase). You're not suffering like this because you fear Him.

   b. No, it is because of your endless iniquities (vv. 5-9)
      i. The statement (v. 5)

   The following verses indicate that Eliphaz is not referring to the sinfulness of all men, which could apply to Job as well.

He accuses Job of specific sins of oppression, which Job would later deny and could not be proven. Eliphaz asserts that there is no limit to Job's "iniquities."

This accusation is blatantly slanderous, but Eliphaz is convinced. It serves as a warning to us all about assuming the worst in others when we see tragedy befall them.

   ii. The sampling of iniquity (vv. 6-9)

Exodus 22:25-27 codified the Law of love for the poor in Israel, shedding light on the specific accusations Eliphaz is making against Job:

> *If you lend money to My people, to the poor among you, you are not to act as a creditor to him; you shall not charge him interest. "If you ever take your neighbor's cloak as a pledge, you are to return it to him before the sun sets, for that is his only covering; it is his cloak for his body. What else shall he sleep in? And it shall come about that when he cries out to Me, I will hear...him, for I am gracious.*

See also Deuteronomy 24:6, 17; Ezekiel 18:12. Job will answer these accusations in 29:12-16; 31:13, 16-17, 21.

Verse eight may reflect Eliphaz's interpretation of *Job's* mindset, which he claims underpins Job's supposed crimes. However, we know from chapters 1-2 that these charges were patently false. But in Eliphaz's watertight theology of retribution and reward, Job's suffering serves as sufficient evidence to implicate him in sin.

   c. *This is why you are suffering, terrified, in darkness, and danger (vv. 10-11)*

In 18:9, Bildad told Job that "A snare seizes [the wicked] ..." And Job had already acknowledged experiencing dread or "terror" (3:25). Eliphaz is merely confirming that this has indeed befallen Job.

"Darkness" is frequently mentioned in the book to signify God's judgment. Here, it highlights the fear of the unknown and the potential for sudden catastrophe. Imagine being engulfed in a flash flood—something plausible in the regions of Edom. Eliphaz says, *You are a despicably wicked man, Job—that's why you are suffering.*

3. You don't seem to think that God sees your sin (22:12-20)

   a. Do you think God doesn't see? (vv. 12-14)

Believers generally agree with the theology presented in verse 12—God is the transcendent ruler of creation. He is exalted above all. But in verse 13, Eliphaz seems to project his own interpretation onto Job's earlier musings about God, framing them as rebellious accusations, despite the fact that Job's previous speeches do not contain such statements. In 23:8-10, Job will complain that God is inaccessible, yet he still believes that God knows his way (cf. Alden, p. 234). In verse 14, Eliphaz imagined that Job believed that God could not "see".

   b. Do you continue to ignore the evidence that God sees and judges the wicked? (vv. 15-16)

In verse 15, Eliphaz asks if Job will persist on the path that wicked men have taken. Verse 16 states that wicked men of old have died "before their time," and what they based their lives on was washed away "with a flood" or "by a river."

   c. Will you think lightly of the kindness and common grace He extends to the wicked? (vv. 17-18)

Even though the wicked of old told God to "leave [them] alone" and questioned what the Almighty could do, it is He who blessed them "with good" (v. 18a). Much like Job in 21:16, Eliphaz distances himself from such wicked reasoning, stating, "So I will have nothing to do with that kind of thinking" (NLT).

d. *The righteous rejoice when the wicked are judged (vv. 19-20)*

In this context, Eliphaz suggests, whether knowingly or not, that the "righteous" are "glad" about what has happened to Job. Those whom Job has undoubtedly wronged are celebrating and mocking the "fire" that consumed his possessions (remember 1:16).

In verses 12-20, Eliphaz essentially claims: *You don't seem to think that God sees your sin,* but He does, and you are suffering for it while good people rejoice. Unlike Zophar's previous sermon, Eliphaz still believes there is hope for Job. Thus, in verses 21-30, he urges his wayward friend to repent.

4. Repent and know the blessings of God! (22:21-30)
    a. Repent now, and God Himself will be your treasure (vv. 21-25)
        i. Submit to God and good will come to you (v. 21)

The NIV captures the thought well: "Submit to God and be at peace with him; in this way prosperity will come to you." Good things will follow if you become a faithful steward under God's authority.

   ii. Listen to God's Word and repent—and you will be restored (vv. 22-23)

"Please receive the torah of His mouth, and set His words in your heart." Job will address this in 23:12.

In verse 23, Eliphaz assures Job that if he "turns to the Almighty," he will be "built up"—if he "removes iniquity" from his "tent." *Listen to God's Word and repent—and you will be restored.*

   iii. Regard riches as nothing compared to knowing God, and He will be your treasure (vv. 24-25)

Taken apart from their context, these words are a brilliant call to treasure God above all else. Jesus appropriately used such a call to the rich young ruler in Luke 18:22. But in this context, Eliphaz is merely reaffirming his belief that Job is a covetous idolater who does not genuinely value God.

Verses 26-30 catalog some of the great blessings that Eliphaz asserts will follow repentance.

b. *Receive the blessings of repentance (vv. 26-30)*
   i. You will have a relationship with God (vv. 26-27)

Zophar previously offered Job similar counsel in 11:12-15. Psalm 37:4 reads: "Delight yourself in the LORD; and He will give you the desires of your heart." Job will address this in 27:10. The phrase "lift up your face" signifies acceptance with God and the end of humiliation. Verse 27 promises answered prayer.

   ii. He will direct your paths in blessing (v. 28)

This verse promises that God would grant Job his heart's desire. As the *New Living* paraphrases: "You will succeed in whatever you choose to do, and light will shine on the road ahead of you." Eliphaz is promising that if Job repents, he can have his best life now.

   iii. You will become a minister of blessing and salvation for others (vv. 29-30)

The Hebrew in verse 29 is challenging. Some English translations suggest that Job will help others, while others indicate that God will save Job; still others interpret it as a warning that God casts down the proud but lifts the humble. Taken together with verse 30, I interpret Eliphaz's words as a promise that if Job repents, God will use him to minister blessing and salvation to others. The NET Bible captures this idea: "When people are brought low and you say 'Lift them up!' then he will save the downcast; he will deliver even someone who is not innocent, who will escape through the cleanness of your hands."

We should not overlook that while Eliphaz may have exaggerated the benefits of repentance somewhat, Jesus Himself affirmed that those who remove the log from their own eye will be able to help others with the splinter in theirs (Matt. 7:1-11). If we trust, obey, and pray, God will accomplish remarkable things through us (cf. Mark 11:23-24; cf. Alden's comments on p. 238). Eliphaz tells Job—*I've heard enough—repent and be saved.* Though some of Eliphaz's theology seems orthodox in a theological vacuum, it is woefully misapplied and actually harmful in counseling Job.

N. Job—I can't find God, but I believe; I'm terrified but I speak (23:1-24:25)

1. If I could find God, I would argue my case—but I can't find Him (23:1-9)

   a. I am still contentious in my complaint (vv. 1-2)

   The word translated "rebellion" could be rendered "bitter". And the second phrase may express weakness due to his pain. Thus, Job might be stating that he is in pain or that he will continue to complain bitterly—holding on to what his friends deem "rebellion" since God had not yet answered his "complaint," his plea for help.

   b. I wish I could argue my case before God (vv. 3-5)

   Jeremiah 12:1 echoes a similar sentiment: "Righteous are you, O LORD, that I would plead my case with you; Indeed I would discuss matters of justice with You. Why has the way of the wicked prospered? Why are all those who deal in treachery at ease?" "It is precisely because Jeremiah believed implicitly in the Lord's justice that he had the courage to question Him about it, and to hold out for an answer" (Mason, p. 246).

   Here, Job speculates on what he would do and how it would unfold if he could find God and "come to His seat." He would argue his case (v. 4) and then "learn the words" that God "would answer." Job longs to hear and understand God's words concerning him. He will finally "hear" from God in chapters 38-41, and he will choose not to argue his case. In these verses, however, Job asserts: *I wish I could argue my case before God*. In verses 6-7, we see another glimmer of faith in God's goodness and grace.

c. *I know He would pay attention and I would be delivered (vv. 6-7)*

Some may accuse Job of pride in thinking he could justify himself before God. However, given Job's character, it is more likely that he believed in a fundamentally good and gracious God. As Alden writes:

> Job anticipated a friendly court and a beneficent judge because he knew himself to be innocent of known sin and very devout. Those who truly fear God are not afraid to meet him ... As it turns out, [Job] never had the opportunity (or the need) to state his case at God's tribunal, but nevertheless he did win, simply because he endured the suffering and did not deny his God (Matt 10:22; 24:13; Heb 12:7) (Alden, p. 240-241).

Job still believed that God would do what's right—if he could somehow present his case. Yet our beleaguered hero felt utterly exiled—unable to find God no matter how hard he tried.

d. *But I can't find Him (vv. 8-9)*

Job employs poetic language to describe his futile search—east and west, north and south—"forward ... backward ... on the left ... on the right." Yet he cannot seem to find God anywhere.

If I could find God, I would argue my case—but I can't find Him. Then, in verses 10-12, he reaffirms his faith, however frustrated it may be.

2. I believe God knows what He's doing, and I will ultimately be vindicated (23:10-12)

   a. God knows what He's doing [and where I'm going], and I will shine forth as gold (v. 10)

Job may not be able to perceive or find God, but he trusts that God knows the "path" Job took. And "after I have been tested I will come out like gold" (BBE). "Job believed that God knew his situation ... that God was testing him ... [and] that he would emerge a better man" (Alden, p. 242). James 1:2-4 and 1 Peter 1:7 encourage New Testament believers to adopt this same perspective.

   b. I have walked in His ways (v. 11)

God knew that Job's "path" aligned with His "path," and that His servant had "not turned aside."

   c. I have delighted in His Word (v. 12)

Job had not "gone back from the commandment" of God's lips (KJV). In fact, he "treasured the words of His mouth." The Hebrew can be interpreted to mean either "more than my portion" or "in my bosom." Thus, it can be read as "In my bosom, I have hidden the words of His mouth" or "More than my portion, I have stored up the words of His mouth." Regardless of the translation, Job's point remains clear: *I have delighted in His Word.*

Thus far, Job has expressed: *If I could find God, I would argue my case—but I can't find Him;* and *I believe God knows what He's doing, and I will ultimately be vindicated.* Yet we know from his earlier speeches that he sometimes questions this belief. Job now puts his glorious statement of faith into perspective. He believes, yet he is simultaneously terrified by God's ways.

3. God does whatever He please and it terrifies me (23:13-17)

   a. *God is sovereign—He does whatever He wants and does not turn from it (vv. 13-14)*

Job confesses in verse 13 that God is "unique," immutable, and sovereign. In verse 14, he acknowledges that God is sovereign over his life and circumstances. He understands the truth of Psalm 115:3: "But our God is in the heavens; He does whatever He pleases." Contemplating God's unique, immutable, sovereign character leads Job to consider what it would be like to actually stand before Him and argue his case.

   b. *God's sovereign presence would terrify me (v. 15)*

In one sense, Job was not afraid to face God. He was a believer, a man in right standing with Him through faith, and he walked in integrity. Yet, to actually argue before the One true, unchanging, sovereign God would be rightly terrifying. Ultimately, Job would have very little to say in God's awesome presence.

   c. *God's sovereign ways terrify me now—but I am not cut off (vv. 16-17)*

Even now, Job's heart was "faint" or "feeble." His courage was waning. God's almighty power had terrified Job, yet he had not been "silenced" or "cut off"—terminated—by the darkness and gloom that covered him. Though he felt confident in God while simultaneously terrified by Him, and enveloped in gloom and darkness, he was not yet dead or silenced in the grave. So he would continue to speak, much like the Psalmist who said, "I believed when I said, 'I am greatly afflicted'" (Ps. 116:10; cf. 2 Cor. 4:13).

Thus, Job continued to wrestle with these two realities—faith in God while being utterly mystified and terrified by His sovereign governance of the universe and his own life.

4. Why do the wicked prosper and others get oppressed—and God doesn't seem to do anything? (24:1-17)

   a. *Why doesn't God set a court date, so His people will see Him act in judgment? (v. 1)*

In light of the following context, Job is asking why God doesn't take action against the injustice in the world—or at least allow His people to understand His plans.

   b. *Look at the injustice (vv. 2-12)*
      i. Thieves and oppressors (vv. 2-3)

Some seize land and flocks that do not belong to them (v. 2; cf. Deut. 19:14; Prov. 22:28; 23:10); they oppress orphans and widows (cf. Deut. 10:12-19). These heartless oppressors and swindlers often prosper. "Why?" Job asks. In verses 4-8, he chronicles the plight of those whom these thieves oppress.

      ii. The plight of those they oppress (vv. 4-8)

The oppressed are pushed aside and must hide from their oppressors. They wander like donkeys searching for food and work as servants of the wicked. They lack proper clothing and shelter. This continues, and God seems unresponsive.

      iii. Slave masters (v. 9)

Here, Job references slavery, particularly the enslavement of children. This occurred in Job's day, and it persists today. He chronicles the perplexing wickedness that the sovereign God, whom we believe in, somehow allows, and there is no court date for these people in sight.

      iv. The plight of those they enslave (vv. 10-12)

The poor have nothing, yet they are enslaved and labor to produce oil and tread the wine presses—while remaining hungry and thirsty. There is groaning and crying—yet there seems to be no divine reckoning.

c. *Look at the iniquity (vv. 13-17)*
   i. Rebels against the light (v. 13)

The world is filled with God rejecters who refuse to walk in the "light"—in the truth and holiness of God. The contrast between light and darkness, day and night, is framed and repeated in verses 13-17.

   ii. The murderer (v. 14)

Some individuals get away with murder, rising "before dawn" to kill innocent people—"the poor and the needy."

   iii. The adulterer (v. 15)

In Job's day and ours, the world is filled with adulterers who believe that no one sees their actions.

   iv. They do not know the light, but operate in darkness (vv. 16-17)

A whole culture of wicked people lives at night and sleeps during the day, preferring the "terrors of thick darkness," going to sleep in the morning. They steal at night and then get some shut-eye in the daytime.

Job's point is clear—*Why do the wicked prosper and others get oppressed—and God doesn't seem to do anything?* In verses 18-25, he presents the opposing viewpoint—either declaring that it won't last forever or, more likely, articulating his counselors' perspective regarding the wicked.

5. [But you say,] "The wicked get their just reward" (24:18-25)
   a. *The wicked are short-lived and not blessed (v. 18)*

As just mentioned, either Job experiences a drastic change of heart on the subject, and considers the ultimate end of the wicked, or he is expressing hope—or perhaps citing his friends' position in verses 18-25.

In verse 18, the imagery of "foam" or debris floating down a river suggests that they come and are really nothing but trash. They are cursed rather than blessed.

b. The wicked are overtaken by death (vv. 19-20)

In verse 19, the imagery of "drought and heat" overtaking the "snow waters" symbolizes "Sheol" overtaking "those who have sinned." They will soon be consumed by death.

In verse 20, it states that "the womb" forgets the sinner and that the "worm feeds sweetly until he is no longer remembered." Or as the *New Living* puts it: "Maggots will find them sweet to eat." Ultimately, "Wicked people are broken like a tree in the storm" (NLT). Verses 19-20 combine to say that soon enough the wicked are gone and forgotten—like snow that melts, and like a body that is buried in the grave and eaten by worms, and like a tree that is broken off. *The wicked are overtaken by death.*

c. The wicked may feel secure in their wickedness, but God sees and cuts them off (vv. 21-24)
   i. The violence of the wicked (v. 21)

Once again, we see a reference to violence and oppression. The wicked have no compassion for the needy.

   ii. The justice of God [or the violence of the wicked continued] (vv. 22-23)

These verses can be interpreted as either a description of the justice of God that comes upon the wicked or a continued description of the wicked themselves. Most English translations interpret the Hebrew as referencing God's justice against the wicked. Verse 24 may support this interpretation.

iii. The justice of God in regard to the wicked summarized (v. 24)

The wicked may be exalted for a time, but they will eventually be gone. They are destroyed and cut off like a head of grain.

After questioning why the wicked prosper while God appears inactive (vv. 1-17), Job includes this section on the judgment of the wicked (vv. 18-25). Again, he is either wrestling with both truths—or making the point that his friends' arguments do not measure up with reality in this life.

6. Who can prove me a liar [that God's friends don't always get to see Him act in judgment, but He will judge the wicked]? (v. 25; cf. 24:1)

Job's friends seemed to believe that the wicked always face swift judgment—in this life. Job argued that this perspective does not align with reality. He undoubtedly believed in God's ultimate justice; otherwise, he would have cursed God and died. But Job presented a more honest case for the injustice in the world than his friends did. No one could "prove [him] a liar or "render [his] words of no account."

Application

In chapters 22-24, we have yet another round of dialogue that reveals how a godly man—tested to his limits—sought to persevere in faith—in spite of the faulty counsel of a friend. Job felt abandoned by God, yet he knew he wasn't. He understood the sovereignty of God and acknowledged that it both comforted and confused him. He trusted in God's sovereignty (albeit with much difficulty), and yet it terrified him.

For his part, Eliphaz spoke many things that would have been true if his premise that sin was the root of Job's suffering were true. But he was wrong about Job, making all his counsel foolish and harmful to his friend. Job refused to conform to his friends' views merely to see if his circumstances would change. To Job, God was not a cosmic genie; He was a friend who seemed to be nowhere to be found. Job questioned, pleaded, trusted, argued, and speculated, but he kept waiting and holding on in faith, that God would one day reveal the truth and vindicate both Himself and his friend.

The Book of Job cautions us against misapplying proverbial wisdom. It confirms that human theological speculation can be futile and dangerous, even when true statements are made without all the facts being known. Genuine comfort and help come to the sufferer only when God reveals His awesome power and trustworthy nature with clarity through His Word. The suffering may not be removed, but through God's comforting self-revelation and presence in the midst of the pain, the sufferer's faith is strengthened.

God's dealings with Job are meant to encourage believers to persevere in the faith, knowing that the Lord is full of mercy and compassion—even when it doesn't seem that way (James 5:11). We may not understand or *feel* blessed. We can cry, pray, argue, debate, and speculate. But in the end, God is trustworthy, a lesson Job learned, and one we must learn as well.

Bildad—God is Majestic and Man is a Maggot
Job—God is Awesome; I Am Innocent; and May God Do to My Enemies as You have Described
Job 25:1-27:23

Have you ever been involved in an argument that seemed impossible to resolve? What usually happens? Eventually, one party stops talking, believing that further discussion would be futile. In this lesson, we witness Job's three friends finally cease their attempts at dialogue. Bildad delivers a brief final speech, marking the end of their contributions.

Notably, Bildad's final word is to call man a filthy magot. He was evidently under the impression that in order to exalt God, he needed to so over-state man's depravity so as to undermine the biblical truth that man is made in the image and likeness of God.

Unlike his three friends, however, Job is not yet finished; he will respond at length. Following Job, a young observer named Elihu will offer his two cents *for six additional chapters*. And only then, finally, and graciously, God will put an end to the speculation, accusations, and exhausting dialogue.

Job 25:1-27:23

In Job 25-27, we will examine Bildad's closing remarks and Job's response, both of which contribute to a frustrating web of thoughts about God's dealings with humanity. This leaves us yearning for God Himself to speak so we can know with surety, how we are to think about Him.

O. Bildad—God is infinitely majestic, and man is a filthy maggot (25:1-6)

1. God is infinitely majestic (25:1-3)

a. God's rule is absolute and awesome (vv. 1-2)

This marks the final speech of Bildad the Shuhite (cf. 8:1; 18:1) and the last recorded words of any of Job's three friends introduced in the prologue. Elihu, a younger observer, will speak in chapters 32-37. As Bill Cotton observes:

> The argument at this point is clearly running out of steam. It has, in any case, been a dispute of closed minds. No one is willing to budge an inch. The combatants are clearly exhausted and the speeches in a deadlock. Bildad's response to Job's latest speech is the briefest of all, and Zophar, whose turn it should have been at the end of chapter 26, can't think of anything to say (Cotton, p. 109).

This is Bildad's final attempt, short and to the point—only five verses. It begins well—with the majesty of God. But it ends rather abruptly with a reference to man as a maggot. Bildad has nothing new to contribute.

Unlike his earlier speeches, which were filled with insults and irony (Alden, p. 255), Bildad opens with an eloquent declaration of God's majesty: "Rule and dread are with Him—He imposes peace in His heights." God is in complete control, regardless of Job's circumstances. *God's rule is absolute and awesome.*

b. God's resources are limitless and His glory universal (v. 3)

These rhetorical questions expect a negative answer. God's "troops" or "armies" are beyond counting, and "His light" shines on everyone and everything. This may refer to general revelation being universal—everyone is aware of God's glory—or perhaps to God's universal awareness of all.

The combined point of verses 2-3 is that *God is infinitely majestic*. He is so great, so sovereign, so fearful, so powerful, and so glorious that man cannot fully comprehend His greatness. Most would agree on some level. Yet, Bildad's application becomes evident in verses 4-6.

2. Man is a filthy maggot (25:4-6)

a. How then can a man be just with God? (v. 4)

In context, Bildad asserts that God's majesty is so overwhelming that man can never claim to be "right" or "clean" before Him. While this is a valid theological point in precept—echoing Romans 3:23, "For all have sinned and fall short of the glory of God"—we know from the prologue that Job was blameless, upright, and in right standing with God (1:1, 8; 2:3).

Notably, Bildad simply reiterates what Eliphaz asked in his opening speech in 4:17: "Can mankind be just before God? Can a man be pure before his Maker?" (see also 15:14). In 6:29, Job did assert his righteous standing before God. See Bildad's similar approach in 8:3, 6. No doubt, Job understood the doctrine of depravity (9:2; 14:4), and the apparent paradox of his righteousness (9:15, 20). He believed that in the end, he would be proved to be right with God (13:18).

Once more, Bildad overstated the doctrine of depravity to somehow help Job see his need to repent. In verses 5-6, Bildad employs two poetic images to illustrate man's status before such a majestic God.

b. Heavenly light in the darkness cannot begin to compare with God's glory—much less, man who is a maggot by comparison (vv. 5-6)

Verse five describes the "moon" and the stars, which usually shine brilliantly against the night sky. However, God's radiance far exceeds theirs. These bright creations have no brightness compared to God. Then, in verse six—"How much less man, a maggot, and the son of man, a worm." Compared with God, man is a lowly, disgusting worm.

In 7:17ff, Job asked God why He chose to focus His scrutiny on a lowly creature as man. Yet, Job's used language reminiscent of Psalm 8:4-5, which actually exalts man as a creature under God. Bildad's description here is such an overstatement that it tacitly denies man's uniqueness as a creature, that he is made in the image of God (Gen. 1:26-27).

Here, then, is the final counsel offered by Job's dear friends come to comfort him. *God is infinitely majestic, and man is a filthy maggot.* Job thus begins his reply by essentially saying— "thanks for nothing."

P. Job—Thanks for the help; I know God is awesome; I swear I am innocent; and may God do to my enemies as you have described (26:1-27:23)

1. How in the world has your instruction helped, and where in the world did it come from? (26:1-4)

   a. *How in the world has your instruction helped? (vv. 1-3)*

   "And Job answered and said ..." (cf. 3:2; 6:1; 9:1; 12:1; 16:1; 19:1; 21:1; 23:1; 26:1).

   The pronouns in verses 2-3 are singular, indicating that Job is responding directly to Bildad, marveling at his maggot reference. With great sarcasm, Job essentially says: "What great help you bring to the powerless! What deliverance to the arm without strength! Such wonderful advice for a man lacking wisdom! So much common sense you've expressed!" (CJB). Or as the New Jerusalem Bible reads: "To one so weak, what a help you are, for the arm that is powerless, what a rescuer! What excellent advice you give the unlearned; you are never at a loss for a helpful suggestion!"

b. *Where in the world has your instruction come from? (v. 4)*

Notably, Eliphaz had received a similar revelation about man's depravity in 4:12-17, from a spirit in the night. Here, Job questions Bildad, as the NIV renders it: "Who has helped you utter these words? And whose spirit spoke from your mouth?" Or the *New Living*: "Where have you gotten all these wise sayings? Whose spirit speaks through you?"

Depravity without hope, without the image of God and His grace, is damning and demonic. And Job senses this. *How in the world has your instruction helped?* and *where in the world has your instruction come from?* To eloquently speak of God's majesty only scratches the surface of the true knowledge of God, and Job demonstrates that he can do this as well.

2. I too can describe God's amazing power and majesty (26:5-14)
   a. *God's power and majesty extends not only in the heavens, but also in Sheol (vv. 5-6)*

Job here shifts from his questioning of Bildad, to a section describing God's power and majesty. The connection between questioning the origin of Bildad's advice and stating that God knows and judges the "departed spirits" subtly implies that Bildad's advice comes from hell.

Notably, in verse five, "the departed spirits" is literally "*rephaim*"—"giants" or "great men"—with some translations using "ghosts." This term has been associated with the "sons of Anak" in Numbers 13:33, and the Anakim are regarded as "Rephaim" in Deuteronomy 2:11. There may also be an allusion to the judgment of the demonic world during Noah's flood (Genesis 6:4).

"Abaddon" in verse six is the place of "destruction", and is often used in parallel with "Sheol." Verses 5-6 together indicate that God's power and authority extend not only to the heavens, as Bildad claimed, but also to hell. As Hebrews 4:13 states: "...all things are open and laid bare to the eyes of Him with whom we have to do." Job touches on the reality of the demonic realm but he doesn't grasp that it is directly involved in the trials that he is experiencing.

b. God created space, the atmosphere, and the celestial phenomena (vv. 7-10)

Job continues his reflection by echoing Genesis 1. "Empty space" in verse seven corresponds to the word "formless" in Genesis 1:2. "Job's assertion that the earth hangs on nothing is amazingly accurate ..." (Alden, p. 259).

Job was intrigued, knowing clouds were made of water and how heavy water was, that the clouds did not always "burst" forth rain (Alden, p. 259). As the Holman Bible reads: "He enfolds the waters in His clouds, yet the clouds do not burst beneath their weight." God controls the shining of the moon and the place of the horizon (v. 9-10). Notably, Job seems to understand the earth and sea as contained within a "circle"—where light and darkness meet.

c. God controls the storms and their origins (vv. 11-13)

Verse 11 may poetically refer to thunder or possibly to mountains that quake. Creation trembles under God's authority. In verse 12, the verb has two possible meanings, which are opposites. Either He "calmed" the sea with His power or He stirs the sea with His power. Either way, God's power is vividly depicted. "Rahab" was a mythical sea monster associated with the chaos of the churning sea. God is able to subdue the sea.

In verse 13, God's Spirit or breath makes the heavens clear or fair, and His hand pierced the "gliding serpent," possibly referring to the clouds. Job may also be implying that God is greater than the demonic forces that might be influencing Bildad's counsel. Again, Job may have stumbled upon the reality of chapters 1-2 without fully grasping its significance.

Job poetically depicts God's supremacy over the phenomena that the world attributes to various legends and powers. God is supreme, but this only begins to capture the truth about Him, as verse 14 confirms.

d. God's power and majesty are beyond our full comprehension (v. 14)

The Jewish Bible reads: "These are but glimpses of His rule, the mere whisper that we perceive of Him..." Job then asks, "But who is able to grasp the meaning of his thundering power?" The things we perceive and stand in awe of are merely whispers of God's true power and majesty. The fullness of His power remains incomprehensible.

So, in verses 5-14, Job demonstrated that he too could describe God's power and majesty. But it didn't begin to reveal the depth of the Almighty's powerful ways.

With no response from his friends, Job continues in chapter 27 to defend his innocence once again.

3. I know I am innocent, and will go to my grave holding fast my integrity (27:1-6)

   a. Job continued (v. 1)

Verse one differs significantly from the previously repeated formula: "Job answered and said." Here, the text literally reads: "And Job again lifted up his proverb and said..." The Jewish Bible states: "And Job again took up his theme and said." He may have waited for a response and received none; thus, "Job continued his discourse." His "proverb" or "parable" that follows consists of words meant to once more affirm His innocence and warn his friends.

b. Job continued to maintain his innocence (vv. 2-6)
   i. Under oath (v. 2)

Here, Job uses the language of an oath, presenting sworn testimony. He would be guilty and damned if it weren't true. He identifies God as the "living God" and the One "who has taken away my judgment"—the "Almighty who has embittered my soul." Andersen's comments are helpful:

> The most arresting feature of Job's oath is that he swears by the God 'who has denied me justice' (2a, NEB), who has made my soul bitter (2b, RSV; cf. 7:11; 10:1; 21:25). What he says is a fact, and Job has consistently maintained it. His high trust in God becomes quite audacious in this paradoxical appeal to God against God. Many since Elihu (34:5) have been shocked by it. But Job is not shaking his fist at God. By his solemn gesture he stakes everything on a justice beyond this injustice. It is up to God to set right the wrongs which, in a world of which He is the sole Maker and Owner, must, behind all secondary causes, be His full responsibility. Just how responsibly God would take up this burden and, in the person of His Son, Jesus Christ, would carry, absorb and quench 'the sins of the whole world' (1 Jn. 2:2), Job could not know. But his faith is leaping the vast distance into God as 'righteous ... and a Saviour' (Is. 45:21) (Andersen, pp. 220-21).

Job was placing himself under oath before God, even the God who had thus far denied him his request for a hearing; but Job still believed that God was living and Almighty.

   ii. For as long as I live (v. 3)

Job maintained his innocence—under oath, and for as long as he still lived. The living God is the giver of "life." As long as God sustained his life, he would testify to his innocence, speak honestly, and maintain a clear conscience.

iii. In utter honesty (v. 4)

Job's oath was binding till death, before a sovereign God, that he would speak in utter honesty. No "falsehood" or "deceit" would come from his "lips" or "tongue".

iv. I maintain my righteousness with a clean conscience (vv. 5-6)

Job would never declare his friends to be "right." Young's literal translation reads: "Pollution to me—if I justify you. Till I expire I turn not aside mine integrity from me." In other words, Job said that he would be defiled, unholy, and worthy of damnation if he affirmed that his friends were right, that he had some wickedness in his life he would not let go of. Their reward-retribution theology, applied in reverse, was indeed damning. Job could never admit to something untrue in order to somehow regain God's blessing.

Job pledged to maintain his "integrity" and hold fast his "righteousness" without letting it go. He had a clean conscience—"my heart shall not reproach me as long as I live" (NKJV).

4. May God do to my enemy as you have all described (27:7-23)
   a. *May my enemy be as the wicked (v. 7-10)*
      i. The imprecation (v. 7)

Verse seven is an imprecatory prayer of sorts. Job calls on God to deal with his "enemy ... as the wicked" and his "adversary" like one who deviates from justice. How does God deal with the "wicked" and the "evil-doer"? Verses 8-10 outline the implications.

   ii. The implications (vv. 8-10)
      aa. The wicked will not escape God's justice (vv. 8-9)

The word translated "cut off" can also mean to "gain by violence." Verse 8 is quite similar to Mark 8:36: "For what does it profit a man to gain the whole world, and forfeit his soul?" Verse nine asserts that God will not "listen to" the cry of the godless in that day. *The wicked will not escape God's justice.* Why?

    bb. The wicked have no relationship with God (v. 10)

The wicked—in this context, Job's enemy—does not "delight in the Almighty" or "call on God at all times." It is again frightening to note that none of Job's friends are recorded as speaking to God—calling upon Him—only speaking for Him. But over and over again, even when vexed and angry, Job called on God "at all times." Why? Here the contrasting parallel points to his "delight in the Almighty."

In verses 7-10, Job prays—*May my enemy be as the wicked, who do not escape God's justice because they lack a relationship with Him.* In the rest of the chapter, Job reminds his friends of what they claimed to have seen regarding the end of the wicked. A summary of their own teaching should serve as a warning to *them.*

b. May I remind you of what you have seen concerning the end of the wicked (vv. 11-23)
  i. This you have seen—it is your instruction and mine to you (vv. 11-12)

 Job's friends had repeatedly lectured him about God's dealings with the wicked. Here, Job reminds them of what they already knew about the "hand of God" and the things of the "Almighty." He exclaims in verse 12: "Behold, all of you have seen it; Why then do you act foolishly?"—literally, "And why this breath of your vanity?" As the NET Bible puts it: "If you yourselves have all seen this, Why in the world do you continue this meaningless talk?"

> ii. This is the portion of the wicked man from God (vv. 13-23)
>> aa. The wicked man will have an inheritance from the Almighty (v. 13)

In 20:29, Zophar spoke these words: "This is the wicked man's portion from God, even the heritage decreed to him by God." Job uses essentially the same words to remind his friends of what they already knew. But in context of his speech, he warns them against opposing him as if they were enemies. To do so would identify them as wicked men. And as they knew, *the wicked man will have an inheritance from the Almighty*—Zophar said so.

>> bb. The wicked man will lose all his family (vv. 14-15)

Bildad said of the wicked in 18:19: "He has no offspring or posterity among his people, Nor any survivor where he sojourned." Listen to Zophar's words in 20:26: "... unfanned fire will devour him; It will consume the survivor in his tent." Here, Job adds the image of "widows" who are unable to weep—either because of the justice of it or because they do not care. As his friends had so callously told him, *the wicked man will lose all his family*.

>> cc. The wicked man will lose all his wealth (vv. 16-19)

Bildad alluded to the misplaced trust of the wicked using similar language in 8:13-15: "So are the paths of all who forget God; And the hope of the godless will perish, Whose confidence is fragile, And whose trust a spider's web. He trusts in his house, but it does not stand; He holds fast to it, but it does not endure." In 22:24, Eliphaz had told Job to place his "gold in the dust" and make the Almighty his treasure. Job articulates the same basic proverbial wisdom that his friends had. In fact, Proverbs 13:22 does indeed state: "...And the wealth of the sinner is stored up for the righteous."

> dd. The wicked man will be taken away in sudden terror (vv. 20-22)

Eliphaz had said in 22:10-11: "Therefore snares surround you, And sudden dread terrifies you, Or darkness, so that you cannot see, And an abundance of water covers you." Zophar used the same term "flee" to denote inescapable judgment in 20:24. The picture is of the wicked being taken away in sudden terror—a motif repeatedly used by Job's friends.

> ee. The wicked man will be the object of ridicule and scorn [or perhaps the wind claps its hands and hisses him from his place] (v. 23)

Job describes enduring similar ridicule in 17:6 and 30:9-14. However, this may complete the thought of verses 21-22—the east wind carries him away; whirls him away; hurls him; he tries to escape but it "claps its hands" at him and drives him from his place with sounds of hissing.

Application

Chapters 3-27 have left the reader and Job's friends exhausted—and largely speechless. The argument is so tangled that one often loses track of who is saying what. Where can wisdom be found? Chapter 28 will pose that very question (v. 12)—and answer it (v. 23-28). It is found only in God and is obtained solely through faith—the fear of the Lord.

Chapters 29-31 will contain Job's closing arguments in the case he wishes to present before God. Again, it reflects on his circumstances and pain. In chapters 32-37, another human attempt at wisdom is offered, with the cumulative effect being that we are even more thoroughly exhausted by men talking. Finally, in chapter 38—God speaks, and we can be sure we can trust what He says. Only in God's self-revelation can we find rest and truth that we can know to be infallibly trustworthy. In that self-revelation, we learn why He is to be feared and trusted.

For now, let's remember a few lessons from the preceding argument. Job's friends overstate and misapply their theology, which often sounds very orthodox to us. Job speaks honestly, sometimes makes shocking statements, pledges his innocence, declares his faith, then his despair, and he prays often. He persevered in faith, even if it was a rocky road.

We learn that we ought not judge people based on their circumstances or even how they might talk in an argument. If we don't listen closely to everything they say, we might mistake some of their emotional language as indicating more sin than might actually be there.

Beyond this, Job's pain and his struggles with friends and God have been recorded for our instruction, so that we might have hope (Rom. 15:4) and find examples to avoid at times and emulate at others. From the Book of Job, we understand that God may be doing things in the heavenly realm in ways we do not comprehend. This gives us hope to trust, and persevere, and seek Him, even when we feel abandoned and treated unjustly. As James 5:11 states, "You have heard of the endurance of Job, and have seen the outcome of the Lord's dealings, that the Lord is full of compassion and *is* merciful."

Where Can Wisdom Be Found?
Job 28:1-28

In chapters 3-27 of the Book of Job, the reader encounters a series of speeches filled with human reasoning and theology—sometimes orthodox but often misapplied. The overwhelming amount of dialogue leaves us grappling with the poetic portraits of God's majesty, interwoven with a lethal dose of retribution theology, painful rebuttals, and speculations.

In chapter 25, Bildad issued a final call to repentance, encapsulated in the statement, "God is majestic, and man is maggot." In chapter 26, Job spoke, and his friends evidently chose not to respond. So, in chapter 27, Job resumed his discourse.

Chapter 28 appears to originate from Job, yet it presents a distinct poetic form as a self-contained unit. It seems that, for a brief moment, Job reflects on true wisdom after cautioning his friends in chapter 27. Where can wisdom be found? In chapter 28, we find welcome relief from the misapplied theology of Job's friends and Job's emotionally charged responses. This chapter serves as the chiastic center of the book—an ode to the value and source of wisdom, providing a moment of respite before the emotional turmoil resumes with Elihu's final attempt at humanly interpreted wisdom.

In Job 28, we will explore three movements that offer a refreshing contrast to the human wisdom often highlighted in the preceding speeches.

III. Job's poem considering divine wisdom (28:1-28)

A. Wisdom is harder to obtain than precious metals and priceless jewels [God's wisdom is beyond human effort and ingenuity] (28:1-12)

1. Man, through human effort and ingenuity, has found the source of all that is precious in the temporal realm (28:1-11)

    a. The minerals man seeks after (vv. 1-2)

      i. Silver and gold (v. 1)

"Silver and gold," even the most precious earthly materials, have a *source* that man has been able to find.

   ii. Iron and copper (v. 2)

Deuteronomy 8:9 speaks of Israel as a "land whose stones are iron, and out of whose hills you can dig copper." Although "iron" and "copper" are less precious than gold or silver, they remain valuable due to the implements made from them. Thus, man has learned how to extract them "from the dust" and pour them "from rock."

Man goes to great lengths to find and extract precious or useful minerals from the earth.

   b. The mines where treasure is found (vv. 3-6)

      i. The mine and mining pictured (vv. 3-4)

When one digs into the earth for these materials, he "puts an end to darkness," bringing light into the deep recesses of the mine. Even with a lamp or torch, the mine walls are "rock in gloom and deep shadow." The focus is on the great lengths to which man goes, "to the farthest limit he searches out" these treasures.

In verse four, we see the reality that mines are often dug in inaccessible places—"far from habitation, forgotten by the foot." The picture is of a miner lowering into a cavity, swinging "back and forth, far from men."

   ii. The produce of the earth (vv. 5-6)

It seems that Job and his contemporaries understood that not only did the earth produce "food" on its surface, but they also had some knowledge of geology. Perhaps from active volcanoes or exploration into mines, they recognized that "underneath" the earth "it is turned up as fire," and "its rocks are the source of sapphires." The mention of "gold" here (cf. v. 1, 15, 16, 17, 19 [6 times in English, four different Hebrew terms]) underscores the precious value of the "stones" referred to here in English as "sapphires."

It is possible that the "fire" underneath the earth refers to the torches that miners use underground, but it may also be understood as molten rock from which precious stones are formed.

  c. The manmade genius of finding such treasures (vv. 7-11)
   i. The keenest and strongest animals could never find such hidden treasures (vv. 7-8)

The "bird of prey" and the "falcon's eye" reference animals with exceptionally keen vision. Yet, despite their optical prowess, they have not seen the source of the precious metals and stones found underground. However, man has. Man's intellectual prowess and insight into earthly wealth, even geology, are unmatched.

Though the "proud beasts" and "lion" possess fierce strength and hunting ability, they cannot match man's relentless pursuit of hidden treasures. Lions have never dug into the earth, swung on ropes, and extracted gold, silver, stones, iron, and copper. Some suggest this verse may allude to Satan and the demonic realm. "Proud beasts" is more literally rendered "sons of pride" (cf. 41:33-34). It is true that Satan and his minions can never find true wisdom, as they do not fear the LORD, except for the cringing fear of certain judgment. But that this verse alludes to the demonic realm may be debatable.

Verses 9-11 reveal the ingenuity and power that man has for such treasure-seeking expeditions.

   ii. The cleverness and strength of man is incredible in finding precious, earthly treasure (vv. 9-11)

This paragraph highlights man's efforts, and by implication his cleverness, in finding "anything precious" (v. 10). He assaults the flinty rock (v. 9) and can "overturn the mountains at the base" with his strength and ingenuity. He carves out tunnels "through the rocks" to find treasures (v. 11). Man "can even dam up rivers so that the riverbed can be exposed and exploited for resources" (Longman, p. 329).

2. Man, through human effort and ingenuity, has not found the source of wisdom (28:12)

Notably, "wisdom" is not further defined or explained. It is assumed that the audience has some grasp of the meaning, though not the fullness of its content or source. The word itself implies "skill." Perhaps it can be paraphrased: "But where can skill to live and cope and understand life—where can it be found?" "Understanding" is a synonym that refers to the "insight" into something, enabling one to make use of it. Where can the skill to live, cope, and thrive in life—and perceive how to respond to life's circumstances—be found?

Here lies the summary point of this opening section of chapter 28. In spite of man's capabilities, even wisdom in uncovering precious treasures beneath the earth, he has not unearthed "wisdom" or found the source of "understanding." No amount of effort or ingenuity can lead men to true "wisdom" or "understanding."

This serves as a succinct commentary on the previous dialogue. Eliphaz, Bildad, Zophar—and perhaps to some extent Job—all crafted highly skilled literary and poetic expressions of theology and application. Yet they have largely missed the mark. No one is much wiser than when they began the dialogue.

Verses 1-12 combine to confirm: Wisdom is harder to obtain than precious metals and priceless jewels [God's wisdom is beyond human effort and ingenuity].

B. Wisdom is more valuable than precious metals and priceless jewels [God's wisdom is beyond price] (28:13-22)
   1. The price of wisdom is beyond human comprehension (vv. 13-19)
      a. *Wisdom's value is not understood (v. 13a)*

Man has no understanding of even how to estimate the worth of wisdom or rank it in order of importance.

   b. *Wisdom is not found in man's realm—in earth or sea (vv. 13b-14)*

Wisdom is not "found in the land of the living" (v. 13). Moreover, in verse 14, it is not found beneath the sea. Wisdom is not found in man's realm—whether in earth or sea.

   c. *Nothing can compare to the surpassing value of true wisdom (vv. 15-19)*
      i. Not pure gold nor the price of silver (v. 15)

There are four different Hebrew words for "gold" in this section, with this one meaning something akin to "solid gold."

Wisdom cannot be bought with even "pure gold" or "silver." Proverbs 16:16 states: "How much better it is to get wisdom than gold! And to get understanding is to be chosen above silver." The most precious metals cannot compare to wisdom. At this juncture in the story, both Job and the readers long for God's wisdom after the confusing debate. For the believing sufferer, nothing is as valuable as God's wisdom.

   ii. Not the gold of Ophir, onyx, or sapphire (v. 16)

"Ophir" is believed to be located in southern Arabia, near the Red Sea, and was renowned for its "gold." The text adds "onyx" and "sapphire." The combined thought of verses 15-16 echoes Proverbs 8:10-11, 19, where Lady Wisdom calls out: "Take my instruction and not silver, and knowledge rather than choicest gold. For wisdom is better than jewels; and all desirable things cannot compare with her ... My fruit is better than gold, even pure gold, and my yield better than choicest silver."

   iii. Not gold or glass, or gold jewelry (v. 17)

The NIV reads: "Neither gold nor crystal can compare with it, nor can it be had for jewels of gold." The term for "glass" or "crystal" is rare but clearly refers to some precious or semi-precious jewel.

   iv. Not coral and crystal or pearls (v. 18)

"Coral" is not strictly a gemstone, but it was evidently prized. "Crystal" here is translated "quartz" by some versions or "jasper," or possibly even "pearls." Some translations interpret the last jewel as "rubies," while others say "pearls." Proverbs 3:15 describes wisdom as more precious than "jewels." "And nothing you desire compares with her."

   v. Not topaz from Ethiopia or pure gold (v. 19)

Here, the "topaz of Cush" and "pure gold" (the same term as in verse 16) conclude the list of incomparable treasures.

The point is clear—nothing can compare to the surpassing value of true wisdom. So why don't we value wisdom above all else? The poetic expressions in verses 13-19 emphasize that the price of wisdom is beyond human comprehension.

2. The place of wisdom is beyond human discovery (12:20-22)

   a. *Where does wisdom come from? (v. 20; cf. v. 12)*

This verse is nearly identical to verse 12, differing only in the verb. Like verse 12, it encapsulates the reality that the source of wisdom is beyond human ability to discover. And much like verses 13-14, the next verse says with poetic flair that wisdom cannot be found in creation.

   b. *The answer is not found with the living, even from the vantage point of the birds of the sky (v. 21)*

Verse 13 indicates that wisdom is not found "in the land of the living." Here, it is described as hidden from the eyes of all living." In verse 14, wisdom can't be found in the deep. Here, those who have a bird's eye view can't find it. In verses 13-14, wisdom's source cannot be discovered in earth or sea; in this verse, it remains unseen in earth and sky.

   c. *The answer is not found in death—though there is a report of it there (v. 22)*

"Abaddon" represents the place of destruction. Here, destruction and death are personified as testifying that they do not ultimately know the source of wisdom, but have merely "heard a report of it." Humanity has searched for and mined every precious earthly treasure, but neither the living nor the dead, in earth, sky, or sea, knows the treasure and place of wisdom.

Wisdom is harder to obtain than precious metals and priceless jewels [God's wisdom is beyond human effort and ingenuity]; Wisdom is more valuable than precious metals and priceless jewels [God's wisdom is beyond price]; yet in verses 23-28, Job affirms that man is not without hope, as he writes ...

C. Wisdom is found only in God and known only in the fear of the Lord [God's wisdom is begotten only in God and revealed to man as inextricably bound to the fear of the Lord] (28:23-28)

1. Wisdom is known by God alone (28:23-27)

a. The reality—God knows wisdom (v. 23)

"Elohim perceives its path, and He Himself knows its place." God alone knows wisdom. Here is the starting point: humanity possesses no wisdom and can find no lasting wisdom; but God knows wisdom. That's the reality—God knows wisdom. In verses 24-27 we see the reasons that God has such knowledge, poetically stated.

b. The reasons (vv. 24-27)
  i. He sees everything (v. 24)

"Because He Himself views the ends of the earth and everything under the heavens sees." Nothing is hidden from God's sight—not even the place of wisdom.

  ii. He created everything (vv. 25-26)

There is an allusion to creation here. "Wind ... waters ... rain ... and thunderbolt" may foreshadow God's revelation introduced in chapter 38, where Yahweh speaks from the "storm" or "whirlwind." Proverbs 8:22-31 employs similar imagery of wisdom personified in conjunction with God's creative work.

Here, the point is that humanity does not truly understand the value or source of wisdom. But God does. He sees everything. He created everything. And in verse 27 ...

iii. He established wisdom (v. 27)

The verbs are "saw," "counted," "established," and "searched." The word "declared" may refer to evaluating something. No human can see, count, establish, or search out wisdom, but God can and did.

As a short haven of relief, Job eloquently expresses that man does not value or know wisdom. Wisdom is known by God alone. But since God is intimately and perfectly acquainted with wisdom, there is hope. Note the conclusion in verse 28.

2. Wisdom is made known by God in the proverb: "Behold, the fear of the Lord, that is wisdom; and to depart from evil is understanding" (v. 28)

This affirms that divine wisdom must come from divine revelation—divine self-disclosure alone. Nothing can be known about "wisdom" apart from the all-knowing, all-seeing Creator, who establishes wisdom and reveals it.

The term "Adonai" is used here for Lord. The similar phrase, "fear of Yahweh" is used repeatedly in the Psalms (Psalm 19:9; 34:11; 111:10) and Proverbs (1:7, 29; 2:5; 8:13; 9:10; 10:27; 14:26-27; 15:16, 33; 16:6; 19:23; 22:4; 23:17); not to mention the commands to "fear God" or "fear the Lord."

A study of "the fear of the Lord" leads to the conclusion that it embodies a trembling reverence and awe that is both humbling and yet comforting. First John 4:16-18 confirms that perfect love casts out fear—that is, the horror of divine condemnation and punishment. Love casts out such fear of condemnation, but it does not cast off the trembling awe, reverence and admiration of the Holy One, who alone is God (cf. Longman, p. 334). To fear God is to love and trust Him.

Reverence, trust, and loving admiration for the Sovereign Master—that is wisdom; it provides the skill to live, cope, and thrive in any circumstance. To depart from evil is true perception. God alone knows wisdom, and He reveals it to humanity. Fear the Lord and turn away from evil.

> The "man" who had been looking for wisdom inside mountains and who would, if he could, buy it with this world's wealth now hears the simple but profound truth—wisdom consists in fearing the Lord on the one hand and shunning evil on the other. "The fear of the LORD" appears at the beginning of Proverbs (1:7), at the end of Ecclesiastes (12:13), and here in the middle of Job" (Alden, p. 277).

Many have noted that it is often easier to intellectually grasp the fear of the Lord than to embrace it practically—especially in the midst of excruciating trials or while trying to help those who are suffering through them.

Application

For a brief moment, we feel a sense of relief as the writer of Job provides a chapter that extols true wisdom, free from the pejorative language, misapplied theological half-truths, and emotional twists of the previous debates. In the flow of the book, Job grasps this truth, at least intellectually. He will ultimately embrace it more fully as God reveals His grandeur and majesty afresh to him in chapters 38-41. Then he will acknowledge his ignorance and rest in the fear of God, thereby embracing the wisdom of God.

This too was part of Job's journey in persevering in faith: reciting the truth that God's wisdom is more precious than anything else and is revealed only to those fear Him.

Where do you search and what is your treasure?

> *My son, if you will receive my words And treasure my commandments within you, Make your ear attentive to wisdom, Incline your heart to understanding; For if you cry for discernment, Lift your voice for understanding; If you seek her as silver And search for her as for hidden treasures; Then you will discern the fear of the LORD And discover the knowledge of God. (Prov. 2:1-5)*

Job's Closing Testimony
Job 29:1-31:40

In Proverbs 1:33, Lady Wisdom says: "But he who listens to me shall live securely and will be at ease from the dread of evil." Proverbs 3:2 promises "length of days and years of life and peace." Proverbs chapter three continues:

> *How blessed is the man who finds wisdom and the man who gains understanding. For her profit is better than the profit of silver and her gain better than fine gold ... Long life is in her right hand; in her left hand are riches and honor. Her ways are pleasant ways and all her paths are peace. She is a tree of life to those who take hold of her, and happy are all who hold her fast ... Keep sound wisdom and discretion, so they will be life to your soul and adornment to your neck. Then you will walk in your way securely and your foot will not stumble. When you lie down, you will not be afraid; when you lie down, your sleep will be sweet. Do not be afraid of sudden fear nor of the onslaught of the wicked when it comes; for the LORD will be your confidence and will keep your foot from being caught ... He blesses the dwelling of the righteous.*

The rewards of wisdom are plentiful. Yet Job, the epitome of a man of wisdom, suffered like no other, save our Lord Jesus Christ (Who is wisdom incarnate, yet suffered violence, injustice, and unspeakable pain). Perhaps the Book of Job helped men like Simeon (Luke 2:34-35), or later Nicodemus (John 7:46-52; 19:39), understand that the Messiah would suffer under the blessing of God, though most interpreted Jesus' suffering as a sign of God's curse.

Job teaches us that we ought to always trust in God's goodness and wisdom, even when our circumstances seem to contradict these truths. Ultimately, God determines the consequences and rewards of fearing Him and turning away from evil. His promises of life, peace, happiness, and prosperity extend beyond this life and world. Jesus is exalted in heaven above every name, and Job is now enjoying paradise until his resurrection, where His body, life, peace, and prosperity will be perfect for eternity.

In Job 29-31, the three movements in Job's final speech illustrate the contrasts between his past glories and present pain, culminating in his testimony of innocence regarding any hidden sin. In Job's last speech, we find his closing arguments and final words before God's revelation in chapters 38-41.

IV. Job's perspective concerning his suffering and pledge concerning his innocence, and Elihu's painstaking response (29:1-37:24)
  A. Job—His closing testimony (29:1-31:40)
  1. I long for the days and honor of the past (29:1-25)
    a. *I was blessed by God (vv. 1-6)*
      i. The longing expressed (vv. 1-2a)

This same introductory phrase was used in 27:1. It may indicate that Job's friends remained silent after the song of wisdom in chapter 28.

Job expresses his longing for a life "as in months gone by." The following verses describe his perspective on life before the calamities that befell him.

ii. The love-relationship described (vv. 2b-4)

Note the poetic allusions to God's loving care that Job once cherished but now feels is absent—"the days when *God watched over me*"; "*His lamp shone over my head*, by *His light* I walked through darkness"; "the *friendship of God* was over my tent.*"* Job recalls that God protected, directed, and fellowshipped with him. He longs for that relationship to be restored. See Psalm 121:3-8 for a song about the LORD's care.

iii. The life of blessing described (vv. 5-6)

God's "Almighty" presence was evident to Job in months gone by. Job's children "around" him testified to God's blessing and grace. "Butter" or "cream" and "oil" were evidence of material blessings that Job knew were from the Giver of every good and perfect gift. No doubt, Job's reflection aligns with Satan's depiction of his life in 1:9-10: "Then Satan answered the LORD, 'Does Job fear God for nothing? Have You not made a hedge about him and his house and all that he has, on every side? You have blessed the work of his hands, and his possessions have increased in the land.'"

b. *I was respected by others (vv. 7-10)*
   i. The respect of young and old (vv. 7-8)

The "gate of the city" and the "seat in the square" refer to where city leaders conducted business and held court. Job was a respected leader. In verse eight, it states: "The young men saw me and stepped aside, and the old men rose to their feet" (NIV). "Young" and "old" respected Job's wisdom and leadership.

   ii. The respect of princes and nobles (vv. 9-10)

Other leaders stopped talking and began listening when Job spoke. He commanded utmost respect among the chief men and highest officials. Job asserts—he was blessed with intimacy with God and respected by all.

c. I was a blessing to others (vv. 11-25)
  i. My godliness and wisdom were obvious (v. 11)

Others affirmed Job's wisdom and godliness. When they heard him speak, they recognized he was blessed by God (cf. Ps. 1). When they "saw" how he lived, they testified to Job's character, godliness, and wisdom. Verses 12-24 elaborate on what people heard and saw in Job's speech and actions.

  ii. My compassion brought blessing to the orphan and widow (vv. 12-13)

Job was a defender of the defenseless and brought joy where there was sorrow. With no governmental welfare, the "poor," the "orphan," the needy, and the widow had to rely on the benevolence of private citizens. In the past, Job could provide tangible compassion and blessings to these individuals. Now, he finds himself in their position, without anyone to help or bring him joy.

  iii. My justice brought blessing to those who were oppressed (vv. 14-17)

In verse 14, Job portrays himself as clothed in "righteousness" and "justice." The context reveals his thinking. Job treated the disabled with dignity, rather than neglecting or exploiting them (v. 15). He dealt justly with the needy—providing assistance rather than taking advantage (v. 16). Job even took time to investigate "the case which [he] did not know" and delivered the oppressed from their unjust oppressors (v. 17). As Alden observes: "The self-portrait Job painted is one of tenderness, generosity, service, justice, and bravery, an admirable assortment of attributes that all God's people would do well to own" (Alden, p. 284).

iv. My outlook was hopeful and confident (vv. 18-20)

The metaphors in these verses indicate provision and safety. Job believed he would live securely in his "nest" with a long life (v. 18). He would flourish like a well-supplied plant (v. 19) and continue to be honored and strong in life and ministry (v. 20). Essentially, Job embraced the promises of Psalm 1! He says—*my outlook was hopeful and confident.*

v. My words were respected and brought hope (vv. 21-24)

In verses 21-23, Job's counsel was coveted and satisfying. The picture of people opening their mouths as for the spring rain symbolizes refreshment for the thirsty. Job's words were respected, sought, and brought hope and satisfaction to those in need. Verse 24 highlights the reverence people had for Job. As the NIV reads: "When I smiled at them, they scarcely believed it; the light of my face was precious to them."

vi. My leadership was unquestioned (v. 25)

Everything Job said was followed. The Jewish Bible reads: "I decided their course and presided over them; I lived like a king among his troops, Like one who consoles mourners." Job provided direction and comfort, earning respect and love.

Chapter 29 records Job's poetic cry: *I long for the days and honor of the past.* This is the way it was. In chapter 30, he recounts the way it now is.

2. I lament the degradation and humiliation of the present (30:1-31)
   a. I'm not respected—I'm an object of ridicule (vv. 1-15)
      i. The description of those who now mock Job (vv. 1-8)
         aa. Their fathers were worthless men (v. 1)

In 29:8, young men hid themselves, and old men stood in respect when Job came to the city gate. "But now," Job laments, "those younger than I mock me." These mockers are the dregs of society, as verses 1-8 illustrate in great poetic detail. "Job has exchanged the respect of the most respectable for the contempt of the most contemptible" (Andersen, p. 235). Those who mock Job came from a lineage of untrustworthy vagrants, their fathers unworthy even to be compared to his sheepdogs.

  bb. They are without strength and food (vv. 2-4)

The mockers of the once-great Job are neither strong nor hardworking (v. 2). Instead, they are scavengers (v. 3) who consume the food of the destitute (v. 4). They barely survive—yet they view themselves as better off than Job. So, they laughed at him in scorn.

  cc. They are without a home (vv. 5-7)

In verse five, Job's mockers are depicted as outcasts of society, the very opposite of those who sit at the city gate—the princes and nobles. The great men once revered Job; now, the homeless vagabonds who sleep among the bushes "cry out" against him.

  dd. They are without any honor (v. 8)

God-rejecting "fools"—people without "name" or honor—as the Jewish Bible reads: "Scoundrels, nobodies, Stricken from the earth." These people mock Job, the most honorable, righteous, God-fearing man on earth, as per Yahweh's own estimation (1:8). Verses 1-8 describe the mockers. Verses 9-15 describe their mocking.

  ii. The description of their mocking attacks (vv. 9-15)
    aa. They sing and talk about me (v. 9)

The word "taunt" refers to a vulgar song. Job says: "And now I'm what they sing and talk about." Ancient Near Eastern vagrants sing and joke about Job. But that's not all.

bb. They spit at my face (v. 10)

The *New Living Translation* states: "They despise me and won't come near me, except to spit in my face." Even the outcasts "stand aloof" and "detest" the beleaguered Job, confirming their disgust by "spitting" in front of him or in his face.

cc. They are unrestrained in their abuse (v. 11)

Job suggests that either God has become unrestrained in His affliction of him, leading the mockers to similarly act without restraint, or that the mockers justify their unrestrained abuse by reasoning that since God has loosed His bowstring, they are free to attack Job as well. In either case, the notion of unrestrained abuse is clear.

dd. They join together to attack me (v. 12)

Job perceives this "brood" of young attackers as an army laying siege to him, depicted as taking his feet out from under him and then mobbing him.

ee. They are unrestrained—no one stops them (vv. 13-15)

The repetition of the idea of no restraint is notable. In verse 13, no one restrains them; in verse 14, they come as through a wide breach; in verse 15, they pursue my honor as the wind, and my prosperity has vanished like a cloud. The wind is relentless, and clouds disappear quickly. Job was not only devastated emotionally and physically—he was under unrestrained attack from even the most despicable men, with no one intervening to stop the mockery and ridicule.

b. *I'm afflicted, opposed, alone, and dying (vv. 16-31)*
   i. I am afflicted and dying (vv. 16-19)

"And now my life ebbs away; days of suffering grip me" (v. 16; NIV). "At night my bones are filled with pain, which gnaws at me relentlessly" (v. 17; NLT). The Hebrew poetry in verse 18 has been interpreted in various ways. The Jewish Bible states: "With great effort I change clothing; The neck of my tunic fits my waist"—suggesting that Job has lost significant weight due to his affliction. The *New Living Translation* reads: "With a strong hand, God grabs my shirt. He grips me by the collar of my coat." Both interpretations convey the idea of suffering.

In verse 19, the pronoun "He" may refer to God. Nevertheless, Job's main point is that he is afflicted, in pain, and his life is being poured out.

As previously noted, Job often turns directly to God in prayer in the midst of his anguish and pain. He does so in verses 20-23.

> ii. I cry out to You, O God, for help—but You oppose me (vv. 20-23)

The singular second-person pronouns indicate that Job is directly addressing God, as only He can help. In verse 20, Job exclaims to God—"I cry out to You for help, but You do not answer me." When Job "stands up," it only invites divine scrutiny or a silent gaze. He continues in verse 21, telling God that He had attacked him. In verse 22, Job prays: *You've hung me out to dry, swinging in the wind.* In verse 23, he laments: *You're killing me. I cry out to You, O God, for help—but You oppose me.*

In verses 24-26, Job contrasts his previous responses to those in need with what he perceives to be God's response to his cry for help.

> iii. I am not suffering due to my own lack of compassion (vv. 24-26)

In verse 24, Job poses a rhetorical question, asserting that the right action when "in a heap of ruins" is to reach out for help and "cry out for help." This is what he has done, as noted in verse 20. Then in verse 25, he emphasizes that he has wept with those who weep, showing compassion for those "whose life is hard." He thought he too might have sympathy, someone would bring light and good, but only evil and darkness came.

   iv. I am agitated, without comfort, alone, sick, and full of sorrow (vv. 27-31)

In verse 27, Job expresses, "I am seething within," which is literally rendered in the KJV as "My bowels boiled." Job is at least extremely agitated and possibly suffering from severe digestive issues. He finds no relief from his physical and emotional distress, with no one to comfort him, though he cries for "help" in verses 28-29. He feels abandoned, except for the jackals [older translations, "dragons"] and ostriches/owls—creatures that no other animals associate with. Job felt utterly alone.

In verse 30, he says "My skin grows black and falls from me; My bones burn with fever" (NKJV). He had some horrible skin ailment causing significant discoloration and peeling. Alden notes: "These last symptoms of Job's malady must be taken with others to complete the picture of his intense physical discomfort. He had scabs and festering sores over his entire body (7:5), malnutrition (17:7; 19:20), a repulsive appearance (19:19), bad breath (19:17), and pain day and night (30:17)" (Alden, p. 297).

He poetically ends chapter 30 by stating that he only hears sad songs (v. 31). He is agitated, without comfort, alone, sick, and full of sorrow.

Chapter 29—*I long for the days and honor of the past*; chapter 30—*I lament the degradation and humiliation of the present*; And next in chapter 31 ...

3. I legally testify to my honesty and innocence under oath (31:1-40)
    a. *I'm innocent of lust, deceit and adultery (vv. 1-12)*
        i. I am not guilty of lust (vv. 1-4)
            aa. I have made a covenant with my eyes (v. 1)

Here, Job begins by stating—"I am not guilty of lust." Throughout the chapter, he employs oath language as a final testimony to his innocence. "I have cut a covenant with my eyes"—I have made a legally binding agreement with my eyes; how then could I look at a virgin? This is emblematic of his purity of heart. No one could prove or disprove this but God, and Job believes that God sees even his innermost desires, as verses 2-4 confirm.

      bb. Because God sees—and there are devastating consequences (vv. 2-4)

These verses convey that if Job were to break his covenant regarding lust, he would face God's judgment. The oath language throughout the chapter indicates that Job does not believe he is guilty of these sins. He asserts that God sees and takes account of his paths. Here he confirms that he had not committed the heart sin of lust, because God sees—and there would be devastating consequences. *I am not guilty of lust.*

  ii. I am not guilty of deceit (vv. 5-8)
    aa. If I have walked with deceit—God knows the truth (vv. 5-6)

The New Living Translation says: "Have I lied to anyone or deceived anyone?" Job wanted to be weighed on honest scales, knowing that God is aware of his integrity. Lest we are tempted to charge Job with self-righteousness, we ought to remember that God did indeed know Job's integrity (1:8; 2:3).

> bb. If I have strayed—then let me face the consequences (vv. 7-8)

Job expresses that if he were guilty of falsehood, he invites a curse upon himself. If he has deviated from the path of truth, if any "spot" could be found on his "hands," he declares: "Let me sow and another eat, and let my crops be uprooted". I deserve to be defrauded and my livelihood taken away. If I have strayed—then let me face the consequences. *I am not guilty of deceit.*

> iii. I am not guilty of adultery (vv. 9-12)
>> aa. If I have committed adultery—may my wife serve others (vv. 9-10)

Job pledges his fidelity in marital matters as well. His oath concludes with a startling curse. If he were guilty of coveting another man's wife, then he called for his wife to be at the service of others.

>> bb. I have not committed adultery, for that would bring the grave and the loss of everything (vv. 11-12)

While it would be shameful for one's wife to serve others, Job articulates even graver consequences. In verse 11, he states he would legally deserve capital punishment (Lev. 20:10; Deut. 22:22-24). In verse 12, he notes that adultery leads to the fire of Abaddon and the loss of everything. "Abaddon" is used elsewhere as a synonym for the "grave" (26:6; 28:22; Ps. 88:11; Prov. 15:11). Thus, Job declares, "I'm not guilty of adultery."

> b. I'm innocent of injustice (vv. 3-23)
>> i. If I have committed injustice in business, how could I answer to God? (vv. 13-15)

Job listened to the grievances of his employees and took action (v. 13). If he had not, what could he say when God called him to account? He believed he would stand before the righteous Judge of all the earth to answer for his actions and how he treated even his servants (v. 14). Verse 15 reveals that Job believed there is no partiality with God; He is the Creator of both master and slave—employer and employee. If I have committed injustice in business, how could I answer to God?

  ii. If I have withheld charity from the needy ... (vv. 16-21)

Verses 16-23 again contain oath language with a curse if Job were guilty. This paragraph focuses on loving one's neighbor, especially the poor and needy. In verse 16, Job asserts that he has cared for the poor and the widow. In verses 17-18, he states he has supported the orphan, even in his youth. In verses 19-20, he mentions giving clothing and shelter to the needy. Verse 21 refers to legal decisions that might have adversely affected the fatherless. Job always stood up for those who had no defender, even when it wasn't politically convenient. If he hadn't cared for the defenseless, he utters the curse of verse 22 ...

  iii. Let my arm be broken off by God, because I did nothing to help those with outstretched arms (vv. 22-23)

If Job had "raised his arm" against the helpless, then he calls for his "arm to be broken off from the bond of the upper arm and it to fall off at the shoulder." However, it is God's displeasure, according to verse 23, that Job fears most. This again demonstrates Job's faith rather than self-righteousness.

c. *I'm innocent of greed and idolatry (vv. 24-28)*
  i. I have not turned to the idolatry of wealth (vv. 24-25)

A man like Job, who was once wealthy, may have been tempted to trust in his "gold" or boast about his "great wealth." In fact, in 1:3, after listing Job's possessions, the text states that Job was the "greatest of all the men of the east." Even the godly Hezekiah fell into this temptation (Is. 39), but Job claims he has not trusted in his wealth.

ii. I have not turned to the idolatry of paganism (vv. 26-28)

Verses 26-27 address the worship of the sun and moon associated with paganism. Nevertheless, Job's fear was God, as verse 28 confirms. It appears he was reflecting on true wisdom and openly affirming that he feared the Lord and turned away from evil. Yet his dire circumstances did not align with his understanding of what a life of wisdom should produce. *He asserts, "I'm innocent of greed and idolatry."*

d. *I'm innocent of hatred, blame shifting, and bad stewardship (vv. 29-40ab)*
   i. I have not rejoiced in the calamity of my enemy (vv. 29-30)

Romans 12:14 instructs, "Bless those who persecute you; bless and do not curse." Job lived hundreds of years before this was written. Proverbs 24:17 advises, "Do not rejoice when your enemy falls, and do not let your heart be glad when he stumbles." Job states, "I have not rejoiced in the calamity of my enemy." He did not harbor hatred for his enemy; in fact, he extended hospitality to all.

   ii. I have not refused hospitality to anyone (vv. 31-32)

Job's servants could testify that no one had been turned away from Job's hospitality, even strangers. Romans 12:13 encourages believers to "practice hospitality." Job's faith in the Lord was lived out.

   iii. I have not covered my sin—but rather confessed it publicly (vv. 33-34)

While "Adam" may refer generally to mankind, the first man, Adam, fits well within Job's argument here. Using a rhetorical question, Job asserts that he is not a man who covers his sin, but rather one who confesses it publicly. Job is not claiming to be sinless; but he is claiming that he maintains his integrity. He didn't hide iniquity in his heart/bosom, not even if it meant shame in front of a multitude or even possible reprisal by "families."

Some may find Job's claims in verses 33-34 to be anticlimactic compared to issues like lust or deceit. However, it seems he recognized that his assertions could appear somewhat self-righteous, and he wanted to emphasize that he was known for publicly acknowledging his sins, regardless of social consequences. He was not a proud, self-righteous man. Yet, as we see in verses 35-37, he was confident he could refute charges in a heavenly court.

> iv. I have confidence I can refute any indictment before God (vv. 35-37)

Job longed for a hearing with God. In words, Job poetically signed his legal oath (literally, "Look, my mark") and wanted the "Almighty" to respond. He wanted a written indictment or document from his "prosecutor."

When Job received his list of alleged crimes, he would "carry it" on his "shoulder" and "bind it to himself like a crown." He would not be ashamed, because his life would refute any accusations. There is debate over whether Job or his prosecutor is the one likened to a prince, but the main idea is that Job would not shrink from the charges against him. As Archer notes: "Such a prosecutor he would welcome like a prince, for this man would at least be open and above-board, rather than operating by baseless inferences and insinuation as his three critics have been doing" (Archer, p. 90).

Though Job's assertions may make us uncomfortable, it is clear that he has contemplated true wisdom (28:28), evaluated his life as honestly as he knew how, and concluded that he did fear God and did indeed turn away from evil. As far as his conscience was concerned, Job could confidently stand before God.

v. I have not defrauded the land or its tenant farmers (vv. 38-40ab)

In what may seem like yet another anticlimactic moment, Job makes one final oath/curse: "If I have defrauded the land or its tenant farmers—let me bear the curse of briars and stinkweed instead of wheat and barley." He may have recalled one last area he had not addressed—misusing God's creation, which would also harm those who worked it. Alternatively, this may relate to the curse upon the ground that Adam (Gen. 3:17) and Cain (4:11) faced for failing to fear God and turn away from evil. As Andersen writes:

> The list of crimes in Job's negative confession is neither systematic nor complete. It was not drawn up by an articled clerk. It is a poem, recited by a miserable outcast on the city rubbish dump, not by a prisoner in the dock. It is Job's last passionate outburst, and the author has given it an earnestness and a torrential quality by composing it with a measure of incoherence. This effectively conveys Job's persistent indignation. This effect is lost when the loose ends are tidied up and the speech is made like a page from a barrister's brief (Andersen, p. 239).

Finally, the last phrase of verse 40 concludes Job's speeches.

e. I rest my case—the words of Job are ended (v. 40c)

"Complete are the words of Job." Notably, the term "ended" shares the same root as the word "integrity." Could this be a play on words? Whatever else, it signifies the conclusion of Job's testimony and the debate cycle.

One now expects perhaps God to answer. But, as in much of Job, we must endure the anti-climax of yet another lengthy and convoluted speech from the young Elihu in chapters 32-37, which only heightens our desire for clarity from God Himself, which Job and the readers ultimately receive in chapters 38-41.

Application

Chapter 29—*I long for the days and honor of the past*; chapter 30—*I lament the degradation and humiliation of the present*; chapter 31—*I legally testify to my honesty and innocence under oath*.

It seems that 28:28, the chiastic center of the book, should inform our understanding of Job's final speech. He was a man who feared the Lord and turned away from evil. His past bore witness to a life characterized by godly fear, wisdom, and understanding. His present circumstances, however, seemed to contradict this reality. Yet, under oath and the threat of a curse, Job testified to his innocence.

When God finally does speak, He does not indict Job but instead poses a series of questions that reveal Job's innate human limitations. Job is never compelled to recant his defense of his integrity (cf. 42:1-6). As Andersen observes:

> Job's pride in his achievement should not be misunderstood. It was legitimate, not self-righteous. For Job to have adopted the posture of a cringing sinner would have been a species of self-righteousness for him. We need to keep this in mind when reading 42:2-6, for even then Job does not go back on the present speech by admitting to any known fault (Andersen, p. 231).

Can we also testify that we have turned away from evil because we believe in the true and living God? Job could. Yet, what Job still needed to fully embrace is that fearing God and turning away from evil does not guarantee respect from others, good health, or earthly prosperity. While the Bible's wisdom literature often associates such rewards with wisdom, these outcomes are not absolute guarantees in this life. Instead, God's perfect wisdom may lead us down inscrutable paths.

We can trust Him. Yes, we can be honest. We can proclaim our integrity. We can lament our pain, even if we must confess later we spoke in ignorance. Ultimately, the Book of Job calls us to trust God and His perfect wisdom, whatever our circumstances. When, through pain and disappointment, we gain a clearer vision of God's greatness, it will be more than enough to satisfy our souls in Him.

Will you and I trust our Savior even when we are humiliated, suffering, and wrongly accused—and no one but God knows the truth?

Elihu's Introduction and First Speech
Job 32:1-33:33

In the final portion of Job's dialogue section, before the LORD speaks, Elihu, a young man who has remained silent until now, has much to say. He gives his advice though no one solicits his opinion. After he is finished, we do not hear from him, or of him, again. What should we make of Elihu and his counsel?

Commentators have varying perspectives on the significance of Elihu's remarks, their value, and his role in the overarching message of the Book of Job. Some view Elihu as a human mediator preparing the way for God's speech. Others see him as a prophetic figure foreshadowing Christ. Still, others consider him as the greatest of Job's tormentors, an anti-Christ-like figure, that many might mistake for a man of wisdom, but in reality, they believe he is even more dangerous in disguising but recycling the demonic rationale of retribution theology.

In this section, we will begin to analyze Elihu's introduction and initial speech.

Job 32-33 presents the first two sections of Elihu's monologue, showcasing yet another human attempt to help Job, which ultimately only intensifies our desire for God to speak and clarify our understanding of how we ought to think about the entire ordeal.

B. Elihu—The angry young man, full of words (32:1-37:24)
1. Elihu's introduction—the angry young man and his opinion (32:1-22)
a. *The explanation of Elihu's motive in prose (vv. 1-5)*
i. The absence of an answer that solicited the young man to speak (v. 1)

After Job's final arguments in chapters 28-31, we long for God to answer and give divine clarity to all that has transpired. But what follows seems to be an inspired anti-climax—another human attempt to clarify the situation, which only heightens our desire for God to reveal Himself, answering Job and all of us.

Here, the author breaks from poetry to provide a brief introductory explanation of the context surrounding the next speech. Job's words ended in 31:40. There was no reply from his three previously named friends. The reason is clearly stated in verse one: "... these three men ceased to answer Job, because he was righteous in his own eyes." The *New Living Translation* reads: "Job's three friends refused to reply further to him because he kept insisting on his innocence." After the prolonged argument, the silence must have been deafening. It was this silence, the lack of an answer to Job, that compelled the next man to speak.

ii. The anger that motivated his speech (vv. 2-5)
aa. His anger toward Job (v. 2)

The name "Elihu" means "my God is He." There are five individuals in Scripture named "Elihu," including the prophet Samuel's great-grandfather (1 Sam. 1:1); a man from the tribe of Manasseh who supported David in the wilderness (1 Chron. 12:20); a gatekeeper from the Korahites (1 Chron. 26:7); and notably, one of King David's brothers (1 Chronicles 27:18). Thus, we see a well-attested Jewish name in the text of Job, even though Job and his friends were from the region of Edom, with non-Jewish names.

"Barachel" is a Hebrew name meaning "Blessed of God" or "God blesses." According to Genesis 22:21, a man named "Buz" was a nephew of Abraham. Furthermore, according to Ruth 4:19, "Ram" was in the lineage from Judah to David.

While Eliphaz, Bildad, and Zophar had dubious connections in their lineages, it is possible that Elihu came from a Jewish heritage, even though Jeremiah 25:23 lists "Buz" alongside Dedan and Tema, regions south of Israel.

The phrase "anger burned" is repeated four times in verses 2-5 to describe the compelling emotion driving Elihu's subsequent speech. The Hebrew may be rendered literally as "his nose burned."

Specifically, verse two states that Elihu was angry because "Job justified his soul rather than God." He was incensed that Job declared himself "right" instead of God. Like Job's friends, Elihu believes that Job was being self-righteous, which angered the indignant young man. However, Elihu's anger is not solely directed at Job.

    bb. His anger toward Job's three friends (v. 3)

The Jewish Bible states: "He was angry as well at his three friends, because they found no reply, but merely condemned Job." The ESV reads: "They had declared Job to be in the wrong." *The New Living* reveals another interpretation of the Hebrew: "He was also angry with Job's three friends, for they made God appear to be wrong by their inability to answer Job's arguments."

Regardless of which interpretation aligns more closely with the original thought, it is clear that Elihu is angry at both Job and his friends. In verse four, we see that he is an angry *young* man, and his age is the reason he waited so long to vent his frustration.

Job 32:1-33:33

cc. His attention to cultural protocol (v. 4)

In 12:12, Job acknowledges: "Wisdom is with aged men; with long life is understanding." The Hebrew allows for this to be interpreted as a question: "Is wisdom in the aged, And understanding in the long-lived?" (TNK). In other words, *Age should bring wisdom [but you have proved otherwise]*. As well, Eliphaz references the importance of respecting the wisdom of one's elders in 15:10. So here, Elihu "waited to speak to Job because they were older than he." Job and his friends had lived longer than Elihu, so he paid attention to the cultural norms and conventional wisdom, remaining silent—until now.

dd. His anger over the absence of an answer (v. 5)

The repetition here may indicate that the preceding argument caused Elihu's nose to burn toward Job and his perceived self-righteousness. But "when Elihu saw that there was no answer in the mouth of the three men, his nose burned."

b. *The exhortation of Elihu in poetry—listen to my unbiased opinion (vv. 6-22)*
  i. Listen to me—I too will tell you what I think (vv. 6-10)
    aa. I waited because of my youth and your age (vv. 6-7)

Verse 6a introduces the beginning of Elihu's poetic response to the entire argument. "I am young in years, and you are old; that is why I was fearful, not daring to tell you what I know. I thought, 'Age should speak; advanced years should teach wisdom'" (NIV). Verses 6-7 reinforce the narrator's comments in verse four. *I waited because of my youth and your age.*

bb. But God hasn't given you wisdom (vv. 8-9)

Verse eight appears to reference God's Spirit as the true source of wisdom, rather than age. Thus, in verse nine,

"Great men are not always wise, Nor do the aged always understand justice" (NKJV). The implication is that the older men had no spiritual, God-given wisdom to contribute to this situation. However, in verse 10 and onward, it becomes clear that Elihu believes he has much wisdom to offer.

    cc. Now listen to me and I too will tell you what I think (v. 10)

The NET Bible reads: "Therefore I say, 'Listen to me. I, even I, will explain what I know.'" Notice the frequent use of first-person pronouns in this verse and throughout this section. The angry young man has a propensity for talking about himself. *Now listen to me and I too will tell you what I think.*

Next, Elihu directly rebukes Job's friends for their failure to refute Job's arguments.

    ii. You never refuted Job's arguments (vv. 11-14)
        aa. I waited and listened carefully (vv. 11-12)

In verse 11, the use of the first-person pronoun "I" stands out again. Here, we gain insight into the prior dialogue. These men took time to formulate their arguments; they "pondered" or "searched" for what to say. Elihu asserts that he paid close attention to the three counselors' arguments, but none of them addressed Job's words or refuted him. *I waited and listened carefully,* yet you did nothing to answer Job.

        bb. Don't claim that you have answered Job, and now God will rout him (vv. 13-14)

In verse 14, Elihu seems to claim that his logic is superior to that of Job's friends: "If Job had been arguing with me, I would not answer with your kind of logic!" (NLT).

Elihu argues that their arguments are inadequate and that their silence, allowing God to handle Job, is a cop-out. Job did not directly argue with him, but Elihu insists he would not have used their reasoning if he had. In fact, though no one has asked his advice, Elihu will continue to speak for the next five and a half chapters.

> iii. I am full of words—let me speak, and I will answer without bias (vv. 15-22)
>> aa. Words have failed them—but not me (vv. 15-16)

Elihu comments on Job's friends in verse 15: "They are baffled; they have nothing more to say; words have failed them." The expected answer to his rhetorical question in verse 16 is—"No, I must be allowed to speak now that everyone else is at a loss to resolve this impasse." *Words have failed them—but not me.*

>> bb. I too will give my opinion (vv. 17-18)

As he stated in verse 10, Elihu reiterates in verse 17: "I too will explain what I know." Why? Because he is "full of words," and the "wind/spirit within [him] is pressing on [his] belly." His need to speak is further detailed in verses 19-20.

>> cc. I must speak or burst (vv. 19-20)

Jesus wasn't the first to use the imagery of new wine and bursting wineskins; Elihu uses it to express his urgent need to respond to the arguments of these men. Relief will only come if he opens his lips and addresses Job and his friends.

>> dd. I will be partial to no one (vv. 21-22)

"I won't play favorites or try to flatter anyone" (NLT). In 13:8 and 10, Job accused his friends of showing partiality toward God to gain His favor. Elihu asserts in verse 22 that he doesn't even know how to do that. If he did, his Maker would put an end to him. *I will be partial to no one. I am full of words—let me speak, and I will answer without bias.*

This serves as Elihu's introduction. His motives are outlined in verses 1-5, and his exhortation. even if belabored, was: *Listen to my unbiased opinion.* In chapter 33, he turns to address Job directly.

2. Elihu's first speech: Here's where you're wrong, Job—God is gracious [in allowing you to suffer] (33:1-33)
   a. *I'll speak for God (vv. 1-7)*
      i. Listen to me now, Job (vv. 1-2)

Using two imperatives—commands to listen and give ear—along with the word "please," Elihu demands Job's attention. In verse 2, he adds more words to essentially say, "I'm going to talk now." As the NIV reads: "I am about to open my mouth; my words are on the tip of my tongue."

   ii. I speak honestly and sincerely (v. 3)

Again, the *New Living Translation* succinctly captures Elihu's intent: "I speak with all sincerity; I speak the truth" (NLT). Listen to me, Job—I speak honestly and sincerely. In verses 4-7, he presents a lofty challenge.

   iii. I'll speak for God—and you try to refute me (vv. 4-7)
      aa. I'm a creature—try to refute me if you can (vv. 4-6)

It is unclear whether Elihu is claiming to possess inspired wisdom or simply stating that he, too, is a creature. Verses 6-7 seem to confirm the latter. His wording here is at least patronizing to hint that Job might be overwhelmed by him (cf. Longman, p. 385). God made me (v. 4), and His breath gives me life. In verse 6, Elihu claims that God owns him and that he is made of dust, just like Job. Verse 5 states: "If you can, answer me; Argue against me, take your stand" (TNK).

      bb. I should not scare you since I'm a man and not God (v. 7)

In 9:34 and 13:21, Job expressed that God's presence terrified him. Here, Elihu asserts that Job should have no such concern with him, since he too is a creature. At the risk of being as judgmental as Elihu and the others (no doubt this comment alone tips my hand as to my assessment of Elihu's comments), it seems incredible that he would be so cavalier in his comments concerning Job's fears in light of Job's suffering (even though he was not aware of God's assessment of Job in chapters 1-2).

  b. *Job, you claim you are sinless [innocent] and that God is acting unjustly [opposing you without cause] (vv. 8-11)*
    i. I've heard you claim that you are sinless [innocent] (vv. 8-9)

Here, Elihu confirms that he has listened to Job's testimony and arguments, and the following context reveals that he is not happy with Job's assertions.

The angry young Elihu here evidently paraphrases his understanding of Job's argument, claiming, "I am pure, without transgression; I am innocent, and there is no guilt in me."

The term "pure" can mean "clean" or possibly "righteous." However, Job used that term only once, in 16:17 when he stated: "*My prayer* is pure" (emphasis added). He never claimed *he* was "pure," at least not using that specific term. Bildad and Zophar used it (8:6; 11:4) to imply or assert that this is what Job claimed. In reality, there is no record of Job using the word except to describe his prayer as "pure."

A study of the term translated "transgression" or "rebellion" in Job suggests the opposite of Elihu's assertion. Job never claimed to be "without transgression." He desired God to reveal and forgive his transgressions (7:21; 13:23; 14:17). In fact, in 31:33, Job stated he was known as a man who publicly acknowledged his transgressions. But no doubt, Job did maintain he had no hidden sin that caused the calamities he experienced. Elihu understood that much but perhaps overstated Job's cries of innocence.

The term "innocent" appears only here in Scripture and is believed to mean "clean" or "without guilt," likely based on its context. The word "guilt" is sometimes translated as "iniquity." Job prayed in 13:23 for God to reveal his iniquity. This could be construed, perhaps, as an arrogant assertion of being guiltless—but rather it is a plea from a suffering, despondent believer asking God to help him see. In 13:26, Job considers the possibility that he was somehow now suffering for the iniquities of his youth. And in 31:33, he admitted he did not hide his "iniquity" but instead confessed it. Therefore, he was not claiming perfect guiltlessness.

To be fair to Elihu, he may have understood that Job was not claiming complete sinlessness but was asserting his innocence concerning the calamities and accusations from his friends. But Elihu's verbosity, seeming self-importance, and his assertion of accurately representing Job's words—though perhaps not as precisely as he believes—lead us to question whether Elihu possesses the revelation Job needs to begin thinking clearly about God again. In verses 8-9, Elihu states—*I've heard you claim that you are sinless [innocent]*.

  ii. I've heard you claim that God opposes you [without cause] (vv. 10-11)

The Jewish Bible translates verse 10: "But He finds reasons to oppose me, considers me His enemy." Again, the term translated "pretexts" or "opposition" is not found in any of Job's speeches.

Job did pray in 13:24: "Why do You hide Your face and consider me Your enemy?" (see also 19:11). In 13:27, Job cried: "You put my feet in the stocks and watch all my paths." Elihu has again closely paraphrased Job's argument, except he used a summary term that Job never employed.

We know, however, what Elihu did not: in 2:3, Yahweh Himself told Satan: "For there is no one like him on the earth, a blameless and upright man, fearing God and turning away from evil. And he still holds fast his integrity, *although you incited Me against him to ruin him without cause*" (emphasis mine). Job's words may not have been as egregiously wrong as Elihu and the three friends might have assumed.

In verses 8-11, Elihu states—*Job, you claim you are sinless [innocent] and that God is acting unjustly [opposing you without cause]*. In much of the remaining chapter, he will attempt to respond to his interpretation of Job's accusations.

  c. *God is greater than man, yet He graciously reveals Himself (vv. 12-18)*
    i. You are not right in your claims—because God is greater than man (v. 12)

After a chapter and a half of verbiage, Elihu finally attempts to help Job see where he is "not right." However, somewhat anticlimactically, he asserts what Job, Eliphaz, Bildad, and Zophar already acknowledged—"God is greater than man." It is not "righteous" to claim that God opposes you while you are innocent, as God is indeed greater than man. In light of God's forthcoming revelation to Job in chapters 38-41, Elihu is correct. However, it will not be until God unveils Himself that Job—or we—will be convinced.

Unlike the three previous counselors, Elihu does not immediately attack Job's integrity. Instead, he urges Job to stop complaining about God's silence, noting that God does reveal Himself in various ways. This is evident in verses 13-18.

    ii. Why do you complain that God does not give an account of His actions, when He is gracious to reveal Himself to man at all? (vv. 13-18)
      aa. The question (v. 13)

The word translated, "give an account" refers to providing an "answer." In 19:7, Job proclaimed: "Behold, I cry,

'Violence!' but I get no *answer*; I shout for help, but there is no justice." In 30:20, he said: "I cry out to You for help, but You do not *answer* me; I stand up, and You turn Your attention against me." In 31:35, Job exclaimed: "Oh that I had one to hear me! Behold, here is my signature; Let the Almighty *answer* me! And the indictment which my adversary has written."

Here, Elihu asks, "Why do you complain against Him that He does not answer you concerning all His doings?" (my paraphrase). In verses 14-18, Elihu will go on to say that God *does* speak in different ways. The implication might be that Job perhaps hasn't been listening.

    bb. The revelation (vv. 14-16)

Verse 14 poetically conveys that God communicates in many ways. Elihu will provide two specific examples of divine revelation: dreams (v. 15) and pain (v. 19). In verse 15, Elihu assumes that God speaks "in a dream, a vision of the night." In verse 16, he states that God opens people's understanding. Job, indeed, experienced terrifying dreams, as noted in 7:13-14. Elihu may be implying that Job has not been attentive to God's messages.

    cc. The reason for God's revelation (vv. 17-18)

Elihu seems to suggest that God gives men dreams to "keep man from pride" and to prevent their death or destruction. In verses 19-22, he will refer to God's gracious revelation through pain and how one should respond to it.

Elihu argues that Job is not right in his claim that God is opposing him for no reason. Instead, Job needs to understand that *God is greater than man, yet He graciously reveals Himself* through dreams or visions to protect man from death and destruction. Although somewhat convoluted, verses 19-30 capture Elihu's perspective on the appropriate response to God's revelation through pain.

> iii. God hears those who hear His voice in pain, come to realize their sin, and then turn to Him in prayer (vv. 19-30)
>> aa. When chastening comes (vv. 19-22)

Job had said in 30:17: "At night my bones are filled with pain, which gnaws at me relentlessly" (NLT). Here, Elihu asserts that God speaks through "unceasing complaint in [the] bones." In 3:24, Job mentioned groaning at the sight of his food. Elihu interprets this as God's gracious revelation. Job's severe weight loss is noted in 16:8 and 19:20—which parallel Elihu's words in v. 21. And in reading verse 22, we remember that Job often spoke of the nearness of his death.

Elihu seems to be implying that Job's circumstances are actually God's gracious revelation to him, meant to keep him from sin rather than being a consequence of it. Psalm 30 indicates that there is a measure of truth in this assertion. However, though perhaps true in a larger theological discussion, we know from the introduction of Job that this was not God's stated purpose. Rather, Job was suffering as a witness to God's glory.

Next, Elihu discusses a mediator and repentance in verses 23-26.

>> bb. If there is a messenger-mediator to turn him to repentance and bring restoration (vv. 23-26)

In verse 23, "angel" could be translated as "messenger." The term "mediator" can refer to an "interpreter." Ironically, it more commonly means "mocker." It might speak of one who must condescend to interpret something.

Andersen notes, "The designation one of the thousand rules out the idea that there is one angel who is a specialist in such negotiations. It implies rather that God has a large team available for such a task" (Andersen, p. 250). Others suggest it may refer to the rarity of such an individual.

Job desired a mediator in 9:32-35 and 16:19. Here, Elihu may be subtly identifying himself as that rare messenger and interpreter who reminds Job of "what is right for him." Alternatively, he may be indicating that God sends such a messenger to man in his pain.

This messenger-mediator would be gracious, interceding for the sufferer and pleading a ransom (v. 24)—a term related to "atonement." From this side of the cross, this sounds quite Christ-like. But the "ransom" is left unspecified. In verse 25, the messenger-mediator would ask God to restore the sufferer's health.

Verse 26 reveals the results of this mysterious mediator's ministry. The sufferer seeks God and is restored: "Then man prays to God, and he accepts him; he sees his face with a shout of joy, and he restores to man his righteousness" (ESV).

Elihu's speech here is cryptic at best. Some interpret it as prophetic, while others see it as demonic. Again, as so many times in the speeches section of Job, we are left longing for God Himself to speak so we might know for certain what to think.

What is clear is that Elihu sees this messenger-mediator as bringing repentance to the sufferer.

>   cc. Then the chastened one will sing praise and confess his sin (vv. 27-28)

Once the angel-interpreter, who brings the unspecified ransom, has done his work, the restored sufferer "will sing *to men* and say, 'I have sinned and perverted what is right, and it is not proper for me. He has redeemed my soul from going to the pit, and my life shall see the light'" (emphasis mine). Job would indeed experience a change after God's self-disclosure (42:6). However, we have no explicit record of Job confessing to men—though perhaps the canonical book serves as such a confession.

> dd. God chastens man oftentimes to bring him to repentance (vv. 29-30)

"These" in verse 29 evidently refers to dreams, the chastening of pain, and the sending of an angel-interpreter. The purpose of God's revelation through these means is "to bring back [the sufferer's] soul from the pit, that he may be enlightened with the light of life."

Again, there may be some truth to Elihu's overall argument. Job's ordeal and God's revelation will indeed bring Job to a place of consolation. And Job did eventually confess to speaking ignorantly before God. But God Himself was the messenger-interpreter who led Job to this conclusion.

To some, Elihu's demeanor appears self-important thus far. His words could be interpreted as prophetic of Christ's ministry, a grandiose self-portrait, or worse, an attempt to solicit false repentance from Job (cf. Morris, pp. 75-82). His counsel remains enigmatic, and again, only when God speaks and reveals His character do we find something before which we can truly humble ourselves and trust.

In verses 31-33, Elihu concludes his first speech with ...

> iv. Hold your peace and I will teach you wisdom (vv. 31-33)
> aa. Pay attention, Job—listen to me (v. 31)

The direct address to "Job" may suggest that he appeared inattentive or distracted. Verse 32 could be interpreted as an implicit call to repentance.

> bb. Respond to my instruction—I want to help you (v. 32)

It seems unlikely that Elihu is asking Job to continue declaring his innocence. The young arbiter wants to "justify" Job—declare him right based on how he responds to this new perspective (that suffering is God's way of protecting him from deadly pride). But if Job disagrees, Elihu calls for further silence.

    cc. If not—keep silent and I will teach you wisdom (v. 33)

The language and grammar are striking, especially in light of Job's privileged position in God's plan, as revealed in the first two chapters of the book. If Job has nothing to say in agreement with Elihu, then Elihu's statement literally reads: "If nothing, you listen to me; keep silent, and I will teach you wisdom."

Application

In chapter 32, we see *Elihu's introduction—the angry young man and his opinion*; and in chapter 33, we see *Elihu's first speech—Here's where you're wrong, Job—God is gracious [in allowing you to suffer]*. He will continue for four more chapters.

As we have noted repeatedly, Elihu's role in the final form of the book is debated. I contend that he adds to the confusion and heightens the believer's longing for God's wisdom to be revealed, free from human opinion and error. Notably, however, God does not rebuke him as He did Job's other three counselors (42:7). The reason for this is also a subject of debate among scholars. Elihu remains an enigma—I believe, by divine design.

Had the Lord responded immediately to Job's closing arguments after chapter 31, we might have been tempted to think that if we demand God reveal Himself or claim our innocence loudly enough, God is obligated to speak. But the Elihu section reminds us that sometimes God allows even more time to elapse and more enigmatic advice to come before revealing His glory to those who seek Him. We cannot force God to respond to our oaths of innocence—He is sovereign over when and how He responds to our prayers for help (cf. McCabe, Robert V., "Elihu's Contribution to the Thought of the Book of Job," *Detroit Baptist Seminary Journal*, Volume 2, pp. 77-78).

Elihu may serve as a warning that the words of an angry young man, even when he thinks he has something new to say, all too often serve only to heighten everyone's desire for God to speak through His Word. May the Lord encourage us to *wait* on Him and continue seeking Him in humility—rather than responding in anger during our trials or toward others who express themselves with windy words in their suffering.

Elihu's Second and Third Speeches
God is Righteous
Job 34:1-35:16

In chapter 31, Job delivered his closing testimony and called upon the Almighty to speak (31:35). However, instead of hearing from God, Job (and we) must endure another six chapters filled with human opinions about his situation and words. It is in the middle of this section that we encounter the poetic monologue of Elihu—the angry young man out to set Job and his friends straight about their understanding of God.

In Job 34-35, Elihu delivers his second and third speeches, which aim to defend God's righteousness but ultimately lead us to question whether he accurately represents Job and God.

3. Elihu's second and third speeches: Here's where you're wrong, Job—God is righteous (34:1-35:16)
   a. *Hear my words, you wise men (vv. 1-4)*
      i. The Elihu speeches continue (v. 1)

It is difficult to determine how much time passed between Elihu's speeches, but the language here suggests a new section, even if he is continuing from his previous monologue. This pattern will be repeated in 35:1 and 36:1.

ii. The exhortation to listen (v. 2)

As he had in 33:1 and again in 33:31, 33—and will do again in 34:10, 16 and 37:14—Elihu commands his audience to "listen" to him.

The phrases "you wise men" and "you who know" seem to refer, perhaps sarcastically, to Job and his three friends. It is possible that he is using these terms rhetorically or addressing anyone in the crowd who may have witnessed his speeches.

iii. The evaluation of what is right and good (vv. 3-4)

In verse three, Elihu may be alluding to Job's earlier statement in 12:11: "Does not the ear test wisdom, as the palate tastes its food?" This proverb asserts that reasoning will be self-authenticating as wise. Verse four calls for an evaluation of "what is right" and "what is good," as Elihu lays out what he believes Job's argument to be and contrasts it with the wisdom he intends to share.

b. *Job claims it profits a man nothing to delight in God (vv. 5-9)*
  i. The quote from Job (vv. 5-6)

As in 33:8-9, Elihu does not quote Job verbatim, but rather summarizes what he believes Job has stated. As Andersen writes: "Elihu represents Job's position by means of a mixture of identifiable quotations (such as 27:2) and summaries which are harder to trace to Job's reported words, and which, perhaps, distort his views" (Andersen, p. 252). Other commentators, however, suggest that Job would not quibble over Elihu's paraphrases (Alden, p. 333; Longman, p. 391). Likely, it is not so much the wording, as the interpretation that Job may have objected to—though there is no record of Job ever responding to Elihu.

The only explicit record of Job using the term translated "I am righteous" appears in conditional sentences in 9:15 and

10:15. These are not direct assertions—though they may imply as much. But as we have stated previously, Job's nuanced claims of being "right" or "righteous" do not imply absolute sinlessness. Rather, they are made in response to accusations from his friends that he must be guilty of some hidden sin that corresponded to his suffering. Elihu seems to be referencing Job's statements in 27:1-6 (see the commentary there for an explanation of Job's statements).

So, while Job had made these statements as Elihu claims, it seems likely that Elihu misunderstood Job's intent and overlooked the context in which they were spoken.*

The NIV presents an alternative translation of the Hebrew: "Although I am right, I am considered a liar." The word "wound" is literally "arrow." In 6:4, Job stated: "For the arrows of the Almighty are within me ..." And yes, Job had proclaimed his innocence (explicitly or implicitly) in 10:7; 13:23; 16:17. It is understandable, given the prolonged argument filled with speeches and counter-speeches, that Elihu would piece together a close quotation or paraphrase of Job's words.

Verses 5-6 are *the quote from Job*—of sorts. Verses 7-8 reveal Elihu's opinion of Job's words.

ii. The question that condemns Job (vv. 7-8)

Verse seven is akin to the proverb—"water off a duck's back" (Alden, p. 333). "Scorn" or "derision" did not sway Job from his position; he drank it like water, unaffected. Verse eight places Job among those who work "iniquity" and walk "with wicked men" (cf. Ps. 1). These rhetorical questions express Elihu's disdain for Job's response to his friends and his

---

* It is not lost on me as I write this that I could be guilty of misunderstanding or misrepresenting Elihu and Elihu's meaning here and throughout the section (much like I am accusing Elihu of doing to Job and Job's words). But again, I believe the uncertainty and the corresponding longing for divine certainty seems to be part of God's purpose in the human dialogue portion of the book.

circumstances, particularly Job's stubborn pride, which associates him with the wicked. As a compound poetic sentence, verses 7-8 record *the question that condemns Job.*

iii. The quote used to support that conclusion (v. 9)

The New Living Translation has: "He has even said, 'Why waste time trying to please God?'" Again, these words are not found in Job's mouth, at least not in the inspired record of this book. In 9:29-31, Job may reflect the sentiment Elihu is alluding to: [There Job said] "I am accounted wicked; why then should I toil in vain? If I should wash myself with snow and cleanse my hands with lye, yet You would plunge me into the pit, and my own clothes would abhor me."

It is important to note that in 9:29-31, Job was expressing his feelings and fears directly to God. There is no record of Job's friends—including Elihu—ever praying, only preaching. Later, in 21:14-16, Job states that the thinking, "what would we gain if we entreat [God]?" is counsel he rejects.

Elihu may have grasped some of Job's struggling words and thoughts through his paraphrastic quotes, but he interprets them as rebellious charges against God's righteousness, not understanding Job's overall argument. This type of misunderstanding, where certain statements are scrutinized while others are excluded, often occurs in disagreements and does not contribute to genuine wisdom. The two speeches in the remainder of chapters 34-35 are spent correcting what Elihu assumes Job believes: that God is unjust.

c. God is not wicked (vv. 10-15)
  i. He is perfectly just (vv. 10-12)

In verse 10, Elihu addresses the "men of understanding" in the crowd, or perhaps sarcastically refers to Job and his friends. Much like Abraham in Genesis 18:25, he asserts, "far be it from God to do wickedness and ... the Almighty to do wrong." In verse 11, Elihu states that God is perfectly just in His dealings with humanity. Verse 12 reinforces this notion: "It is unthinkable that God would do wrong, that the Almighty would pervert justice" (NIV). Elihu affirms that *God is perfectly just*. Alden comments:

> Here Elihu articulated the doctrine of retribution as clearly as it is done anywhere in the book. The problem is not with the truth of the principle because it is taught from the beginning to the end of the Bible. The problem is in the way these four friends applied it to Job, without exception, with no eye to eschatological retribution, and void of mercy and compassion (Alden, p. 335).

    ii. He is the sovereign Creator and Sustainer of all (vv. 13-15)

God Himself will affirm the same truth in chapters 38-41. *He is the sovereign Creator and Sustainer of all.* Elihu's words abound with allusions to Genesis 1-3, the creation of man, and the dust of death. Genesis 2:7 reads: "Then the LORD God formed man of dust from the ground, and breathed into his nostrils the breath of life; and man became a living being." Genesis 3:19 states: "By the sweat of your face you will eat bread, till you return to the ground, because from it you were taken; for you are dust, and to dust you shall return." Ecclesiastes 12:7 describes death in this way: "then the dust will return to the earth as it was, and the spirit will return to God who gave it."

Elihu is of course correct in saying that God is perfectly just and the sovereign Creator and Sustainer of all. He assumes that Job denies this, but it is not clear that Job has blatantly accused God of injustice.

d. God judges sinners (vv. 16-30)
    i. Wise men will listen to the sound of my words (v. 16)

The angry young man continues: "If you are wise, you will listen to me." Or perhaps: "If you would understand, listen to this; Give ear to what I say" (TNK). Were the others showing an obvious lack of interest in Elihu's monologue?

  ii. Would you condemn the righteous mighty One? (vv. 17-20)
    aa. The implicit judgment against Job (v. 17)

Elihu may be insinuating that Job desires to be sovereign and govern, or else Elihu makes the logical leap that one who is wicked could never govern. In the latter part of the verse, Elihu clearly believes Job is condemning the "righteous mighty One." However, as Longman notes, "Job certainly does not question God's might (e.g., 9:4-10), though he does have questions about God's righteousness in terms of his own suffering" (Longman, p. 395).

    bb. The impartiality of the righteous mighty One (vv. 18-20)

In these verses, Elihu declares that God shows no partiality, a principle confirmed elsewhere in the Scriptures (Rom. 2:11). God is the Creator of both kings and commoners, the rich and the poor. Verse 20 illustrates that all men are equal in God's eyes because all will die—regardless of their social status. All lives are in God's "hand."

  iii. Wicked men cannot hide and do not escape His judgment (vv. 21-30)
    aa. He sees everything—nothing escapes His omniscience (vv. 21-22)

"God watches how people live and sees everything they do" (NLT). There is no place for evildoers to hide. *He sees everything—nothing escapes His omniscience.*

    bb. He does not need to have a court hearing to establish the facts (vv. 23-24)

Job wanted a legal hearing with God. However, Elihu says here, in essence, God does not need to investigate further—He does not require a court hearing to establish the case's facts.

cc. deals justly with the wicked (vv. 25-28)

This passage reflects standard retribution theology. Because God is all-knowing and perfectly just, "He knows their works, and He overthrows them in the night, and they are crushed." The wicked get what they deserve—publicly, according to verse 26. Why? "Because they turned aside from following Him, and had no regard for any of His ways" (v. 27). They oppressed the poor, and their cries reached God (v. 28). Elihu's point is that *God deals justly with the wicked*. Verses 29-30 provide his caveat.

dd. He does this in His own way and timing—not always discerned by men (vv. 29-30)

These verses may seem contradictory to the previous statements: "But if he chooses to remain quiet, who can criticize him? When he hides his face, no one can find him, whether an individual or a nation. He prevents the godless from ruling so they cannot be a snare to the people" (NLT). As Alden writes, "Has Elihu never seen or heard of a wicked king, an unjust judge, or a deceitful leader?" This may explain the Septuagint translation of verse 30: "Causing a hypocrite to be king because of the waywardness of the people" (LXX).

Despite some apparent contradictions, it is evident that in verses 16-30, Elihu asserts: *God judges sinners*. Something he believes Job is denying—but he also seems to believe that Job's very existence serves as evidence of it.

e. *God does not answer to rebellious fools like you, Job (vv. 31-37)*
   i. The proper approach to God suggested (vv. 31-32)

Here, Elihu suggests a proper way to approach God: "Suppose a man says to God, 'I am guilty but will offend no more. Teach me what I cannot see; if I have done wrong, I will not do so again'" (NIV). Rather than proclaiming his innocence,

Job should assume his chastisement indicates his guilt and ask God to teach him his sin and pledge not to do it again.

ii. The problem of Job's approach (v. 33)

From Elihu's viewpoint, Job has "rejected" a humble approach to God by not acknowledging his sin—expecting God to respond on his own terms. But God does not answer on human terms. Therefore, Elihu believes Job "must choose" since Elihu could not choose to repent for him.

iii. The prudent will agree with me—Job speaks ignorantly and rebelliously (vv. 34-37)

Verse 34 asserts that Elihu's forthcoming words align with the wisdom of "men of understanding." Elihu believed that wise individuals will concur with his assessment that "Job speaks without knowledge, and his words are without wisdom." God may also agree with this assessment if we apply 38:2 to Job and not Elihu. Certainly, Job himself will agree in 42:3 after God speaks.

In verse 36, Elihu expresses that Job should be tried to the limit because he answers like wicked men. Elihu's words seem to have no hint of grace or forgiveness offered. Verse 37 reinforces his reasoning: "For he adds rebellion to his sin; he claps his hands among us, and multiplies his words against God." "For you have added rebellion to your sin; you show no respect, and you speak many angry words against God" (NLT).

Many a reader and preacher has felt that Elihu is, in many ways, right about Job. Job has appeared rebellious and has blamed God. And God will rebuke Job for assuming he could instruct Him, and Job will agree with God about speaking ignorantly about things he didn't understand. Yet, Elihu seems to suggest that such ignorant and foolish words are only a part of Job's sin, implying that there is something more. If this is the case, then Elihu is wrong.

In verses 31-37, Elihu states—*God does not answer to rebellious fools like you, Job*. However, as we will see, God will answer Job out of the whirlwind, because God is not only just, He is gracious and compassionate.

At this point, Elihu may have given Job an opportunity to respond. If so, there was evidently no response. Chapter 35 presents another speech, but it is devoted to the same theme—defending God's righteousness against what Elihu perceives to be Job's accusations regarding God's justice.

> f. Job claims to be more righteous than God and that it is worthless to be righteous [The third speech—but continues the defense of God's righteousness] (35:1-3)
>
> i. Another speech (v. 1)

This phrase marks the beginning of another speech by the young Elihu (cf. 34:1). His approach and subject largely remain unchanged, as we will see.

> ii. Another interpretative paraphrase of Job (vv. 2-3)

There are two possible types of translations here: "Do you think it is right for you to claim, 'I am righteous before God'?" (NLT); or "Do you think this is right? Do you say, 'My righteousness is more than God's'?" (NKJV). It is clear that Job did assert his innocence and believed he was "right" before God. At times, his rather bold language seemed to hint at the idea that his understanding of justice seemed to surpass what was occurring under God's oversight (10:2-7; 13:18-19; 27:5-6).

Clearly, Elihu does not believe it is right for Job to assert his righteousness and question how God could allow such unrighteousness.

This is essentially a restatement of the charge made in 34:9, which may arise from a misunderstanding of Job's words in 9:29-30. Again, according to 21:14-16, Job flatly denied this type of thinking. In fact, this is the very crux of the satanic challenge to God in 1:9 and 2:4—that man serves God only for the temporal blessings. Job did not embrace this, but his trials were severely testing his faith.

It appears that Elihu was either misquoting or misinterpreting Job's intent. The young man says: *Job claims to be more righteous than God and that it is worthless to be righteous.* While some of Job's statements may have sounded like this, they were not, it seems, intended to convey such a message within the context of his broader argument. Elihu is bent on setting Job straight on the distinction between God's righteousness and man's righteousness.

> g. Man's righteousness or wickedness is relative to others—but God's ways are higher than man's (vv. 4-8)
> > i. You and your friends have too low a view of God (vv. 4-5)

Based upon Elihu's following instruction, it appears that he believed that not only Job, but also his "friends", had too low a view of God. No doubt, in principle, all could agree on that in regard to all men.

Elihu acknowledges that the "heavens" declare God's glory. Nahum wrote that God is great, and that the "clouds" are the dust beneath His feet (Nahum 1:3). Yet what is dust under God's feet is "higher" than man. The implication is that Job and his friends have an inadequate view of God, leading them to perceive themselves as more important and perhaps more influential than they truly are.

> > ii. Your sin and your righteousness do not influence God (vv. 6-7)

In verse 6, Elihu suggests that man's sin does not really affect God. And in verse 7, he asserts that man's righteousness similarly does not influence God. He portrays God as basically unconcerned with human sin or righteousness, except in the context of judgment.

However, we know from chapters 1-2, and will see in chapters 38-42, that God is deeply concerned and touched by man's righteousness or sin. He cares so much that He will take on Satan over it; and condescend to address His suffering servant at the proper time. And we, as New Testament believers, know He cares so much about man's sin and righteousness that He sent His own Son to bear our sins and reckon us as righteous before Him.

Elihu, however, does not seem to grasp this this concept of God's gracious concern for man and desire for man to be right before Him.

> iii. Your wickedness or righteousness is relative to other men (v. 8)

A man's wickedness or righteousness has a direct influence on himself and other men. It is relative to humanity, not to God—so Elihu seems to believe.

> h. *Oppressed people's prayers are not answered because of pride, empty talk, and lack of patience (vv. 9-14)*
> i. Some cry for help, but not in faith (vv. 9-11)
> aa. Because of their circumstances (v. 9)

This verse refers to oppression and those who "cry for help" due to that oppression. Yet, instead of speaking of God answering with compassion and justice for the oppressed, Elihu takes an unexpected turn. Verse 9 may suggest that such individuals cry out—but not to God.

> bb. But not because they trust God (v. 10)

Elihu asserts here that these cries for assistance do not stem from a recognition of who God is. They do not seek genuine joy—"songs in the night" that God "gives." They merely desire relief from their circumstances. *Some cry for help because of their circumstances but not because they trust God.* Verse 11 expands on this.

cc. And not out of humility (v. 11)

This verse continues the idea introduced in verse 10—No one says, "I want God and His joy—because He has made us in His image and teaches us more than the beasts and makes us wiser than the birds of the heavens." In other words, no one cries out seeking wisdom from God; they simply want what they want.

Elihu may well describe the cries of some people. Yet, in context, he is rebuking Job—someone who wants God and respects Him more than anyone else, as noted in 1:8 and 2:3. Verses 12-14 further clarify Elihu's point regarding Job.

ii. Surely God will not listen to an empty cry (vv. 12-13)

God does not listen to "an empty cry"—"because of the pride of men." Some English versions interpret this as a refutation: "Surely it is false that God does not listen, That Shaddai does not take note of it" (TNK). However, the next verse supports the more common English rendering: "Indeed, God does not listen to their empty plea; the Almighty pays no attention to it" (NIV). Andersen's comments provide helpful insight here:

> It is always possible to think of a reason for unanswered prayer. The trite explanation, which we hear all too often, is that 'You didn't have enough faith', or 'You prayed from the wrong motive', or 'You must have some hidden, unconfessed sin'. This diagnosis is always applicable. Everyone who prays is aware of the weakness of his faith; everyone with a scrap of self-knowledge knows that his motives are always mixed; everyone who searches his conscience can find no end of fresh sins to be dealt with. If no prayers could be offered and none answered, until all these conditions were satisfied, none would ever be offered and none answered. The Elihus of this world do not care about the cruelty of their perfectionist advice and its unreality. Their theory is saved; that is what matters (Andersen, p. 256-57).

iii. So it is with your supposed faith and hope in Him (v. 14)

In 23:3-16, Job professed to live by faith, not by sight, and he held out hope for God's vindication. In 13:15, he exclaimed, "Though He slay me, I will hope in Him," and in 14:14, he states, "All the days of my struggle I will wait until my change comes" (cf. 14:13-17).

But here, Elihu tells Job that his faith and hope are empty because they are self-centered rather than God-centered. This is essentially the same accusation that Satan made before God (1:9-11; 2:4-5). It should be noted—God will indeed answer Job's cries after Elihu finishes talking.

i. Because God is patient, Job increases his foolish talk (vv. 15-16)
   i. Because God is patient (v. 15)

This could be another paraphrase of Job (9:24; 12:6; 21:17), or simply an allusion to God's patience being misinterpreted and abused by Job. Furthermore, the Hebrew in verses 14-15 is obscure enough to be interpreted as either an exhortation or a reference to Job, as the Jewish Bible reads: "Though you say, 'You do not take note of it,' The case is before Him; So wait for Him. But since now it does not seem so, He vents his anger; He does not realize that it may be long drawn out".

However, most versions and commentators view this as a rebuke to Job rather than an exhortation to hope and wait for God to answer. If they are correct, the implication is that because God does not answer the cries of the faithless who are oppressed or in difficulty—i.e., "He has not visited in His anger, nor ... acknowledged transgression," you speak foolishly.

   ii. Job multiplies words without knowledge (v. 16)

"Therefore doth Job open his mouth in vanity; He multiplieth words without knowledge" (ASV). Notably, the phrase "words without knowledge" will later be used by God in 38:2 when He asks, "Who is this that darkens counsel by words without knowledge?" and again by Job in 42:3: "Who is this that hides counsel without knowledge? Therefore I have declared that which I did not understand, things too wonderful for me, which I did not know." Elihu was evidently correct on this particular point. No, God was not silent because Job was faithless. No, God was not indifferent to Job's righteousness. But yes—Job, it seems, multiplied words without knowledge.

Application

In his first speech, Elihu said—*Here's where you're wrong Job, God is gracious* [in allowing you to suffer]. In his second speech, which we've covered in this lesson, he said: *Here's where you're wrong Job, God is righteous* [and you're speaking ignorantly].

As with the other speeches in the book, there is a confusing mixture of truth and faulty application, which the reader must attempt to untangle. With difficulty we are left to interpret and perhaps at times misinterpret the arguments and intentions. Only when God finally speaks do we find words we can trust to bring real hope and peace in the midst of the pain and confusion.

Elihu's speeches warn us that when we quote or closely paraphrase others, believing we understand their argument, we may be distorting their meaning. Perhaps asking for clarification would be a better approach to counsel and wisdom than delivering monologues and speeches.

In any case, Elihu's many words continue to prepare us for God's revelation to follow—for which, like Job, we eagerly await while we suffer through the young man's lectures.

Elihu's Fourth Speech—God is Compassionate and All-Powerful
Job 36:1-37:24

In this chapter, we conclude the section on Elihu in the Book of Job, which many may find a relief. His speeches only intensify the desire for God's wisdom to be revealed. However, unlike Job's three friends, God does not rebuke Elihu (42:7). Again, it is my contention that Elihu contributes to the confusion and heightens the reader's longing for God's wisdom, which is free from human opinion and error. It should be noted, however, God's lack of rebuke towards Elihu, unlike Job's other counselors, is a topic of debate among scholars. Elihu remains an enigma, perhaps by divine design.

Had the Lord responded immediately to Job's final arguments in chapter 31, we might have been tempted to think that demanding God reveal Himself, or loudly claiming our innocence, obligates Him to respond. The Elihu section serves as a reminder that sometimes God allows more time and more enigmatic advice before revealing His glory to those who seek Him. We cannot force God to speak through our claims of innocence—He remains sovereign over when and how He answers our pleas for help (cf. McCabe, Robert V., "Elihu's Contribution to the Thought of the Book of Job," *Detroit Baptist Seminary Journal*, Volume 2, pp. 77-78).

Elihu's final speech, however, does prepare the way for the divine revelation that follow in chapters 38-41.

Job 36-37 contains three sections in Elihu's final speech aimed at helping Job understand where he had gone wrong. We will encounter much truth, yet we will continue to wrestle with how accurately Elihu interprets Job's specific situation.

4. Elihu's fourth speech: "Here's where you're wrong, Job—God is compassionate and Almighty, not uncaring or impotent" (36:1-37:24)
   a. Bear with me a little longer, because I speak for God (36:1-4)
      i. Wait—there is more to be said on God's behalf (vv. 1-2)

34:1 states: "Then Elihu answered and said." The wording differs slightly here: "Then Elihu added and said" (similar phrasing is used for Job in 27:1; 29:1). Again, there may have been a pause for Job to respond, but we have no record of Job saying anything. Instead, Elihu extends his monologue another two chapters.

Alden comments on Elihu's use of the word "little," suggesting: "The 'little' is another of Elihu's hyperboles because this is the longest of his four speeches." Since Job evidently did not respond, Elihu felt compelled to continue defending God's character for a "little" longer. Perhaps Job, his friends, and the other listeners (which could include us) were showing signs of impatience (cf. Longman, p. 400). Thus, he asserts: *Wait—there is more to be said on God's behalf.*

   ii. My words are the very truth of God (vv. 3-4)

These verses are reminiscent of 33:3-5. In verse three, Elihu claims to "fetch [his] knowledge from afar" to "ascribe righteousness to [his] maker," implying supernatural, perhaps even divine, inspiration. Verse four boldly asserts: "For my arguments are without flaw; one who has perfect knowledge is with you" (CSB).

Elihu claimed to speak for God and to present inerrant truth, with "complete knowledge" (cf. the similar expression in 37:16). Since the pronoun "you" is singular, he evidently addresses Job directly. Together, verses 1-4 communicate— *Bear with me a little longer, because I speak for God.* Thankfully, the LORD Himself will soon speak. Nevertheless, Elihu declares some profound truths about God throughout the remainder of his speech.

b. *God is compassionate, even in affliction (vv. 5-21)*
   i. He uses affliction to instruct and lead men to repentance (vv. 5-11)
      aa. God is mighty, but not uncompassionate or unjust (vv. 5-7)

Psalm 113:7-8 affirms: "He raises the poor from the dust and lifts the needy from the ash heap, to make them sit with princes, with the princes of His people." The entirety of revelation points toward an eschatological fulfillment. Elihu spoke truth, but it is unlikely that he understood what we know from the prologue—God *is* exalting Job, even as he presently sits in humiliation. *God is mighty, but not uncompassionate or unjust.*

      bb. God uses affliction to teach men of their pride and lead them to repentance (vv. 8-11)

Notice the "if—then" statements in these verses. A summary would be: "if affliction comes, then God is teaching through it; and if man responds properly (v. 11), God will restore prosperity." This may be a new slant to the old retribution-reward theology. Yes, it involves retribution for sin, but it is also educational—because God is compassionate. But then again, Job's other friends said that if Job would learn and just repent, he would be restored.

ii. If men refuse to see His compassion and repent, they die—so be careful how you respond to affliction (v. 12-21)

    aa. Those who harden their hearts die in their sin (vv. 12-14)

Verse 12 presents the final "if ... then" clause, highlighting the negative consequences of failing to learn from affliction: "But if they do not obey, they will cross the river of death and die without knowledge" (CSB). Verse 13 indicates that the godless become enraged by their suffering and refuse to "cry for help." As a result, they die young, akin to those used and abused as "male cult prostitutes." Elihu paints a brutal and sickening end for those who refuse to learn from suffering. Job, in his suffering, must have marveled at the analogy. What Elihu said may be true in some sense, but seemingly irrelevant in respect to Job's situation. Job was godly, a man of faith—not godless.

Elihu's message is clear—*Those who harden their hearts die in their sin.*

    bb. If you listen, you will be saved and restored (vv. 15-16)

The *New Living Translation* reads: "But by means of their suffering, he rescues those who suffer. For he gets their attention through adversity. God is leading you away from danger, Job, to a place free from distress. He is setting your table with the best food." Elihu seems to echo the words attributed to C.S. Lewis: "God whispers to us in our pleasures, speaks in our consciences, but shouts to us in our pains. It is his megaphone to rouse a deaf world." There is much truth here; it would prove true in some measure with Job. When God eventually speaks, He has Job's attention because of the adversity and the false accusations.

Yet it would seem from his previous accusations and misquotations that Elihu does not have a handle on Job's integrity as we do from the prologue. Here, Elihu's words seem more like an accusation than comfort. *If you listen, you will be saved and restored.*

cc. Your zeal for "justice" is blinding you to God's compassion (vv. 17-21)
- You are consumed with your idea of justice (v. 17)

Essentially, Elihu tells Job: *You are consumed with your idea of justice.* Observationally, we might agree. After God speaks, Job will confess that he spoke in ignorance and retract his demand to a hearing before God. No doubt Job's—and all men's—understanding of the wisdom, righteousness, and justice of God is limited and, in some respect, faulty.

- Your anger has led you astray (v. 18)

The Hebrew is challenging to translate here (and throughout the paragraph). Smick notes: "There are few verses in the entire OT that are more difficult to translate than 17-20 in this chapter. The difficulty does not arise from the individual words but from the fact that they are so difficult to put together" (Smick, p. 1022). Some English versions connect Job's anger at the prosperity of the wicked with his being ensnared. The Jewish Bible states: "Let anger at his affluence not mislead you; Let much bribery not turn you aside."

The *Geneva Bible* states: "For God's wrath is, lest he should take thee away in thine abundance: for no multitude of gifts can deliver thee." This context may favor the idea of Job's anger over the prosperity of the wicked.

- Your own resources cannot deliver you (v. 19)

Alden notes that "all versions must rearrange the seven Hebrew words and add English ones to produce a translation that makes sense" (Alden, p. 351). Essentially, the message conveys that Job's own resources cannot rescue him from the dire circumstances he faces, which is indeed true.

- You must not long for vengeance (v. 20)

This could serve as a warning against wishing for death (cf. chap. 3) or perhaps for desiring the judgment of others through death.

- You must not turn to evil, but rather let affliction teach you humility (v. 21)

Here, Elihu evidently offers a warning and plea. Again, the Hebrew text is difficult and has been translated in various ways. But the core message seems to be a plea for Job to allow his affliction to teach him humility instead of leading him toward evil.

From a human perspective, it would be easy to agree with Elihu. Job's complaining has seemed evil and more beloved to him than God. Yet in light of the prologue, and the epilogue, we hesitate to fully affirm what seems to be Elihu's perspective. Admittedly, however, Job will confess his ignorant speech and will find consolation in God's self-revelation, though still in dust and ashes (42:1-6).

In his final speech, Elihu has said: *Bear with me a little longer, because I speak for God* (vv. 1-4); and *God is compassionate, even in affliction* (v. 5-21). Next, he turns to the power of God to seek to convict Job. Notably, his approach is strikingly similar to God's own revelation to Job in chapters 38-41.

c. *God is almighty; thus you should exalt His work (36:22-37:24)*
   i. Who are you to question Him? (vv. 22-23)

A transition seems to occur here. After warning Job against preferring evil over affliction, Elihu begins to extol the greatness of God. Mason observes:

> Particularly startling is the fact that immediately prior to this (in 36:17-21) we have been seeing Elihu at his very worst: pompous, sententious, irrelevant, judgmental. Clearly he has run out of things to say, and what he does say is so tactless that we cringe in embarrassment for him.
>
> But then all at once, at verse 22, the wind shifts and Elihu comes alive. He becomes incredibly enthusiastic ... This young fellow whose faith all along has had a certain authentic

vibrancy, yet who at the same time tends to be a crashing bore, suddenly begins to speak with great beauty and power, and moreover with authority. So impressive is the latter part of Elihu's speech, clear through the end of Chapter 37, that it stands out as one of the most exalted passages in the book, comparable in grandeur even to the speeches of the Lord Himself (Mason, p. 369).

Though I might not so wholeheartedly affirm Elihu, there is a clear shift that finishes out his speech. The greatness and grandeur of God is his theme, and he seems to be much more in line with God's own revelation in the chapters that follow. Though perhaps God himself has to interrupt him.

"Look, God is all-powerful. Who is a teacher like him? No one can tell him what to do, or say to him, 'You have done wrong'" (NLT). Elihu's statements and rhetorical questions in verses 22-23 echo God's approach in chapters 38-41. In 38:3, Yahweh tells Job: "Now gird up your loins like a man, and I will ask you, and you instruct Me;" and in 40:2: "Will the faultfinder contend with the Almighty? Let him who reproves God answer it."

Elihu asks—*who are you to question Him?*

   ii. Rather, you should exalt His work (vv. 24-26)

Elihu urges Job to remember the proper response to God's greatness—songs of exaltation. Psalm 92:5 states: "How great are your works, O LORD!" Verse 25 aligns with Romans 1—"All men have seen" the work of the Lord. Verse 26 extols God's transcendence. One critique of Elihu's words may be that he does not speak of God's nearness and concern. But indisputably, no one can search out the years of an eternal and infinite God. "See, God is greater than we can know; The number of His years cannot be counted" (TNK).

iii. His power demonstrated in the storm—introduced (vv. 27-33)
aa. God's power over the rain (vv. 27-28)

Alden remarks: "This is not a scientific treatise on meteorology, but it is interesting that Elihu began at the beginning of the cycle—water is drawn up. Then he proceeded to the next step, precipitation" (Alden, p. 357). Elihu's point is that God is the one who controls the hydrological cycle, upon which man is completely dependent for water, food, and thus life. He calls Job to consider *God's power over the rain*.

bb. God's power over the clouds (vv. 29-30)

The inner workings of "clouds," "thunder," and "lightning" associated with the rainstorm are ultimately under God's command. Meteorologists may have theoretical knowledge, but only God understands them perfectly. He controls them.

Not only does God have power over the rain and storms, but He also directs them for His sovereign purposes.

cc. God's power to use them for His purposes (vv. 31-33)

He brings judgment upon people through rain and storms while also providing "food in abundance." He is sovereign over where lightning strikes (v. 32). Verse 33 presents another challenging Hebrew text, suggesting that the "noise"—i.e., thunder—proclaims the approaching storm under God's control, as do the "cattle."

God is in control of the rain, the thunder, and the lightning, and He uses them for His sovereign purposes. In chapter 37, Elihu expands on this.

iv. His power demonstrated in the storm—expanded (vv. 1-13)
aa. Elihu's personal response to God's power (v. 1)

Elihu confesses that the lightning and thunder also make his heart tremble. Perhaps an actual storm was approaching, prompting Elihu to go down this path. Elihu calls Job to respond appropriately to God's power, rather than question and accuse Him.

bb. God's power demonstrated in the thunder (vv. 2-5)

Personifying God's "majestic voice" in the thunder, which is accompanied by "His lightning to the ends of the earth," Elihu vividly illustrates God's Almighty and terrifying power. See John 12:27-29 for God's voice and thunder, and Psalm 29:3-9 for another picture of the Lord's grandeur. God Himself will speak in a similar fashion in 38:25-28.

In verse five, Elihu stresses that God's power and wisdom are beyond our full comprehension.

cc. God's power demonstrated in the snow (vv. 6-10)

Transitioning from the thunder, lightning, and rainstorms typically associated with summer, our young theologian discusses the snow and ice of winter. God controls the "snow," the "downpour," and the "rain." It is His "seal" or signature "that all men know His work". Alternatively, the snow might keep men "sealed" inside their homes, unable to work. "Ice" is formed by the very "breath" of God—His Word governs it. See 38:22, 29-30 for God's question to Job concerning the ice and "snow."

Verses 11-13 connect God's power over the storm with His purposes in the storms.

dd. God's purpose in directing the storm (vv. 11-13)

Verse 11 again mentions the "clouds" and the "lightning," highlighting God's control over them. For what purpose? "That they might accomplish all that He commands them throughout the inhabited earth" (TNK); "Whether for a rod, or for His land, or for kindness (love)—He doth cause it to come" (YLT).

God's sovereign control of things too great for man to fully comprehend can serve for "correction" or for some other purpose in "His world" or for "mercy." There is a purpose. But His power demands a proper response, as outlined in verses 14-24.

> v. His power demands that men fear Him (vv. 14-24)
> aa. Listen and stand in awe, O Job (v. 14)

In 36:24, the pronoun "you" is singular, evidently referring to Job. In 37:2, the imperative is plural—addressing all. Here, Elihu once more exhorts Job directly to "give ear ... stand ... and discern." *Listen and stand in awe, O Job.*

> bb. Can you explain God's almighty ways? (vv. 15-20)
> - Can you explain the inner workings of the clouds? (vv. 15-16)

"While modern scientists can explain much about lightning, there remains a certain unpredictability about it, which shows that God has ultimate control" (Alden, p. 363). No man fully understands the weather, the clouds, the lightning—"the wonders of one perfect in knowledge." Notably, the phrase "perfect in knowledge"—referring to God—is very similar to the wording Elihu used of himself in 36:4.

> - Can you change the weather? (v. 17-18)

Job did not fully "know" God's ways, power, and wisdom in the weather, nor could he change it. Verse 17 suggests that Job feels the heat but can't control it. In verse 18, Elihu asks if Job could "spread out the skies" like one hammers out molten metal. *Can you change the weather?*

> - Can you really instruct God? (v. 19-20)

Elihu, perhaps somewhat facetiously, challenges Job to "teach us what we shall say to" God, then adds that men wouldn't even know how to present a case before God due to their lack of understanding.

In verse 20, he seems to ask Job if he really believes he could summon God—or if he harbors a kind of death wish. Alden comments on Elihu's grammar here: "The tangled character of the syntax of this verse betrays the unclear thinking and frustration of Elihu who, so confident at the beginning, was now running out of arguments and eloquence" (Alden, p. 364). In verses 21-24, he attempts to clarify himself.

> cc. Men cannot even look directly at the sun—let alone God—He is to be feared, not challenged by men (vv. 21-24)
> - God is more awesome than the sun in full strength (vv. 21-22)

The Hebrew text is once again very difficult—as the varied translations suggest. *The Holman Christian Standard Bible* may best capture the thought: "Now men cannot even look at the sun when it is in the skies, after a wind has swept through and cleared them away." Verse 22 strongly implies that God is more glorious, more radiant, and more majestic than the sun.

> - God is almighty and perfectly just (v. 23)

In 23:3, Job expressed a desire to find God: "Oh that I knew where I might find Him, that I might come to His seat!" Here, Elihu states that God is beyond finding because "He is exalted in power." In grace, God will reveal Himself in the next chapter—potentially qualifying Elihu's perception of divine transcendence. But here Elihu remains focused on God's greatness, affirming that God "will not do violence to justice and abundant righteousness."

> - God is to be feared, and He does not regard the proud (v. 24)

The concluding phrase can be interpreted in two ways: as a warning and condemnation—"He does not look with favor on any who are wise in heart"—or as an encouraging question—"For does He not regard all the wise in heart?" (NIV).

In other words, if you are truly who you say you are, He will look with favor upon you.

As seen throughout our study of the preceding 30-plus chapters, we conclude with another note of ambiguity—uncertain about how to interpret man's attempts to convey God's wisdom.

Application

We have of necessity endured Elihu's words, recognizing that they are inspired (since they are in the Bible), but we remain unsure whether they accurately reflect God's perspective on both God and Job. We agree that God is compassionate, even in affliction, and that He is almighty, thus man should exalt His work. But how should Job respond? At times, Elihu seems to misinterpret the intent of Job's language. Will Job defend himself and answer yet again?

Thankfully—God intervenes and reveals Himself in a way that completely satisfies Job. Thus, God grants Job true wisdom—the fear of the Lord—not by answering his demands or removing his affliction but by renewing his mind concerning the wisdom, power, and goodness of God.

Again, James 5:7-11 reveals that the Book of Job calls us to patiently endure affliction and to wait on the Lord, who is ultimately merciful and full of compassion. We've endured the debate, and now we look forward to the Lord's personal revelation and unmixed wisdom in the following chapters.

God's First Cross-Examination (Part 1)
Job 38:1-38

Before Elihu's lengthy lecture, Job presented his closing statement in 31:35-37. These were his words:

> Oh that I had one to hear me! Behold, here is my signature; let the Almighty answer me! And the indictment which my adversary has written, surely I would carry it on my shoulder, I would bind it to myself like a crown. I would declare to Him the number of my steps; like a prince I would approach Him.

Our righteous, but physically and emotionally distraught hero called on God to speak. Rather than do so, our great, gracious, and wise God chose to have an angry young man speak for six more chapters. However, as the young Elihu turned to the wonders of God's creation in chapter 37, the LORD finally approached Job—speaking out of the storm. Chapters 38-39 reveal God's first cross-examination of His beloved complainant, Job. Job will make a very brief statement in 40:3-5 and then God will conduct a second cross-examination in chapters 40-41.

The Book of Job began with a narrative prologue and concludes with a narrative epilogue. In between, we encounter a poetic dialogue that leaves us bewildered and fatigued by the human speculation and misapplied theology. We are challenged and confounded by Job's abrasiveness and audacity, particularly in his interactions with God. Finally, in God's questioning in chapter 38, we arrive at a speech that is clear and can be unequivocally trusted as appropriately applied.

In Job 38:1-40:5, we will explore four movements in the text that combine to record God's first cross-examination of Job and Job's response, allowing us to recognize our smallness before such a great God and to be humbled into silence before Him. In this section, we will begin with the first two movements.

V. Job's powerful Creator's cross-examination: "Whose wisdom will you trust—yours or Mine?" (38:1-42:6)

A. God's first cross-examination and Job's response of conviction (38:1-40:5)

1. The LORD's call for Job to instruct Him (38:1-3)

a. The LORD answered Job out of the storm (v. 1)

Here, as in the prologue, "Yahweh" is used to refer to God. It was only used once in the speeches—in 12:9, where Job asked: "Who among all these does not know that the hand of Yahweh has done this?" In context, Job was asserting, "even the animals know that the true and living God—the I Am—has done this."

The name "Yahweh" would remind the audience of God's faithful lovingkindness and covenant-keeping nature. We recall that Job's test began after Yahweh spoke to Satan about Job. Now, following a barrage of painstaking speeches and a prolonged monologue by Elihu, the living and true God "answered Job out of the whirlwind."

In Isaiah 29:6 and Jeremiah 23:19; 30:23, the "tempest" or "whirlwind" signifies Yahweh's judgment upon the wicked.

According to 2 Kings 2:11, however, the prophet Elijah was carried to heaven by a "whirlwind." Sailors in Psalm 107:25, 29 feared for their lives and sought the LORD due to the "whirlwind," finding His deliverance. And a "whirlwind" is used to announce the glorious appearing of the LORD and the angels around His throne in Ezekiel 1:4ff (see also Zech. 9:14, noting the context of deliverance in Zech. 9:11-17).

b. The LORD questioned who it was that spoke without knowledge (v. 2)

This first question could refer to the last speaker—Elihu—or Job. Notably, Job uses very similar wording to describe himself in 42:3, "Who is this that *hides* counsel without knowledge?" Most commentators, therefore, see this as God's first rebuke to Job via rhetorical questions. However, Henry Morris suggests it may be the only divine reference to Elihu:

> Since God did not rebuke Elihu as he did Job's three friends, some commentators suggest that Elihu's message was basically correct ... The fact that God did not refer to it suggests not that it was right, but that it did not merit recognition. Although God did not specifically repudiate it, neither did he commend or even acknowledge it.

> The only passing reference to it is found in God's opening question to Job: "Who is this that darkeneth counsel by words without knowledge?" Elihu had claimed to have a message direct from God for Job, but then God acted as though he did not even know Elihu! This was a rhetorical question, for God is omniscient, but it makes it obvious that Elihu didn't know what he was talking about. Unfortunately, the same teachers who eulogize Elihu argue that these words were intended for Job. This is impossible, however, for it was Elihu—not Job—who had been speaking at great length just before God interrupted him out of the whirlwind ... The question, "who is this ...?" was addressed to Job, of course, because God knew Job, but it was about Elihu (Morris, p. 85-86).

Even if God is referring to Elihu with His question, it seems, in light of 42:3, that Job saw himself as guilty of a very similar charge. The pronoun is singular here, but it undoubtedly applies to all human participants in the debate. Interestingly, the word "darkens" was used by Job in 3:4, 5, 9 when he wished that the day of his birth were "darkened"—i.e., blotted out. Job was speaking "words without knowledge" in his first speech, expressing a desire never to have been born. If Job had never been born, we would not have the full revelation of God to man in the Scriptures. He had spoken ignorantly, even if emotionally.

c. *The LORD called on Job to instruct Him (v. 3)*

The pronoun "you" is singular and directly addresses Job. This charge will be repeated nearly verbatim in 40:7 and the second half of the statement in 42:4 in Job's reply.

Notably, the word for "man" here is the same word that Job used in his opening speech to refer to the announcement of his birth: "Let the day perish on which I was to be born, And the night which said, 'A *boy* [literally, a "man"] is conceived'" (3:3). It refers to a "man" in his weakness. Perhaps more significantly, Job used it in 16:21: "O that a man might plead with God as a man with his neighbor!" God was now giving him that opportunity. The questions that follow are meant to humble Job and to call him to renewed trust, but not to demean or humiliate him into subjection. As Andersen writes: "On the contrary, the highest nobility of every person is to be thus enrolled by God Himself in His school of wisdom" (Andersen, p. 269).

2. The LORD's challenge concerning Job's wisdom to rule creation (38:4-39:30)

a. *Were you there at the creation of the earth? (vv. 4-7)*

i. Explain how I created the earth (vv. 4-6)

In verse four, God commands Job to "tell" or "declare" his understanding of what transpired at creation. The word "tell" or "declare" was used by Job in 31:37 when he asserted: "I would declare to Him the number of my steps; Like a prince I would approach Him." If Job would indeed "tell" God about his life, he first needed to "tell" God about his knowledge of how God established creation.

Job had used the same term "stretched" in verse five, back in 26:7, when he said of God: "He stretches out the north over empty space and hangs the earth on nothing." Job needed God to remind him of what he already knew (Job understood it intellectually, for the sake of argument, but did not grasp the implications for his trial).

Job had no idea; in truth, we don't either, as to how the world is established. "Bases" and "its cornerstone" poetically depict the *building* of creation. Proverbs 3:19 states: "By wisdom the LORD laid the earth's foundations, by understanding he set the heavens in place" (NIV). In Proverbs 8:25, divine wisdom alone was present when the mountains were "sunk" in the ground. God essentially asks: "Job, who possesses divine wisdom, which is on display in the creation of the earth?"

ii. Examine the response of angels to such wisdom and power (v. 7)

The phrase "morning stars" may poetically refer to the heavenly bodies or, more likely, to the angels, as suggested by the parallel phrase "sons of God" (1:6; 2:1). At creation, there was heavenly, angelic joy and singing. Mason comments on the word "joy" in this context:

> In Job this sudden mention of joy comes as something of an embarrassment—especially since elsewhere in the book nearly every other use of the word "joy" has a negative connotation. (Typical is 9:25 where Job moans, "My days fly away without a glimpse of joy.") Even for a smiling, healthy Christian, the mere mention of joy in a sermon, along with the reminder that rejoicing goes hand in hand with true faith, may toll like a great sad bell in the heart. For real joy is so scarce

among us. We humans, [because of our sin nature, doing nearly] ... everything out of a neurotic necessity and deadly pragmatism, have a most difficult time laying hold of a spirit of pure, spontaneous celebration (Mason, p. 392).

Notice in verse seven, at the original creation—when everything was very good (Gen. 1:31)—"*all* the sons of God shouted for joy." Every last angelic being "shouted for joy." Job was not there to have heard them extol God's wisdom.

b. *Were you there at the creation of the sea? (vv. 8-11)*
   i. Explain the creation of the sea (vv. 8-9)

"Genesis 1:9 records the gathering of the water to one place and the appearance of the dry land" (Alden, p. 371). God alone created the sea and its mists. In Genesis 7:11, the fountains of the great deep burst open, and the floodgates of the sky were opened. The imagery here depicts the sea as an infant in its crib, wrapped in swaddling clothes (cf. 3:10 for similar language). *Explain the creation of the sea, Job.*

   ii. Explain the control of the sea (vv. 10-11)

In verse 11, God poetically quotes Himself while addressing the sea: "Thus far you shall come, but no farther; and here shall your proud waves stop." A thoughtful consideration of the ocean—and its vast power—is enough to humble the strongest man.

c. *Can you control the morning light? (vv. 12-15)*
   i. Have you ever been in control of the morning? (v. 12)

Yahweh next asks Job if he has "ever in his days commanded the morning." Could Job command a sunrise? But how important is the light of day? Verses 13-15 outline two reasons why daylight is essential.

   ii. Can you see the topography of the earth without the light of day? (v. 14)

As dawn takes hold of the ends of the earth (v. 13), verse 14 says the topography of the earth is revealed. In the darkness the mountains, the valleys, the caves and wells, the cracks, the crevices can't be seen. In the morning, daylight reveals the lines like "clay under the seal." As Alden notes, "In the dark the earth might as well be naked, but with the light it is clothed with colors and shapes" (Alden, p. 373). Furthermore, verses 13 and 15 combine to present another reason the light of day is necessary.

   iii. Can you stop the wicked by making the light shine? (vv. 13, 15)

The "wicked" act most wickedly in the darkness. There is a providential restraint of the "wicked" when the light of morning comes. The dawn is like the shaking of a dust rag, in which the "wicked are shaken out." Their rebellion, their "uplifted arm," must cease in the light of day.

Were you there at the creation of the earth and sea? Can you control the morning light?

   d. Have you ever seen what's under the earth and sea—or over the expanse of the earth? (vv. 16-18)
     i. Do you know what is in the depths of the sea? (v. 16)

Job did not know everything about the "recesses of the deep" and the "springs of the sea" (nor do we today). Although modern scientists have discovered freshwater springs in the ocean's depths, according to Henry Morris (Morris, chapter 3), there are still unexplored areas in the ocean. Do we really want to instruct God on how to rule the world?

     ii. Do you know what is in the depths of the earth? (v. 17)

No one knows what lies beyond the grave or in the earth's depths. There are things we simply do not know, but God does.

     iii. Do you know what is on the entirety of the earth? (v. 18)

Like a view from space, God asks Job if he has seen everything on the "expanse of the earth." Even if Job could not explore the ocean's depths, or the world *under* the earth, did he have a complete understanding of everything *on* the earth? God, with Fatherly irony, challenges Job: "Tell Me, if you know all this."

Were you there at the creation of the earth? Were you there at the creation of the sea? Can you control the morning light? Have you ever seen what's under the earth and under the sea—or over the expanse of earth?

e. Do you understand the way of light and darkness? (vv. 19-21)
  i. Do you understand light and darkness, and can you control them? (vv. 19-20)

Verse 19 poses a playful question: "Where does the light go when it's dark, and darkness live when it is light?" Even if Job could explain it scientifically, he had no ability to control when and where light and darkness exist, to direct them home, so to speak. *Do you understand light and darkness, and can you control them?*

  ii. Do tell me, because of your great wisdom. (v. 21)

Again, we see the Fatherly playfulness, as the *NLT* reads: "But of course you know all this! For you were born before it was all created, and you are so very experienced!"

f. Can you comprehend and control the elements of a storm? (vv. 22-30)
  i. Do you understand the origin and divine weaponry of snow and hail? (vv. 22-23)

Perhaps Elihu was onto something when he extolled God's power in the storm in 37:1-13. Yahweh's discourse on the storm is the longest section in His first speech.

The term "storehouses" is translated as "armory" in Jeremiah 50:25. The imagery of war is appropriate in light of verse 23, where snow and hail are depicted as reserved for the day of war and battle. We know from Exodus 9:13-15 that "hail" was used to deliver divine judgment on Egypt. Hail effectively defeated the Canaanites in Joshua 10:11. "The prophets predicted that God would use these icy missiles to press home his lessons and punish the presumptuous (Isa 30:30; Ezek 13:11), and hundred pound hailstones are recorded in Rev 16:21 as part of the plague of the seventh angel" (Alden, p. 376). "Can you figure out how I use the weather to determine the outcomes of battles?"

Neither Job nor we fully understand God's purposes for snow and hail in fulfilling His divine plans. *Do you understand the origin and divine weaponry of snow and hail?*

   ii. How is lightning dispersed, or the east wind? (v. 24)

This could refer to either "light" or "lightning," but in either case, Job and all people lack the wisdom and knowledge to truly grasp its paths. Man cannot fully explain, let alone control, the light and wind. Snow ... hail ... lightning ... wind.

   iii. Who has ordered the place and uses of the rain? (vv. 25-28)

Who created the canyons through which flash floods water the desert (v. 25-26)? God cares for uninhabited places with rain to "satisfy the waste and desolate land." If God, in His wisdom, watches over a desolate land, might there be some inscrutable wisdom in what He is having Job endure? Who fathers the rain and the drops of dew by which life comes? God alone.

   iv. Can you give birth to ice and imprison the deep? (vv. 29-30)

Continuing the birth metaphor, God asks in verse 29: "From whose womb does the ice emerge, and the frost from the sky, who gives birth to it?" (NET). Verse 30 references frozen bodies of water: "when water becomes as hard as stone, and the surface of the watery depths is frozen" (CSB).

Does Job or do we possess the wisdom and power to freeze the depths? *Can you give birth to ice and imprison the deep?* Collectively, verses 22-30 pose the question—*Can you comprehend and control the elements of a storm?*

g. *Can you rule the stars? (vv. 31-33)*
  i. Can you order the stars? (vv. 31-32)

In 9:9, Job acknowledged that God "makes the Bear, Orion, and the Pleiades." But here God asks him to consider them not just as a talking point, but rather in reference to wisdom and power.

Once, Yahweh chose to prevent the sun from setting (Josh. 10:12-14), and once, to make it go backward (Is. 38:8). Job would be unable to alter the course of the constellations or the sequence of the seasons, nor could any human. God alone possesses the authority and wisdom to do so. *Can you order the stars?*

  ii. Do you fix the heavenly laws? (v. 33)

"No mortal knows 'the laws of the heavens,' either in the astronomical sense or in the theological sense … The question confronted Job with the truth that he had nothing to do with the administration of the earth. It is under divine or heavenly jurisdiction" (Alden, p. 379). With this inquiry about heavenly wisdom and authority, God returns to the "weather," but not merely to emphasize the various phenomena of storms, but to ask Job if he can control the weather.

h. *Can you control the weather? (vv. 34-38)*
  i. Can you command the rain? (v. 34)

Can you command the clouds to rain? Man's wisdom and power are indeed very limited in this regard. Can a person "shout to the clouds and make it rain" (NLT)?

ii. Can you command the lightning? (v. 35)

Does lightning obey your commands? Do lightning bolts respond to your call—saying, "We're ready for service, tell us where to go"? No man tells the lightning where to strike. But God does. His wisdom and power far exceed ours. Verse 36 adds an intriguing twist to the weather lesson.

iii. Can you communicate the weather to animals? (v. 36)

The NASB offers an alternate translation for the very rare word at the end of verse 36. It is likely not the term for "mind," but more likely "rooster" or possibly "ibis"—a long-legged wading bird associated with wisdom in Ancient Egyptian mythology. In this context, Job is not the one who imparts wisdom to birds about the weather. This serves as an initial transition to the questions regarding animals that will follow in verses 39-41 and in chapter 39.

God seems to be asking Job: "Have you ever noticed that animals seem to know when the weather is about to change? Did you give them that wisdom?"

iv. Can you cure a drought? (vv. 37-38)

The NIV reads: "Who has the wisdom to count the clouds? Who can tip over the water jars of the heavens when the dust becomes hard and the clods of earth stick together?" The term "water jars" may be better rendered as "waterskins." God is using vivid imagery to ask Job whether he can bring rain during a drought. Job, who must drink from waterskins, is reminded that God alone owns and meticulously governs every detail of the clouds through His wisdom.

Application

To comfort a chastened Israel, the prophet Isaiah recorded a similar message in Isaiah 40:12-14, 21-22, 25-31. Job was about to learn this as well—"those who wait for the LORD will gain new strength ..."

Take a moment to consider the One who was present at the creation of the earth and heard all the angels shout for joy; who was there at the creation of the sea; the One who controls its boundaries and declared, "Thus far you shall come, but no farther; and here shall your proud waves stop." Reflect on the One who commands the morning and knows the dawn's place; who understands the depths and the gates of death; who knows the paths of light and darkness; who creates and governs the snow, hail, lightning, wind, and rain; who cares for even the blade of grass in an uninhabited place. Think of the One who leads the constellations around on a leash for mankind to observe and discern the seasons. Consider the One who can bring rain and alleviate drought.

This One voluntarily humbled Himself, took on flesh, and lived among us as a man. Jesus knew the answers to every question God posed, yet He limited Himself to experience life like Job, you, and me. Jesus could create food, but He understood, believed, and lived by the reality that man truly lives by every word that comes from the mouth of God. Jesus understood that as He took on humanity, He too would need to wait upon the LORD. Is it a stretch to think that the Book of Job taught Jesus endurance as He experienced suffering as a man? Hebrews 5:8 states, "Although He was a Son, He learned obedience from the things which He suffered." The One who made the world and all things in it, who possessed the wisdom and knowledge of God, chose to suffer as a man, so that He could save His people from their sins.

God was helping Job understand that he didn't need an explanation for his suffering. In fact, he didn't need physical healing or the restoration of his property and family. He didn't even need vindication in front of his friends. What he needed was to find solace in God Himself, who is so wonderfully wise and powerful that He is the believer's consolation, in spite of temporal pain and confusion. In a way, God's lesson to Job about creation parallels Jesus' teaching in Matthew 6:25-34. Look to the birds and the flowers to learn of God's care; do not be anxious; trust Him. This is more directly stated by Jesus in John 14:1: "Do not let your heart be troubled; trust in God, trust also in Me."

God's First Cross-Examination (Part 2)—and Job's Enigmatic Response
Job 38:39-40:5

Throughout our study of the Book of Job, we've observed that Job not only talks to his friends, and talks *about* God, but he also talks *directly to* God. He persistently sought God's presence through prayer. While Job's friends and the young Elihu talk a lot *about* God and *talk to Job* about God, Job alone talks directly *to* God. At the conclusion of this poetic section, the LORD speaks to Job directly, vindicating Job's faith in a way he did not expect.

Job 38:1-40:5 consists of four movements that together capture God's first cross-examination of Job and Job's response. This exchange allows us to recognize our own smallness before such a great God and humbles us into silence before Him.

2. The LORD's challenge concerning Job's wisdom to rule creation (38:4-39:30) [continued]

   i. *Do you feed the lion and the raven? (38:39-41)*

      i. Do you give lions the ability to hunt and satisfy their hunger? (vv. 39-40)

With the mention of the rooster or ibis in verse 36 (see note there), God transitions from the elements of astronomy and weather, to the animal world. He starts with the lion, the chief predator in the animal realm. Was it Job, or any man, who provides for these creatures? Obviously not! God, in His providence, provides "the prey for the lion," granting them their ability to hunt and satisfy their hunger.

But in case the lion is too majestic or rare a creature, God pairs it with the raven in verse 41.

> ii. Do you give ravens their instincts to feed their helpless children? (v. 41)

Notably, the raven's young are depicted as crying out to God for food. Both the "young lions" of verses 39-40 and the "young" of the raven need to be fed by their parents. Did Job bestow upon lions and ravens their instincts to feed their offspring? How does that work? If Job would be so bold as to "tell" God about his ways, he would first need to tell God about God's ways.

Psalm 147:7-11 states: "Sing to the LORD with thanksgiving; sing praises to our God on the lyre, who covers the heavens with clouds, who provides rain for the earth, who makes grass to grow on the mountains. He gives the beast its food, and the young ravens which cry." Jesus also referred to ravens to illustrate God's trustworthy character: "Consider the ravens, for they neither sow nor reap; they have no storeroom nor barn, and yet God feeds them; how much more valuable you are than the birds!" (Luke 12:24). Perhaps Job needed to reflect on this as well!

Here, God asks—*Do you feed the lion and the raven* (and give them their abilities and instincts to hunt and care for their own)?

> j. *Do you know the birthing and nurturing of wild goats and deer? (39:1-4)*
> > i. Do you know the birth cycle of wild goats and deer that live in places man cannot travel? (vv. 1-3)

The King James Bible is very literal here: "wild goats of the rock." Mountain goats and deer are reclusive; and it would be a rarity indeed for a person to witness them giving birth, let alone know exactly their gestation period (v. 2) or how long each will be in labor before "they kneel down" and "bring forth their young" and "get rid of their labor pains." God knows every detail perfectly. How could Job "declare" his own ways to God if he didn't know every detail of creation as God does?

Do you know the birth cycle of wild goats and deer that live in places man cannot travel? But God was not yet finished with the wild goats and deer. Verse four ...

  ii. Do you know when their young are no longer dependent on their mother? (v. 4)

God even knows how long until their offspring actually "leave and do not return" to their mothers and start the whole process over again. Doubtless, this would vary slightly for each. God knows.

k. *Do you set the wild donkey free? (vv. 5-8)*
  i. Who untied the ropes of the wild donkey? (vv. 5-6)

Again, the LORD's question seems almost playful. The "wild donkey" is referenced 10 times in the Old Testament, four of them being in Job (6:5; 11:12; 24:5; here; cf. Alden, p. 383). They were known for their extreme independence and for inhabiting nearly uninhabitable regions. God asks, did you untie his rope? Verses 7-8 continue the spoof.

  ii. Who released him from the hustle and bustle of the city? (vv. 7-8)

"He laughs at the commotion in the town; he does not hear a driver's shout" (NIV). In other words, who gave the wild donkey this natural inclination to live alone in the desert? God does and knows things that are so far beyond our comprehension—and we're just talking about donkeys here! *Do you set the wild donkey free?* Or consider the ox—verses 9-12.

l. *Will the wild ox agree to serve you? (vv. 9-12)*

   i. Can you get a wild ox to serve you and let you take care of him? (v. 9)

Verses 9-12 consist solely of questions. God contrasts the wild with the domesticated ox by outlining the tame ox's responsibilities. The "wild ox" would be intimidating to Job, perhaps comparable to the cape buffalo of Africa, which is considered extremely dangerous.

Job knew full well how outrageous it would be for him to try to domesticate the "wild ox." He would not "consent to serve" Job or "spend the night at [his] manger."

   ii. Would you trust him enough to let him walk behind you in the field, or pull your wagon? (vv. 10-12)

Did Job possess the wisdom and power to harness the strength of this wild ox to plow his field? No, such a powerful creature could not be trusted. Notice in verse 10—"after you." Could Job walk in front of such an animal and trust it wouldn't trample him? And verse 12: "Can you rely on it to bring home your grain and deliver it to your threshing floor?" (NLT). It would be foolish to hitch a cart to a wild ox.

God is the one who created such an animal! The LORD's wisdom and power is so far beyond man's, that it is just as absurd to think one could instruct God about their situation. However, the very fact that God is taking the time to lecture Job, albeit with a touch of humor, tells us that God cares about Job's plight.

God created the goats and deer with their reclusive behaviors, granted the wild donkey or onager its freedom, endowed the wild ox with explosive strength, and even gave the ostrich its apparently silly attributes, as described in verses 13-18.

m. *Consider the silly ostrich (vv. 13-18)*

  i. Consider her anatomy (v. 13)

In contrast to the rapid-fire questions in the rest of God's first interrogation, this section does not contain rapid-fire questions, but rather a somewhat comical description of this unique bird, which God made. Though the King James Version mentions both the "peacock" and the "ostrich," in verse 13, the context seems to be focused on the ostrich. The verse also compares the ostrich's wings to those of the "stork."

Here, the LORD invites Job to *consider her anatomy*—with joyfully flapping wings that, unlike the stork's, cannot lift her off the ground. Why did God create her this way? What purpose do her wings serve in their apparent uselessness?

  ii. Consider her habits in regard to her young (vv. 14-16)

Most commentators suggest these verses best describe the ostrich's behavior. Unlike most birds that lay their eggs in trees, the ostrich buries hers in the "dust." These camouflaged eggs seem vulnerable to being trampled. The ostrich seems to give no thought to her young. Why would God create such a creature? What could be the reason for this behavior? How could Job understand its way? How then could he be sure that he understood his own way and defend it before God?

  iii. Consider Who made her unique (v. 17)

Here, "God" is explicitly identified as the one responsible for the ostrich's seemingly foolish habits.

From the reclusive goats of the rock and deer (vv. 1-4) to the stubborn donkey (vv. 5-8) and the uncontrollable ox (vv. 9-12), to the seemingly silly ostrich, God knows their ways. Does Job? Does Job truly know his own way? Are any of us wise enough to chart our own course and argue that we have a better plan for our lives?

iv. Consider her speed (v. 18)

An ostrich can reach speeds of up to 40 miles per hour, leading to the assertion that "she laughs at the horse and his rider." Why would God make such an animal—what purpose could He have? She's faster than a horse and its rider, yet men don't ride ostriches. God tells Job to *consider the silly ostrich*, highlighting the depth of His inscrutable wisdom. The mention of the "horse" here leads us to the next paragraph.

n. *Do you give the horse his might? (vv. 19-25)*

i. Do you give the horse his strength, beauty? (v. 19)

In stark contrast to the comical ostrich, God now speaks of His wisdom in creating the horse—particularly the warhorse, as indicated in verses 21-25. Did Job or any man design the horse, endowing it with "strength" and clothing its "neck with a mane"?

ii. Do you give the horse his agility? (v. 20)

Watching a horse leap and listening to its snort should remind us of the Creator. Its agility is astonishing given its size; its "nostrils" instill terror in those he opposes. Men can train horses, but they cannot give them their inherent strength, beauty, agility, and courage—only God does, by His own wisdom.

iii. Do you give the horse his courage in battle? (vv. 21-25)

The wild donkey "laughs" at the business of the city (v. 7); the ostrich "laughs" at the horse and rider; and the horse "laughs at fear and is not dismayed." What gives a horse the ability to be trained in such a way that it actually "goes out to meet the weapons" and charge "at the voice of the trumpet"—even when "a quiverful of arrows whizzes by him, and the flashing spear and the javelin?" (TNK) How can such a horse even seem to smell the fight from afar?

Does Job or any man endow the horse with courage in battle, or is it solely the work of God? How? Why?

o. Is it by your wisdom that the hawk flies and the eagle provides for its young? (vv. 26-30)

  i. Is it by your wisdom the hawk soars? (v. 26)

Even though some in the so-called "modern scientific era" may have insights into the flight of the "hawk," it is ultimately by God's "understanding" that they possess such abilities.

  ii. Is it by your wisdom the eagle protects and provides for its young? (vv. 27-30)

The term for "eagle" can also refer to a "vulture." This bird resides "upon the rocky crag "in "an inaccessible place." The final phrase in verse 30, "and where the slain are, there is he" is very similar to Jesus' statement in Matthew 24:28 and Luke 17:37. "Wherever the corpse is, there the vultures will gather," speaking of the judgment at His coming.

The "eagle" may fit better with the context here. Verse 29—who gave the eagle his eagle eyes? Technically, verses 28-30 more fully describe the bird, introduced by the question in verse 27. The eagle/vulture eats blood and feeds its "young ones" with blood. Eagles are known to both hunt for prey and eat carrion ("road kill") (Alden, p. 391).

One might be an expert in the breeding and birthing habits of mountain goats and deer, but who could fully understand meteorology, astronomy, the reproductive cycles of mountain goats, the instincts of lions and ravens, the ability to tame an ox, or the peculiarities of the ostrich, let alone possess expertise on the warhorse *and* birds of prey? God, in His perfect wisdom, has a purpose for all creation, even if man cannot fully grasp it. Might He have a good purpose in Job's trials?

The next time you feel troubled and are struggling in your relationship with God, listen to the croaking frog or observe a bird in flight; remember that God's wisdom is so vast and unmatched, and it is perfectly suited for each creature. We can trust His inscrutable wisdom for our painful circumstances.

In 38:1-3, we see *the LORD's call for Job to instruct Him*. From 38:4-39:30, we witness *the LORD's challenge concerning Job's wisdom to rule creation*. In 40:1-2, we encounter...

3. The LORD's challenge concerning Job's complaint against God (40:1-2)

   a. *The culmination of the first cross-examination signaled (v. 1)*

   Perhaps Job remained silent as Yahweh paused for a moment to allow him to respond. Regardless of the timing, "Yahweh" challenged Job to "answer" in verse two.

   b. *The challenge issued—answer Me (v. 2)*

   A fitting paraphrase might be: "Shall the one who is in need of instruction, strive with the Almighty? Let him who arraigns God answer." The wording echoes sentiments from 9:2-4, 14-16, 32, and 13:18-24; 23:3-17; 31:35-37. Now, Job has his chance. God is not threatening judgment; He is merely calling for an answer to these questions.

4. Job's response to such revelation of the LORD [The LORD's incontestability revealed in Job's first response] (40:3-5)

   a. *I am small, and I will be silent (vv. 3-4)*

   With God's command to "answer," "Job answered Yahweh and said ..."

   The term "insignificant" can imply being cursed, but it literally means "to be little" or "small"—the opposite of being "glorious" or "weighty." Job's only response to God's questions, which reveal the LORD's incalculable wisdom, is "behold, I am little, how can I bring back to [you an answer]?" This first speech brought Job to a realization of his "smallness" before the LORD.

In 29:9, Job reminisced about the days when "the princes stopped talking and put their hands on their mouths." Here, he recognizes that he is the one who must be silent and cover his own "mouth," in view of the unfathomable wisdom and knowledge of Yahweh.

b. I've already said more than I should have (v. 5)

Job's words convey the sentiment—"I've said way too much already." As Alden writes: "Job had out-talked Eliphaz, Bildad, and Zophar; but in the presence of God he was dumbfounded, that is, dumb and confounded" (Alden, p. 392).

Application

Job's words convey a conviction of his own smallness and wordiness and the LORD's incontestability. Yet, we are left to wonder if he has truly changed his perspective. Resignation does not equate to relationship. Did Job still question God's rightness in dealing with him this way—just not out loud anymore? Was he simply overwhelmed, as he thought he might be when speculating about coming before God in chapter nine? Or was Job filled with a silent admiration?

In addition to these questions, from a literary perspective, there is no resolution regarding Job if the book concludes here without the prose epilogue found at the end of chapter 42. Thankfully, God's lecture does not end here. Clearly, Job's acknowledgment of his smallness and silence—and Yahweh's irrefutability—were not all that God wanted to produce in Job. Thus, He would graciously provide His honored servant with two additional chapters of Self-revelation.

Job's vindication was approaching, as God Himself was instructing him. Job was a righteous man, not because he was perfect, but because he believed in the true and living God who has fellowship with those who trust Him. As Hebrews 11:6 states: "And without faith it is impossible to please Him, for he who comes to God must believe that He is and that He is a rewarder of those who seek Him." God's revelation and lecture served as a vindication of that relationship and, consequently, Job's faith. In a sense, it was a reward for Job's faith—but Job needed to recognize it as such. He will (42:6).

Our embattled hero showed signs of conviction at this point, but his response is a bit ambiguous as to whether he was truly satisfied with God's Word. Therefore, a second cross-examination will occur in the remainder of chapters 40-41. God's love is a love that will not let us go.

Consider again the One who was present at the earth's creation and heard the angels rejoice; who was at the creation of the sea, controlling its boundaries; who commands the morning and causes the dawn to know its place; who knows the recesses of the deep and the gates of death; the One who knows the pathways of light and darkness; who creates and governs snow, hail, lightning, wind, and rain; who cares for even the blades of grass in uninhabited places; who leads constellations around on a leash; the One who can make it rain and end the drought; who provides for the lions and ravens; who knows precisely how long it takes for each goat and deer to give birth; who gave the wild donkey its nature, the ox its strength, and the ostrich its speed and peculiarities; who gave the horse its ability to be used in battle; the hawk and the eagle their instincts.

This One voluntarily humbled Himself, took on flesh, and lived among us as a man. Jesus knew the answers to every question God posed—yet He limited Himself to live like Job and like you and me. Jesus knows what it means to trust that His Father knows what is best. He recognized that resignation is no substitute for true rest in the Person and Word of God. Jesus, the incarnate Son of God learned it in the days of His sojourn on the earth. Job learned it. Are we learning to trust and rest in God's sovereign wisdom in our lives?

God's Second Cross-Examination and Job's Consolation
Job 40:6-42:6

As a brief review, recall God's assessment of Job's character in chapters 1-2. In 1:1, we read: "There was a man in the land of Uz whose name was Job; and that man was blameless, upright, fearing God and turning away from evil." In 1:8, the LORD challenges Satan regarding Job's character as a believer: "The LORD said to Satan, 'Have you considered My servant Job? For there is no one like him on the earth, a blameless and upright man, fearing God and turning away from evil.'" To which Satan made the accusation that men only fear God for the temporal benefits—the blessings, if you will—not because God is worthy or because there is a genuine relationship to be experienced (1:9-11). The LORD permitted Satan to destroy all of Job's wealth and to kill all of Job's children (1:12-19). Job responded in faith—yes grief, yet he worshipped God (1:20-22).

In chapter two, we see a similar scene in heaven where God challenges Satan with Job's faith and character. In 2:3, the LORD said to Satan, "Have you considered My servant Job? For there is no one like him on the earth, a blameless and upright man fearing God and turning away from evil. And he still holds fast his integrity, although you incited Me against him to ruin him without cause." To which Satan claimed that Job would turn away from God, curse the

LORD to His face, if his health was taken and his life was in jeopardy (2:4-5). The LORD allowed Job's health to be taken. And he suffered greatly, left with no money, no family—sitting in dust and ashes as he scraped the oozing boils with broken pieces of pottery in the dump in which he sat.

Job's three friends came and sat in silence with him for seven days to mourn. Then, in chapter three, Job spoke. He did not curse God, but he did curse the day of his birth, expressing regret for ever being born. His friends, displeased with Job's words and tone, took to counseling him—accusing him of hidden sin that led to his suffering. Job responded with a mix of anger, prayer, self-defense, and hope in God's redemption. This dialogue continued for some 34 chapters.

At the end of the seemingly endless speeches and rebuttals, we are left exhausted and somewhat perplexed as to how to interpret all that has been said. We understand that Job is a believer, a man in right standing with God, and that his calamities were not due to sin but rather because he was a trophy of God's grace. But we, like Job's friends, struggle with Job's boldness before God and the implications of his words that seem to insinuate that God is in the wrong.

Job's final challenge was for God to answer him. In 31:35-37, he declared:

> *O that I had one to hear me! Behold, here is my signature; let the Almighty answer me! And the indictment which my adversary has written, surely I would carry it on my shoulder, I would bind it to myself like a crown. I would declare to Him the number of my steps; Like a prince I would approach Him.*

Job was so confident of his innocence that he desired God to give an account for why he was suffering so, especially wanting vindication from the wrongful accusations of his friends.

God, however, did not respond immediately. Instead, He allowed Elihu to speak for six more chapters, further exhausting both Job and the audience.

Finally, God answered Job out of the whirlwind in chapters 38-39. He urged Job to observe the wisdom exhibited in creation, the nature of obstinate wild donkeys, the speed yet apparent silliness of the ostrich, the fury of the storm—and to consider whether he truly possessed the wisdom to govern the universe. Job's initial response was essentially, "I've already said too much. I'll be quiet now."

Job had the chance to curse God to His face, but he did not. Yet Job's silence was evidently not the best thing for Job, as God discerned it. So, God continued to instruct His beloved and honored child, aiming to bring about a complete change in perspective. This leads us to chapters 40-42.

Job 40:6-42:6 features four movements that reveal God's power and wisdom in such a way that it brought true and sufficient comfort to Job in the midst of his horrendous suffering. This passage also aims to help us find our sufficiency and solace in knowing God.

B. God's second cross-examination and Job's response of consolation (40:6-42:6)

1. The LORD's call for Job to instruct Him (40:6-7)

a. The LORD again answered Job out of the storm (v. 6)

The wording here is nearly identical to that of 38:1. Notably, the NASB translates 38:1 as "The LORD answered Job out of the whirlwind"—and uses "storm" here. The difference in Hebrew is the absence of a definite article before the word "storm" (cf. Alden, p. 392).

Job's silence was evidently not all that God was seeking. We will witness the satisfactory and glorious response at the conclusion of this lesson in 42:6.

Recall that in 31:35, Job cried out: "Let the Almighty answer me!" Thus, here we read, *Yahweh again answered Job out of the storm.*

b. The LORD again called on Job to instruct Him (v. 7)

This verse is nearly identical to 38:3, differing only by the omission of "and" before "I will ask you." God is repeating Himself, but the differences indicate this is not mere literary repetition.

In our commentary on chapter 38, we noted:

> ... the word for "man" here is the same word that Job used in his opening speech to refer to the announcement of his birth: "Let the day perish on which I was to be born, And the night which said, 'A boy [literally, a "man"] is conceived'" (3:3). It refers to a "man" in his weakness. Perhaps more significantly, Job used it in 16:21: "O that a man might plead with God As a man with his neighbor!" God was now giving him the opportunity. The questions that follow are meant to humble and call Job to renewed trust, but not to demean or humiliate him into subjection. As Andersen writes: "On the contrary, the highest nobility of every person is to be thus enrolled by God Himself in His school of wisdom" (Andersen, p. 269).

The repetition from chapter 38 in verses 6-7 serves to remind Job that his silence is not the final answer to his pain. While he may know he has already said too much, he has not yet found consolation in God's revelation. There remains more to learn, understand, and discover in God's power and wisdom. The revelation of Yahweh's glory moves us beyond mere silent submission in the face of pain—to finding consolation in the midst of that pain.

2. The LORD's challenge concerning Job's complaint against God (40:8-14)

a. Do you still hold to your case? (v. 8)

Combining translations from CSB, NASB, and NLT, we might render this verse: "Will you really challenge My judgment and condemn Me just to prove you are right?"

We have noted that Job never explicitly asserted that God was unjust or should be condemned. However, at times his language seemed to imply such sentiments. In 9:24, he stated: "The earth is given into the hand of the wicked; He covers the faces of its judges. If it is not He, then who is it?" When studying that verse, we concluded:

> Job is lamenting the injustice in a fallen world and asking if God is not sovereign over these things, then who is. Our hero is struggling mightily with his faith—but notably, he is not stating these things as fact, so much as questioning the conventional wisdom that his friends were preaching as his way of escape. Reality does not fully reconcile with a reward and retribution theology. There are injustices and inequities in this world. And without question, God must be sovereign over them—or He is not God. So how are we to view them? (cf. comments on 9:24)

If Job wanted a court hearing with God to vindicate his innocence, then Job needed to consider the implications of what evidence he was going to present. God is essentially asking Job if he truly wishes to challenge His justice and, in doing so, condemn God in order to justify himself.

Perhaps a good summary question might be: *Do you still hold to your case?* If so, Job must have the power and authority to prosecute his case and justify himself. It is essential to remember the context: Job is honored by the LORD in the angelic realm and deeply loved by God. God is not belittling him, but is ultimately seeking to assist him. In light of Yahweh's wisdom, power and authority, it would be of no real and lasting consolation to condemn God in order to prove oneself innocent of sin. Is Job's vision of a court case before God genuinely the solution to his suffering? *Do you still hold to your case?*

  b. *Do you have the power and authority to prosecute your case? (vv. 9-14)*

    i. The question concerning Job's power and authority (v. 9)

In Hebrew thought, the "arm" symbolizes power and authority. Just as "thunder" captures one's attention, God asks if Job possesses a similarly compelling "voice like His." If Job wishes to prove his innocence in a divine court, implying that God's justice is not all that it should be, then Job better be able to present his case with the same power and authority as God's.

    ii. The commands for Job to demonstrate divine power and authority (vv. 10-13)

In essence, God instructs Job to rectify all the perceived wrongs in the world. If Job believes his sense of justice is superior and his plan more perfect, he should go ahead and "adorn [himself] with eminence and dignity, and clothe [himself] with honor and majesty. Pour out the overflowings of [his] anger, and look on everyone who is proud, and make him low. Look on everyone who is proud, and humble him, and tread down the wicked where they stand. Hide them in the dust together; bind them in the hidden place."

In other words, God challenges Job to go ahead and execute justice—humble the proud and bury those deserving of capital punishment. If Job could accomplish this, then Yahweh would agree that Job is able to care for himself.

    iii. The confession that will come if Job can prove himself able to press his case (v. 14)

The term "confess" also implies "praise." "Then I will also praise you, that your own right hand can deliver you." If Job is able to execute justice perfectly, then God will acknowledge that Job can take care of himself.

So, we see *the LORD's challenge concerning Job's complaint against God*. You're silent, Job, but you haven't dropped your case in regard to your self-vindication. Will being vindicated really bring comfort in your pain, or will it yield an empty victory that offers no true consolation? Job needed to find solace in God's power and wisdom, not in personal vindication. Job can either trust in God—or trust in his own ability to vindicate himself. But as we will see, man doesn't possess the power and wisdom to govern creation, let alone justify himself before his Creator.

3. The LORD's challenge concerning Job's wisdom to rule the land and sea creatures (40:15-41:34)

   a. *Are you wise and powerful enough to capture Behemoth? (vv. 15-24)*

   i. The description of Behemoth (vv. 15-18)

   aa. He is a creature (v. 15a)

God urges Job to consider—"Look now" at "Behemoth," a Hebrew term meaning "beast." It signifies the "beast of beasts"—the ultimate "beast." Some scholars suggest that "Behemoth" symbolizes death itself and aligns with the forces of evil (Fyall). The ensuing description of Behemoth reinforces the point that God *made* it just as He made Job. The ultimate "beast" (that Job cannot capture or control) is merely a creature under God's sovereign care, like Job.

Even if this refers to the spiritual forces of death, the key takeaway is that God is the only One who controls it. The following description emphasizes that Behemoth is an herbivore. Thus, it would seem that no matter the spiritual reference, this was truly an animal known to Job.

bb. He is not a carnivore (v. 15b)

The animal depicted in the following verses "eats grass like an ox." The description of this animal as both a "creature" and one that "eats grass" seems to militate against the view that this is some mythical creature (Alden, p. 396). Behemoth is a creature; he is not a carnivore, and in verses 16-18...

   cc. He is colossal (vv. 16-18)

God called Job to consider the "strength" of this creature's "loins" and "his power in the muscles of his belly." Some older commentators want to identify this animal as a hippopotamus or perhaps elephant; but it may be an extinct species, perhaps a dinosaur of some sort. Genesis chapter one clearly states that man and all animals were created on the same day. If dinosaurs did roam the earth as suggested by the fossil record, then humans coexisted with them.

Verse 17 seems to rule out a hippopotamus, as this creature possesses a "tail like a cedar." Those who propose an elephant interpret this description as referring to its "trunk," resembling a cedar. Verse 18 again highlights the creature's strength.

Whatever this animal is, it is a creature, it is not a carnivore, and it is colossal—with a tail like a cedar tree. Verses 19-23 reveal that such a great creature remains dependent on God. And if Behemoth personifies death and spiritual darkness, it is still ultimately under God's authority.

  ii. The dependence of Behemoth as a creature in God's creation (vv. 19-23)
     aa. He is a creature under the authority of God alone (v. 19)

This expression does not suggest that God created this animal "first" in time, but rather that he is the chief, the strongest of God's creatures. Only God can control and determine the life or death of this animal—"Let his maker bring near his sword." Did Job genuinely want to defend himself when he knew full well that he could not defend himself against such an animal?

bb. He is a creature, dependent on creation (vv. 20-22)

According to verse 20, Behemoth seems to feed on the hills or "mountains" among all the beasts. Yet, this animal prefers to lie down "under the lotus plants" and "in the covert of the reeds and the marsh." Verses 21-22 suggest that he spends considerable time in rivers. These verses together confirm that Behemoth is a creature *dependent* on creation.

cc. He is colossal and confident in his habitat (v. 23)

Though he relaxes in rivers according to verses 21-22, Behemoth is unaffected by rapids or strong currents (v. 23). The description of Behemoth serves a specific purpose in relation to Job, leading us to verse 24.

iii. The demonstration of Job's limitations of power and authority in regard to Behemoth (v. 24)

No one can "capture" Behemoth "when he is on watch." Perhaps some had been captured when sick or half-dead, but God's rhetorical question in verse 24 makes it clear that both He and Job knew that no human is a match for such an animal. Did Job really want to make his own defense before God if he couldn't even approach Behemoth, a grass-eating creature of God's?

The LORD does not wait for an answer; He continues His zoology/theology lesson with yet another remarkable creature and asks...

b. *Are you wise and powerful enough to catch Leviathan? (vv. 1-34)*
  i. The demonstration of Job's limitations of power and authority in regard to Leviathan (vv. 1-10)
  aa. Can you catch him? (vv. 1-2)

Speaking of capturing animals, what about "Leviathan"? The term "Leviathan" is transliterated from the Hebrew and refers to a "serpent" or aquatic "dragon." It appears five times in the Scriptures (Job 3:8; 40:25; Ps. 74:14; 104:26; Is. 27:1). Psalm 104:26 seems to reference a literal sea creature: "There the ships move along, *And* Leviathan, which You have formed to sport in it."

Some of the other references are a bit more ambiguous, possibly alluding to Satan (Is. 27:1) or a satanically inspired enemy like Egypt (Ps. 74:14) or a mythical monster (Job 3:8). The detailed description that follows appears to depict a literal animal, yet perhaps it was universally acknowledged as a creature so fierce that it symbolized Satan himself or satanic evil. In this reference, Job might have gained insight into the satanic nature of his trial. If Job did detect an allusion to Satan, the message remains: Job is no match for such a creature. Only the Creator controls Leviathan. Thus, deliverance lies in no one else, *not even one's own integrity and righteousness.*

God's questions in verses 1-2 make it clear that Job could certainly *not* "draw out Leviathan with a fishhook." He could not be put on a stringer with a "rope in his nose" or a "hook" in his jaw. *Can you catch him?*

  bb. Can you tame him? (vv. 3-5)

This animal would not beg for mercy and speak politely to Job. The obvious implication is that this animal is fierce and feared. Job could not tame such a creature and make it his servant (v. 4). Lions, tigers, and apes can be tamed to some extent, while sea creatures like dolphins and whales may be trained for entertainment.

But Leviathan could not be tamed. Many see this animal as a crocodile, perhaps an ancient, giant one. Still, its description aligns more with the stories of dragons of old. But even if it is a crocodile-like creature, "A girl leading on a leash a crocodile that may weigh as much as a ton is a whimsical if not absurd scene" (Alden, p. 401). Clearly, God employed humor to teach Job.

How could Job think he could tell God how things ought to be if he can't tell a creature how it should behave? But the LORD is not finished with the Leviathan illustration.

    cc. Can you sell him? (v. 6)

Verse six paints a picture of a fish market. Can Job catch and butcher the animal so that "traders bargain over him and divide him among the merchants?"

    dd. Would you even dare to try? (vv. 7-9)

Even if one attempted to "fill his skin with harpoons or his head with fishing spears," it would be a devastating fight. So much so that no one would dare try twice (v. 8). One who dared to fight Leviathan has underestimated the cost. This animal's appearance is so rare and fierce, the one who sought the battle would "be laid low even at the sight of him."

Job is a believer but is struggling, convinced that he has a better plan for his life than God does. God essentially asks him: Does Job truly want to save himself and prove his own righteousness? Can he save himself from such a creature as Leviathan? Who, then, is the only One able to govern and administer justice in creation?

ii. The deduction that God alone has sufficient power and authority to judge creation (vv. 10-11)

If "no one is so fierce that he dares approach" Leviathan, "who then is he that can stand before Me?" Is God indebted to anyone? No, He owns everything and everyone. Does Job genuinely believe he can administer a more just, more perfect, more right plan for his life and the world?

But God is not yet done speaking of this elusive and awesome creature.

iii. The description of Leviathan (vv. 12-34)
aa. His body (vv. 12-17)

Leviathan's anatomy is now described poetically. He is both a strong and graceful creature. Alden states of verse 13: "The point of the verse is that the leviathan has a tough hide and an untamable temper."

In verse 14, no one would dare to try to make him smile. Verse 15 describes "rows of shields" as his pride, tightly sealed. His armor-like protection is so secure that "no air can come between" the tile-like scales, which are "joined one to another" and "cannot be separated," resembling a wetsuit (vv. 16-17). This paints a poetic picture of Leviathan's armor-like body and skin.

bb. His breath (vv. 18-21)

Ancient stories of fire-breathing dragons lead one to wonder if humans indeed witnessed such creatures in the past. Here, God reminds Job of Leviathan's breath: "His sneezings flash lightning, And his eyes are like the glimmerings of dawn. Firebrands stream from his mouth; Fiery sparks escape. Out of his nostrils comes smoke As from a steaming, boiling cauldron. His breath ignites coals; Flames blaze from his mouth" (TNK). No known crocodile breathes fire and steam from its mouth and nose.

cc. His impenetrability (vv. 22-29)

He is strong, and dismay dances before him (v. 22)—everywhere he goes, terror follows. He has no soft spots, even where his flesh is joined together (i.e., under the limbs, etc.; v. 23). Some translations render "heart" as "chest." The idea is either that Leviathan cannot be killed by a shot to the heart or that he is utterly hard-hearted (v. 24). The NIV offers a helpful interpretation of verse 25: "When he rises up, the mighty are terrified; they retreat before his thrashing."

Verses 26-30 focus on the futility of using weapons against him. Taking verses 26-27 together, "the sword ... spear ... dart ... or javelin" are useless because "he regards iron as straw, bronze as rotten wood." Slingstones and clubs are like blades of grass to him (vv. 28-29). Attempting to scare him only makes him laugh.

dd. His agility (vv. 30-32)

Leviathan moves through the mud due to his potsherd-like underbelly and leaves a trail resembling farm equipment used to thresh grain (v. 30). The bubbles and churning of lower water layers and the white-capped wake he creates as he moves are described in verses 31-32.

ee. His incomparability (vv. 33-34)

The New Living Translation reads: "Nothing on earth is its equal, no other creature so fearless. Of all the creatures, it is the proudest. It is the king of beasts." The phrase "sons of pride" used here also appears in 28:8, referring to the animal kingdom or possibly the demonic realm. There are clear literary ties between God's speech here and Job's wisdom poem in chapter 28.

Thus ends God's speech. There is no explanation of why Job suffered, no mention of the heavenly courtroom, nor Satan's challenge. Job may have glimpsed the demonic battle in

God's description of Leviathan, but there is no explicit explanation of the heavenly realities we know of as revealed in chapters 1-2. Job didn't need an explanation of those things, he needed to find comfort in the greatness of God, the infinite wisdom of the Creator. The wisdom of God as demonstrated in the storm, and the sea, and the stars, and the mysteries of the animal world silenced Job. The great Behemoth and Leviathan illustrated Job's inability to stand on his own before untamable creatures (perhaps even representing evil spiritual beings), let alone before the Creator.

4. Job's response to the revelation of the LORD [The LORD's consolation revealed in Job's final response] (42:1-6)
   a. [You've called me to answer You—] I know You can do all things and nothing is beyond Your discernment (vv. 1-2)
      i. The call of God to answer, finally answered (v. 1)

In 40:2, God said, "Let him who reproves God answer it." In other words, "Answer Me!" Job's initial response was to say, "I've already said too much." But now, after witnessing God's wisdom, power, and greatness in light of Behemoth and Leviathan, "Job answered Yahweh" and spoke again.

   ii. The confession of Job concerning God's power and discernment (v. 2)

Here, Job confesses that the LORD is "able to do all," and that "nothing from Your purpose will be withheld from You."

In the end, Job returns to God's absolute sovereignty. Yahweh can do whatever He pleases, however He pleases, whenever He pleases. His purposes, His discretion, His discernment will not be withheld in any matter—including Job's life and pain. God was and is in control.

However, this acknowledgment is not made with resignation. Perhaps Job's earlier silence showed good sense, but it did not fully embrace God's wisdom and power in a way that expressed confidence in it. Here he does. First, he says: *I know You can do all things and nothing is beyond Your discernment*. In verse three...

b. *[You've asked, "Who is this that hides counsel without knowledge"?] I have spoken about things I did not know or understand (v. 3)*

   i. The question of God summarized (v. 3a)

Job here seems to be paraphrasing God's question recorded in 38:2, which could have been referencing Elihu or Job. Here Job uses the phrase "*hides* counsel" rather than "*darkens* counsel *by words* without knowledge" (38:2). Job had not "clarified matters by his questioning of God, but rather he has made the situation more difficult" (Longman, p. 449).

Notably, Job had spoken rather theoretically and certainly rhetorically of God's "counsel" and absolute sovereignty in 12:9-13:3 (see specifically 12:13). But now, Job realizes that being able to talk about something, and actually possessing wisdom, are two different things. This is evident in his confession of his own lack of wisdom in 42:3b.

   ii. The confession of Job concerning his own wisdom (v. 3b)

"Therefore" or "Indeed," Job confesses, "I was talking about things I knew nothing about, things far too wonderful for me." Job realized that he spoke without discernment about matters that were "too wonderful for" him.

You are sovereign, and Your discretion cannot be faulty. I have spoken ignorantly about things that are way beyond my comprehension! [*You've asked, "Who is this that hides counsel without knowledge"?] I have spoken about things I did not know or understand*. Finally, Job adds...

c. *[You've called me to instruct you—now that I see] I reject my complaint and I am consoled in dust and ashes (vv. 4-6)*
   i. The question of God restated (v. 4)

Job repeats God's question from 38:3 and 40:7.

   ii. The change in Job's perspective described (v. 5)

Before the storm, Job had "heard" of God "by the hearing of the ear." In 26:14, he said that men hear a faint word from God in creation. Certainly his friends talked a lot about God. Job had obviously "heard" much theology over his years. He expounded it well. He was a believer and a righteous man. But after the revelation from the whirlwind, Job experienced a vision of God that profoundly transformed his thinking, his perspective, and his pain.

It is important to note that we are never told Job saw God physically. Rather, he now "sees" God with a spiritual insight that far exceeds lectures and lessons heard. The nature of Job's changed perspective and perception—his spiritual vision—becomes clearer in verse six.

   iii. The consolation of Job declared (v. 6)

Many translations add the pronoun "myself" after "I reject," but it is absent in the Hebrew. Job simply states, "I refuse" or "I reject." The context suggests that he is retracting his ignorant words and perhaps his desire to defend his integrity before the heavenly court. *The New Living Translation* reads: "I take back everything I said." The Holman Christian Standard Bible states: "Therefore I take back my words."

Job's "words" began in chapter three with his wish that he had never been conceived or born. After witnessing God's self-revealed greatness, Job rejects those foolish words, even though he remains penniless, bereft of his children, and near death.

The next phrase further elaborates on Job's transformation.

And I repent in dust and ashes—The word "repent" here is not the most common term for repentance, which means "to turn" (*shuv*). Instead, it is the term *nahum*, the root meaning "comfort" or "consolation." While this form (niphal) can be and has been be translated as "repent," "regret," or "think differently," the root itself means to breathe deeply. Thus, depending on the context, it conveys a sense of relief or consolation, or perhaps a change of attitude.* In the Book of Job, the same root is translated "comfort" six times (2:11; 7:13; 16:2; 21:34; 29:25; 42:11). The related noun is used in 6:10; 15:11; 21:2—all speaking of *consolation* or *comfort*. The notes in the ESV Study Bible are excellent on Job and comfort:

> God's mercy is pictured further in the humble posture of Job, who in **dust and ashes** finally enjoys the comfort of relational peace that had been withheld from him by his friends: **repent** translates a form from the same root used of the friends' intention to "comfort" Job in 2:11 (see ESV footnote). The translation of the ESV footnote ("I despise myself and am comforted in dust and ashes") finds support in the way it corresponds to Job's search for comfort that runs through the book..., and is consistent with God's declaration that what Job has spoken of him is right (42:7). (Kenneth Laing Harris and August Konkel, "Job Notes," Crossway Bibles, *The ESV Study Bible* (Wheaton, IL: Crossway Bibles, 2008), 932)

The most important key word in the book is the term "comfort"; the book shows where true comfort is to be found. In 2:11 Job's three friends come to comfort him; in 6:10 Job takes comfort in not having denied the words of the Holy One; in 7:13 Job claims that God will not allow his bed to comfort him. In 15:11 Eliphaz claims to be offering the comforts of God,

---

* See Jer. 18:8, 10; 23:6 for the exact same form [all speaking of God; each can be rendered reflexively, "console myself" or passively "be consoled" and preserve the sense within each context]; see also Gen. 6:6-7; 24:67; 38:12; Ex. 13:17; 32:12, 14; 1 Sam. 15:11, 29, 35; 2 Sam. 13:39; 24:16; 1 Chron. 21:15; Is. 1:24; Ezek. 14:22; 24:14; Amos 7:3, 6; Jonah 3:9, 10 and others in the *niphal* that can legitimately be translated "be consoled" or "console [oneself]").

while in 16:2 Job calls his friends miserable comforters, and in 21:34 he declares they are trying to comfort him with empty nothings. In 21:2 Job sarcastically offers to his friends the "comfort" of hearing him out. The key comes in 42:6 (if the reading of the ESV footnote is followed; see note there): now that God has spoken, Job can say that he is "comforted in dust and ashes." When Job's relatives and friends come to comfort him in 42:11, this is probably ironic: Job found the comfort he needed in the vision of God's unsearchable wisdom. (Kenneth Laing Harris and August Konkel, "Job Notes," Crossway Bibles, *The ESV Study Bible* (Wheaton, IL: Crossway Bibles, 2008), 872.)

Yes, Job admitted to speaking in ignorance. If one insists on translating *nahum* "repent" here, then he changed his mind about something he had said—not about any hidden sin or sins his friends were convinced he committed. Yet, in verses 7-8, God twice commends Job for having spoken rightly about [or to] Him. Some may argue that God is affirming Job's words of repentance just spoken. Possibly, but this is not entirely clear—and perhaps not even the most likely interpretation.

In fact, in verse 7, Job's right words in relation to God are set in contrast to those of Job's three friends. They had said nothing because God had been addressing Job, not them. But they had not spoken what was right about God and they needed Job's intercession. In fact, the clear implication is that they had not only falsely accused Job, but they had also misrepresented God.

Could it be that Job spoke rightly to God, and perhaps even about God? If so, what did Job mean when he said: "I retract and am consoled in dust and ashes"?

Recall that Job's passionate speech in chapter three declaring his desire that he had never been born culminated in the cry: "I am not at ease, nor am I quiet, and I am not at rest, but rage comes" (3:26). The term for "rest" is *nuach*—a cognate of *nahum*. In fact, Job used that term three times in his first speech (see also 3:13, 17). In light of the lexical use of the word, and the context of Job's horrific suffering, it seems best to understand Job as telling God: "I had heard of You with the hearing of the ear, but now that I see You—I take back what I've said, and I am consoled [and am at rest] in dust and ashes."

Job was literally sitting in ashes, as noted in 2:8, and his life was described as "dust and ashes" in 30:19, using the same terms. However, after experiencing a renewed vision of God's incalculable greatness, and perhaps even catching a glimpse of His control over creatures associated with death and the satanic realm, Job found comfort even in his "dust and ashes." As one commentator has written: "Everything that Job experienced was worth it because he met God through that experience. Why do the righteous worship? The book of Job shows that the righteous worship God not for what He does, but simply for who He is" (https://myron-kauk.files.wordpress.com/2009/06/why-do-the-righteous-worship.pdf, p. 7).

Application

Job did *not* curse God to His face, as Satan had wagered. Rather, Job demonstrates that knowing God is enough for the believer—more than enough! Job's pain had not disappeared, his children were still gone, his friends may well have still questioned his character—but hearing from, knowing and trusting the LORD and His wisdom brought consolation. This is true wisdom! This is life.

Yes, there are often temporal blessings associated with living in the fear of the Lord, but God is under no obligation to grant us what we think is best for us. His character demands that He does what is in perfect accordance with His own perfectly wise and good discretion. The life of Job calls us to patiently endure in faith and trust the sovereign Lord. Heavenly wisdom continues to hope and rest in Him.

We must never forget the One who *was present* at the creation of the earth and heard all the angels shout for joy; who Himself created the sea and controls its boundaries; who commands the morning and directs the dawn; who knows the recesses of the deep and the gates of death; who understands the paths of light and darkness; who creates and controls the snow, the hail, the lighting, the wind, the rain; who cares for every blade of grass in an uninhabited place; who leads the constellations as if on a leash; who can bring rain and end drought; who feeds the lions and ravens; who knows precisely how long it takes for each goat and deer to give birth; who gave the wild donkey its nature, the ox its strength, and the ostrich its speed and peculiarities; who gave the horse its ability to be used in battle; the hawk and the eagle their instincts; who created Behemoth and controls Leviathan—*this One voluntarily humbled Himself, took on flesh, and lived among us as a man.*

In God's unfathomable wisdom, the LORD became a man (in the Person of Jesus Christ, the Son of God) and died as a substitute—bearing the divine wrath sinners deserved for their sins against an infinitely good and eternally holy Creator. The God-man slain for sinners then rose from the grave on the third day to grant life to all sinners who will trust Him.

Do you believe? Is He enough, or will you turn away when life doesn't go the way you think it should? Believers find their consolation in knowing and trusting the sovereign Lord, who is Himself their redeemer in Jesus Christ.

The LORD is Merciful and Full of Compassion
Job's Faith Withstood the Test of Forgiveness and Reconciliation
Job 42:7-17

If Job were merely a parable illustrating the profound comfort of knowing God, then Job 42:6 would serve as a fitting conclusion. Job learned this lesson and found solace in his relationship with God, even while in dust and ashes. However, Job was a real man who lived, and suffered, and was known as the joke of society. He may be right with the LORD and resting in Him—this is mercy *to Job*. But what about mercy and compassion toward his self-righteous, judgmental friends, or the townspeople and extended family who had forsaken Job and rejected him to live in the dump? What about the drunkards who sang vulgar songs ridiculing him in their taverns, and the jokes, and those who spit on him, and beat him (cf. Cotton, p. 168-69)? How would they come to understand that the Lord is merciful and full of compassion? The epilogue of the Book of Job provides the answer!

The previous chapters have already revealed that Job's final blessings were not earned. They are a gift from the only wise God, who sovereignly governs the universe—who is also glorious generous, good, and delights to bless His people.

In Job 42:7-17, two scenes highlight the LORD's mercy and compassion, encouraging us to persevere in our trials, knowing that in the end, God is full of mercy and compassion.

I. The LORD's rebuke and plan of reconciliation for Job's friends (42:7-9)

A. The LORD's rebuke of Eliphaz and his three friends—Job's vindication (42:7)

1. The record of Yahweh's rebuke (42:7a)

Following Yahweh's ministry to Job, He next extended His compassion to Eliphaz and his three friends. Eliphaz was mentioned first among Job's friends who came to comfort him in 2:11. He was the first to speak to Job (4:1) and was the most restrained and gracious of the three, though his tone became increasingly belligerent as the argument went on (4:1; 15:1; 22:1). But in the end, the LORD showed compassion not only to His faithful servant Job but also to these men who had falsely accused him.

2. The reason for Yahweh's rebuke (42:7b)

Most people live in ignorance of the wrath of God. But here, Eliphaz and his two friends received the sobering yet gracious revelation that God's anger was kindled against them—literally, "My nose is burning at you and your two friends". As the Apostle Paul later affirmed in Romans 1-2, only those who recognize God's wrath against them will see their need for propitiation and salvation from the judgment they rightly deserve. Thus, even Yahweh's rebuke serves as a testimony to His mercy.

Surprisingly to many, the LORD contrasted the misguided words of these men to Job's—and said that Job had spoken what was "right" about Him or unto Him. But didn't God just rebuke Job in the previous four chapters? Didn't Job confess that he spoke ignorantly? How could Job speak what was "right" while his friends did not?

The Hebrew term translated as "what is right" means "that which is grounded" or "established", even "faithfully". The preposition, "of"—in "of Me"—could be rendered "unto". It is possible that God was saying, "Because you have not spoken unto Me what is true". A possible translation would then be, "... you have not spoken faithfully to Me as my servant Job has." Job had indeed spoken honestly and in faith to God and before God.

We have repeatedly observed that Job often talked directly to God about his situation, while there is no record of Job's friends ever addressing God at all, let alone about Job's plight. The Septuagint may suggest this idea as it reads: "Thou hast sinned, and thy two friends: for ye have not said anything true before me, as my servant Job."

Another viewpoint taken by many commentators is that God was telling these men they did not speak the truth about Him, which is evident from their persistent defense of reward-retribution theology. In the context of their conversation, they did not speak any truth about God, as their assertions were entirely misapplied.

In chapters 38-41, it seems God was rebuking Job for the implications of his words. In 42:1-6, Job acknowledged his ignorance and retracted his arraignment of God. Thus, some argue that Job spoke more accurately and honestly about life, suffering, and his situation under God's hand than his friends did. While we might agree with this perspective, it is challenging to ascertain if this was God's intent when He said, "you have not spoken of Me what is right, as My servant Job has".

A third possibility is that God was referring to Job's words of repentance and consolation (42:1-6), indicating that Job's friends did not express any repentance. But clearly God was directly calling on Job to answer and no such divine questioning is recorded of Job's friends. So, one would not expect them to speak.

Evidently God deemed it unnecessary to explain it further. Job is Yahweh's honored servant who, on some level, spoke rightly to and about Him, while Eliphaz, Bildad, and Zophar did not. The surrounding context suggests that these friends concurred with God's evaluation of both their own words and Job's.

An additional question many have raised is regarding Elihu, who was not included in Yahweh's rebuke. Did he speak correctly? Again, we are not told. The narrative and literary flow imply that Elihu's speeches served as a literary foil of sorts (providing an anticlimactic monologue), wherein the reader is left wondering if he is accurate or not, increasing the need and anticipation for God's definitive truth.

Notably, Yahweh was silent in regard to Elihu—neither approving his words, or affirming him as His servant, but neither did He rebuke Him or His words (except perhaps in 38:2, as previously discussed). Ultimately, we know for certain that Eliphaz, Bildad, and Zophar did not speak what was right before the LORD. However, God affirmed twice that Job did (42:7, 8).

3. The rightness of Job's speech and reminder of Job's position as Yahweh's servant (42:7c)

The LORD refers to Job as "My servant" four times in two verses. This repetition serves as evidence of Job's vindication. Despite being in dust and ashes, Job found consolation in recognizing Yahweh's greatness. Here, the LORD chose to vindicate Job before his accusers by repeatedly referring to him as "My servant." The indictment against the three friends and the commendation of Job is reiterated at the end of verse 8. Most witnesses to the debate would have done the opposite, siding with the friends and condemning Job.

However, the divine judge hears more than mere words and perceives more than faces; He understands the thoughts and intentions of the heart (Alden, p. 412).

Regardless of the specific nuances of Job's right words before God, it is clear that Yahweh was vindicating His servant and mercifully rebuking Job's friends. Yet He did not stop at mere rebuke; He graciously provided a means for those under His wrath to be reconciled with Him.

B. The LORD's remedy for their sin—sacrifice and the intercessory prayer of God's suffering servant (42:8)

1. The requirement of a sin offering and repentance (42:8a)

Because of God's wrath—and He is never angry without just cause, unlike men—Eliphaz, Bildad, and Zophar were instructed to take for themselves "seven bulls and seven rams" for a "burnt offering". Interestingly, this was the exact number of "bulls" and "rams" that Balaam offered in Numbers 23. Ezekiel 45:23 also references this same type of offering, though for the entire nation.

Thus, this represents a significant sacrifice for these men, reflecting the seriousness of their offense. The "burnt offering" is described in Exodus 28:18 as "a soothing aroma" to the LORD. It is often associated with fellowship—between God and man, and among men—as well as atonement (Lev. 1:1-17). Notably, neither Job nor Elihu was mentioned as needing to make a sin offering (but again, Elihu is never mentioned at all after his speeches; and for that matter Satan's role is never addressed, either).

2. The restoration of forgiveness and intercession of God's servant (42:8b)

The LORD was calling these men to publicly acknowledge their need for blood atonement and reconciliation with both God and Job, as indicated by the subsequent phrase: "and go to My servant Job, and offer up a burnt offering for yourselves." Job's friends may not have been with him when they received this command, as suggested by God's instruction to "go to My servant Job."

Alternatively, they might have needed to seek reconciliation with someone they had observed in the ash heap, but they had stopped talking to. Whatever their location, they were called to approach this sick and seemingly dying man, trust that Job was indeed God's servant and seek his priestly intercession. From a human perspective, Job was still sickly and homeless. In this era of God's administration, they were permitted to "offer up a burnt offering" for themselves, but the LORD made it clear that His "servant Job" would serve as their intercessor. Restoration would come when they sought Job's forgiveness and intercession, and they would be covered through faith by the blood of the divinely prescribed sacrifice.

The term for "pray" here refers to intercessory, mediatorial prayer. "How little did Eliphaz realize what a prophet he was when he spoke the words of 22:30, 'He will deliver even one who is not innocent, ... through the cleanness of your hands.' If believers do not plead for sinners, who will (cf. Jas 5:15-16; 1 John 5:16)?" (Alden, p. 412). God's omniscient confidence suggests that Job would indeed forgive his friends, as would the LORD. Yahweh's servant's intercession would be accepted.

3. The repeated rightness of Job's speech and reminder of Job's position as Yahweh's servant (42:8c)

In case we missed God's emphasis or Job's friends harbored doubts, Yahweh restates the erroneous nature of Job's friends' theology while affirming the right words expressed by Job. Once again, the true and living God, holy in all His ways, refers to Job as "My servant."

C. The LORD's reception of Job's intercessory worship on behalf of his three friends (42:9)

1. The Faith of Job's friends (42:9a)

Unlike Satan (cf. chap. 1-2) or Cain (Gen. 4:13-14), there was no debate or complaint, only simple obedience to the Word of God. This implies that they had a changed perspective regarding God, His servant Job, and how to be reconciled with Him.

2. The fellowship of Job's intercession—divine and human (42:9b)

Literally, "Yahweh lifted the face of Job." He accepted Job's petition before the throne of grace. This indicates that Job had forgiven his friends, who had also sought his forgiveness. Job prayed for God's grace and forgiveness to be extended to them—and the LORD heard that prayer. Fellowship was now full and unhindered among all involved—both human and divine.

Importantly, all of this occurred even though Job's circumstances had not changed—only his and his friends' perspectives. He remained emaciated and sick, penniless, and bereaved of all his children. Yet he worshipped God, forgave his friends, and sought God's grace on their behalf. They recognized Job as God's servant, with whom they needed to be reconciled, and this was intrinsically linked to their reconciliation with the LORD.

New Testament believers should see a parallel with Christ—Yahweh's ultimate and perfect suffering Servant. He humbled Himself, was despised and rejected, became the sacrifice to make atonement for sinners, and serves as the high priest who makes our repentance and faith acceptable to God. God accepted Christ's suffering and intercession, so believers could be forgiven and brought into full fellowship with Christ and the Father.

In verses 7-9, we see that forgiveness comes through the LORD's rebuke and the plan of reconciliation for Job's friends—blood sacrifice, faith, intercession, and fellowship. Thus, we observe that God is merciful and compassionate toward those who are completely mistaken, self-righteous, and foolish.

II. The LORD's record of compassion in the exaltation of His servant—Job's exaltation (42:10-17)

A. The LORD revealed His compassion and mercy when He turned Job's captivity as he prayed for his friends [note the connection between forgiveness and freedom from captivity] (42:10-11)

1. Yahweh's compassion is revealed in the connection between forgiveness and freedom (42:10)

Some might view this ending as undermining the book's message, which has spent many chapters refuting material retributive justice. As we will see, Job's later financial prosperity will far exceed his previous net worth. How does this align with the preceding 41 chapters? The phrase "restored the fortunes" is a Hebrew idiom that literally means "turned the captivity." Job's experience was metaphorically akin to being in exile, away from the land of blessing. Now, due to Yahweh's compassion, he had returned from exile (which would be instructive for Israel's post-exilic remnant and in keeping with Job's placement in the writings).

Once we understand that "the reward of faith is God, not any of God's [material] gifts" (Blackwood, Andrew Jr., *Devotional Introduction to Job*, Baker, p. 161), we able to see the material blessings as a testimony of Yahweh's overflowing generosity and His character of kindness.

Job did not pray for health or wealth, but for grace and the forgiveness of those who had unjustly and brutally accused him. The Scriptures reveal an undeniable connection between forgiveness and restoration from captivity. Jesus repeatedly taught that forgiving those who wrong us is crucial to our relationship with God and reflective of His forgiveness of our sins (see Matt. 6:12-15; 18:21-35; Mark 11:25-26; Luke 17:3-10).

However, does Job's happy ending undermine the message that God alone is the believer's treasure? Not at all! Instead, it confirmed God's restoration to the world around Job, who did not have the text of Job to clarify God's perspective on Job. Much like Jesus forgave the paralytic's sins—but proved it was so by miraculously healing him (Matt. 9:1-8; Mark 2:1-13; Luke 5:18-26), so Job's restoration and his role as Yahweh's servant, along with the effectiveness of his intercession for his friends, were visibly validated, rather than existing in the realm of unverifiable theology.

As James noted, "You have heard of the endurance of Job and have seen the outcome of the Lord's dealings, that the Lord is full of compassion and is merciful." Job's material restoration displays the Lord's mercy and compassion for all to see, and it gloriously illustrates the connection between forgiveness and freedom from captivity.

The Book of Proverbs rightly guides our understanding of the blessings of wisdom. Job, along with Ecclesiastes, helps us recognize that there are exceptions and apparent contradictions to proverbial wisdom in this life; thus, God is to be our treasure—not the temporal benefits of fearing Him.

See Isaiah 61:1-9 and Zechariah 9:9-12 for the twofold blessings that will come when Messiah arrives to vindicate His people's faith. There will be both temporal and eternal rewards for those who wait on the Lord—who treasure Him above all else.

Those who understand God's mercy are merciful themselves, and they receive abundant compassion and comfort in their suffering.

2. Yahweh's compassion is demonstrated through the arrival of Job's family and friends, who come to comfort and care for him (42:11)

In this verse, the previously suffering servant, who had been abandoned by family and friends, is now surrounded by them for fellowship, consolation, and care. The text emphasizes that the people recognized God's sovereignty in Job's suffering, noting "all the adversities that the LORD had brought on him." Notably, there is no mention of Satan here; God is sovereign over all. It is possible that Job began to rebuild his life with the gifts from "all his brothers and all his sisters and all who had known him before," each giving "a piece of money and a ring of gold." However, as previously stated, it was the LORD who restored Job's fortunes twofold.

B. The LORD revealed His compassion and mercy in doubling Job's fortune, granting him a new family and an extraordinary life (42:12-17)

1. Yahweh's compassion is further confirmed through the doubling of Job's fortune (42:12)

The evidence of Job's restoration is clear in the doubling of his livestock, which can be compared to the original holdings recorded in 1:3. If Job was the greatest of all the men of the East at the start, imagine his status now.

2. Yahweh's compassion is also confirmed through the blessing of a new family (42:13-15)

Did God grant Job's wife repentance? Did she pass away or leave him, allowing Job to remarry? We are not given answers. Perhaps she comforted him along with others, and together they had another "seven sons and three daughters."

Some have wondered why God did not give Job 14 sons and six daughters in his later years, instead merely matching the numbers from 1:2. Could this not hint at the resurrection? Job believed in the resurrection (19:25-27). Abraham believed in the resurrection when he was called to offer Isaac and when he purchased a family tomb in the land promised to him and his descendants (Gen. 22:5; Gen. 23). David also believed in the resurrection and the Messiah (Ps. 16:10-11; 17:14-15).

It is possible that the matching numbers of sons and daughters is meant to convey to the believer, that Yahweh had given Job "twofold"—even in offspring. Now he had 14 sons and 6 daughters. The first set he would not see until the resurrection, but indeed, the LORD granted him double (cf. Alden, p. 413)! There is no doubt that Job cherished his 10 living children. But we can rest assured he still felt the loss of the first 10. Even God's compassionate temporal rewards are limited to this life. Only in eternity will He wipe away every tear (Rev. 21).

Verses 14-15 specifically highlight Job's daughters. "Jemimah" is thought to be related to the word "turtle-dove"; "Keziah" is linked to the fragrant spice "cassia," similar to cinnamon; and "Keren-happuch" is said to refer to a "jar of eyeshadow." It is common for sons to be named while daughters are not. When daughters are mentioned, biblical authors usually do so for a specific purpose.

According to Numbers 27 and 36, a daughter in Israel received a share of the inheritance only if there were no sons. However, Job's offspring, both sons and daughters, would inherit equally. Similarly, Jesus, the Suffering Servant, grants an inheritance to all His followers—men and women alike. The terms "fair" or "beautiful" are used to describe several individuals in the Bible, including Sarah (Gen. 12:11, 14), Rachel (Gen. 29:17), Joseph (Gen. 39:6), David (1 Sam. 16:12; 17:42),

Abigail (1 Sam. 25:3), Tamar (David's daughter; 2 Sam. 13:1), Absalom (2 Sam. 14:25), Tamar (Absalom's daughter; 2 Sam. 14:27), a woman named Abishag (1 Kings 1:3-4), Esther (Est. 2:7), and repeatedly in the Song of Solomon.

God's grace towards His beautiful servant Job transcends conventional expectations. Job's reciprocal grace is exemplified in his exceptional treatment of his beautiful daughters.

3. Yahweh's compassion is evident to others through the grace of an extraordinary life (42:16-17)

Some speculate that Job's lifespan was double that of the first portion of his life. This leads some to assume he was 70 when tragedy struck and that he lived an additional 140 years after being restored from captivity, making him 210 years old at his death. While this is a possibility, we cannot be definitive.

The key point is that Job was blessed with a long life. Verse 17 echoes the statements made about Abraham and Isaac in Genesis 25:8 and 35:29: And according to Genesis 50:23, Joseph was blessed to see the third generation of Ephraim's sons. Here, Job "saw his sons and his grandsons, four generations."

Application

The epilogue of Job teaches us that God's temporal blessings are gifts of grace, not rewards for earned righteousness. Without Job's temporal restoration, the community that had driven him out would never have witnessed God's mercy, leaving us to wonder if God is truly as compassionate as we are told. But God's dealings with Job remind us that He is a God of lavish grace and full of mercy. He does not wound us except for our good and for a future filled with hope and grace.

As stated in James 5:11: "You have heard of the endurance of Job and have seen the outcome of the Lord's dealings, that the Lord is full of compassion and is merciful." It's likely that James had Job in mind throughout his epistle when discussing various trials. In chapter one (1:2-4, 19-20), he addresses the importance of perseverance; in chapter two (2:1-13), he contrasts the perceived blessings of the rich with the struggles of the poor; in chapter three (3:1-12), he warns about the destructive power of the tongue; in chapter four (4:6-7, 10), he emphasizes humility before the Lord and His rightful exaltation; and in chapter five (5:7-11), he encourages patience in waiting for the Lord, who embodies mercy and compassion.

God chose to reveal His glorious compassion and mercy by restoring a significant measure of temporal blessing to Job. However, the Book of Hebrews clarifies that such divine acts are a manifestation of grace, not something to be demanded. Hebrews 11 highlights that figures like Abraham, Isaac, and Jacob all died in faith without receiving the promises, as they looked forward to their heavenly inheritance. Regardless of earthly blessings, the future glory far surpasses any temporary advantages. Hebrews 11:32-40 illustrates that while God sometimes performs miraculous restorations, at other times His purposes lead to mockings, scourgings, chains, imprisonment, and even torturous death.

Even with his restored wealth and new family, Job understood that true consolation is found in Yahweh alone. Only in the resurrection will our pain be completely alleviated. As 2 Corinthians 4:17 states, "For momentary, light affliction is producing for us an eternal weight of glory far beyond all comparison," and Romans 8:18 adds, "the sufferings of this present time are not worthy to be compared with the glory that is to be revealed to us."

Press on, servant of God; your end will be greater than your beginning.

Postscript

The idea is not original to me, though I cannot recall where I heard it. Someone has said that the Book of James can serve as an inspired exposition of the wisdom highlighted in the Book of Job.

James 1—Consider it joy when you encounter trials as it produces endurance and spiritual maturity. Ask God for wisdom—in faith—being quick to hear, slow to speak and slow to anger.

James 2—God is no respecter of persons, whether rich or poor. Love your neighbor as yourself and live out your faith rather than just talk about your faith.

James 3—Let not many of you become teachers, knowing that they will have stricter judgement. And remember that the tongue is small but can set the world on fire with its power. Heavenly wisdom is spoken in gentleness and produces good fruit—but earthly, natural, demonic wisdom produces only bitterness, quarrels and death.

James 4—Quarrels and strife come from unmet expectations and worldly desires. Humble yourself in the presence of God and He will exalt you. Do not speak against one another, because God alone is judge.

James 5—There will be eschatological judgement for the unjust and those that trust in their riches. But those who persevere through suffering like Job will find that in the end, the Lord is gracious and compassionate. Prayer is the path to perseverance in every circumstance—and the salvation of those going astray covers a multitude of sin.

Food for thought at the very least, don't you think?

Selected Bibliography

Alden, Robert L. "Job" *The New American Commentary*, Vol. 11. Broadman & Holman, 1993.

Andersen, Francis I. "Job" in *The Tyndale Old Testament Commentary*. IVP, 1976.

Archer, Gleason L. *The Book of Job*. Baker, 1982.

Atkinson, David. *The Message of Job*. IVP, 1991.

Barrick, William. "Messianic Implications in Elihu's 'Mediator Speech' (Job 33:23-28)" Presented at the Evangelical Theological Society Annual Meeting November 19, 2003; https://drbarrick.org/files/papers/other/job33.pdf

Blackwood Jr., Andrew W. *Devotional Introduction to Job*. Baker, 1959.

Caryl, Joseph. *An Exposition of Job*. Sovereign Grace Publishers, 1959.

Carson, D.A. "Job: Mystery and Faith" *Southern Baptist Journal of Theology* Vol. 4:2.

Constable, Thomas. *Constable's Expository Notes on the Bible*—Libronix.

Cotton, Bill. *Job: Will You Torment a Windblown Leaf*. Christian Focus, 2001.

Davidson, A.B. *The Book of Job*. Cambridge University Press, 1889.

Fyall, Robert. *How does God Treat His Friends*. Christian Focus, 2020.

Genung, John Franklin. "Job" in *The International Standard Bible Encyclopedia*. Hendrickson, 1996 [originally published 1939, 1956 by Eerdmans]

Harris, Kenneth Laing and Konkel, August. "Job Notes," Crossway Bibles, *The ESV Study Bible*. Wheaton, IL: Crossway Bibles, 2008.

Jackson, David R. *Crying Out for Vindication*. P & R, 2007.

Kauk, Myron. "Why Do the Righteous Worship? The Argument of the Book of Job with Special Reference to Job 42:6" Presented at the Midwest Regional Meeting of the Evangelical Theological Society Winona Lake, Indiana, March 23-24, 2001; https://myronkauk.files.wordpress.com/2009/06/why-do-the-righteous-worship.pdf

Longman III, Tremper. *Job*, Baker, 2012.

Mason, Mike. *The Gospel According to Job*. Crossway, 1994.

McCabe, Robert V. "Elihu's Contribution to the Thought of the Book of Job" in *Detroit Baptist Seminary Journal* Vol. 2, Fall 1997; Libronix edition, p. 47-80.

McKenna, David L. *Job/The Communicator's Commentary*. Word, 1986.

Morris, Henry M. *The Remarkable Record of Job*. Master Books, 2000.

Muenchow, Charles. "Dust and Dirt in Job 42:6" *Journal of Biblical Literature*. 108/4. 1989 p. 597-611.

Newell, B. Lynne. "Job: Repentant Or Rebellious?" *Westminster Theological Journal*. Vol. 46:2.

Parunak, H. Van Dyke. "A Semantic Survey of NHM" *Biblica*, Vol. 56 Fasc. 4 1975.

Reitman, James. *Unlocking Wisdom*. 21st Century Press, 2008.

Smick, Elmer B. "Job" in *Expositor's Bible Commentary*. Zondervan, 1988.

Trest, Don. "The Calamity of Job and the Mind of Mankind" in *Biblical Sufficiency Applied*. Tyndale Theological Seminary, 2011.

Stedman, Ray C. *Let God Be God*. www.raystedman.org.

Thomas, Derek. *The Storm Breaks*. Evangelical Press, 1995.

Zuck, Roy B. "Job" in *The Bible Knowledge Commentary*. Victor, 1985.

www.ingramcontent.com/pod-product-compliance
Lightning Source LLC
Chambersburg PA
CBHW050849160426
43194CB00011B/2083